# The Erosion of
# Calvinist Orthodoxy

*The Erosion of Calvinist Orthodoxy* is an invaluable historical case study of the fascinating and complex issues of Christian orthodoxy. In it Ian Hamilton carefully traces the arguments and positions which eventually fed into the theological liberalism of the 19th and 20th centuries that has left the church moribund.

But perhaps the chief value of Ian Hamilton's work is the sobering message it carries for the contemporary church, where some views regarded as new and ground-breaking bear an uncanny resemblance to those that once led to the spiritual wasteland. Ignorance of the past often leads to the repetition of its mistakes. Ian Hamilton here provides an important historical antidote for such theological amnesia.

SINCLAIR B FERGUSON
First Presbyterian Church, Columbia South Carolina

Ian Hamilton's *The Erosion of Calvinist Orthodoxy* is the seminal modern study of confessional subscription in the Scottish tradition. His recounting of the story, and his conclusions, are of direct relevance, not only to Presbyterians, but to all who are committed to confessional fidelity in the great evangelical Protestant tradition. Any further study of this important topic must reckon with Hamilton's account and findings.

LIGON DUNCAN,
Senior Minister, First Presbyterian Church, Jackson, Mississippi

`In an era where the drive in some quarters to watering down confessional commitment precisely as a means of strengthening orthodoxy seems almost irresistible, Ian Hamilton's study of nineteenth century Scottish presbyterianism is a timely reminder: revisions of confessions and terms of subscription have often proved to be anything but friendly towards a robust Christianity, a point made here with scholarly grace and theological acumen. It is good to see this book back in print and made available to a wider audience.'

CARL R TRUEMAN
Professor of Historical Theology & Church History,
Westminster Theological Seminary, Philadelphia

# The Erosion of Calvinist Orthodoxy

## Drifting from the truth in confessional Scottish churches

### Ian Hamilton

Copyright © Ian Hamilton 2010

ISBN 9781845505141

Printed and published in 2010
in the
Mentor Imprint
by
Christian Focus Publications,
Geanies House, Fearn, Ross-shire,
IV20 1TW, Scotland, UK

www.christianfocus.com

Cover design by www.moose77.com

Printed and bound by
Bell and Bain, Glasgow

**Mixed Sources**
Product group from well-managed
forests and other controlled sources
www.fsc.org  Cert no. TT-COC-002769
© 1996 Forest Stewardship Council

# Contents

# Forward

The doctrinal declension of a church or denomination that has subscribed to confessional standards has usually begun with a loosening of the requirements of those standards. When such denominations have ceased requiring full subscription to their confessional standards, they eventually fell into Socinianism or Arminianism. Those that became Arminian in their theology eventually fell into liberalism.

People who do not learn from history are bound to repeat its mistakes and certainly the church today is ignoring the history confessional declension. Pastor Ian Hamilton in *The Erosion of Calvinist Orthodoxy* argues that full subscription to the confessional standards is absolutely necessary to preserve a confessional church from doctrinal declension. He demonstrates from the history of the Scottish Presbyterian secession churches from 1733 to 1892 that decline occurs when the church changes the boundaries of subscription, proving from the 1879 United Presbyterian Church Declaratory Act and the 1892 Free Church Declaratory Act how system subscription leads to the theological declension of the Church.

I first read this book a number of years ago in preparing for a seminar on subscription (full subscription versus system or good faith subscription) in my denomination. I found this book very helpful in establishing the historical case for the relation to loose subscription to theological decline.

The book has been improved with a new introduction that shows the usefulness for the book in our present circumstances, a chapter that details the adoption and effects of the Declaratory Act in the Free Church in 1892, and a concluding chapter, which argues for the importance of confessions in the modern church and answers four objections to the requirement of creedal subscription.

What strikes me most about this revised edition is its relevance to our situation today and Pastor Hamilton's careful research, scholarly precision, and warm style make the book very useful to the scholar and accessible to the ordinary reader. Much of what I read in chapter nine reminds me of the things that are taking place in my own denomination (the Presbyterian Church in America). If you care about the role of the confession in your church or denomination or if you want to study the issue of the importance of confessional subscription, you should read this book.

Dr Joseph Pipa, Jr
April 2010

# 1

# Introduction

Creeds and Confessions have always been thought necessary and valuable by the Church, above all for the contribution they make to the Church's four basic tasks: worshipping, witnessing, teaching, and guarding the truth. These tasks, which J.I. Packer characteristically describes as 'doxological, declarative, didactic, and disciplinary',[1] have, throughout the centuries, been highlighted and identified by the Church's Creeds and Confessions. In fulfilling these tasks Creeds and Confessions have performed the function of 'helps', clarifying and exhibiting what the Church is, what it believes, and what it understands the Christian faith to be.

Because they are at best merely human compilations, Creeds and Confessions have, of necessity, a provisional character. The Westminster Confession of Faith spoke for all the Reformed Confessions when it stated: 'The supreme Judge, by which all controversies of religion are to be determined, and all decrees of councils, opinions of ancient writers, doctrines of men,

---

1. J.I.Packer, *Towards a Confession for Tomorrow's Church* (Church Book Room Press, London, 1975), 4.

and private spirits, are to be examined, and in whose sentence we are to rest, can be no other but the Holy Spirit speaking in the scripture.'[2] They are necessarily provisional because they are the product of a particular moment in history and because they reflect the particular limited insights, however insightful, of mere men.

It should never be forgotten that Scripture alone is *norma normans* (has intrinsic authority), and Confessions are at best *norma normata* (have derived authority). Any Church which believes in *semper reformanda* will ever be ready to redefine and reshape its confessional formulae in harmony with the new insights the Holy Spirit may be pleased to give the Church, and to better commend the faith once delivered to the saints to contemporary society. Sadly, the cry, S*emper reformanda,* has too often been an excuse for ignoring the collected wisdom of the Church over many centuries. At the present time there is a culture of 'chronological snobbery', as C. S. Lewis termed the disease. It is absolutely and undeniably true that the best of Confessions of Faith are inherently inferior to the Church's supreme standard of faith, God's infallible Word. 'Their authority,' argued James Bannerman, 'is inferior, not primary; secondary to the Word of God, and only binding in so far as, and no further than, they are a declaration or exhibition of the meaning of the Word of God...the authority of creeds and confessions is liable at any time to be tried and judged by their conformity or non-conformity with the Scriptures.'[3] However, to engage in confessional revision with no appreciation for the past theological insights of Christ's Church is akin to designing a building with no reference to or appreciation of the history of architecture and the settled truths of design, proportion, perspective, and the axioms of applied mathematics.[4]

---

2. Westminster Confession of Faith I.X in *The Subordinate Standards and Other Authoritative Documents of the Free Church of Scotland* (Edinburgh, 1955), 6.

3. James Bannerman, *The Church of Christ* (first published 1869; this edition Mack Publishing, New Jersey, 1972), vol. 2, p. 305.

4. John MacLeod writes, 'There is a well-worn tag that the Lord has yet much light to break forth from His Word... At the same time as believers have no doubt in

What then is the role of Creeds and Confessions in the Church today? Indeed, do they have a role at all? Few would deny that we live in 'an age of doctrinal unsettlement in which Western culture is drifting away from its historic moorings into a secularised pluriformity'.[5] This contemporary pluralistic confusion in theology has not been conducive to the writing of new confessions. We have reached a point when, for many, 'The two ecumenical creeds are downgraded to the category of Christian gang songs, to be sung as a loyal toast rather than recited as declarations of factual truth.'[6]

The response of the Church towards this doctrinal pluralism and uncertainty in relation to its Creeds and Confessions has been basically threefold:

1.    Relax terms of subscription. In Scotland this was first introduced by the United Presbyterian Church in 1879, when subscription to the Westminster Confession of Faith was no longer expected to be *simpliciter* but to an undefined substance of the faith contained within the Confession (see ch. 5). Although the proposed relaxation of the terms of subscription was to be minimal ('here and there liberty' as it was put), in practice it allowed people to believe almost anything – as the case of Fergus Ferguson proved only too graphically.

2.    Relegate Creeds and Confessions to the status of 'historic', non-binding documents.

3.    Revise the contents to fit the evolution of the Church's thinking. This response is sometimes evoked in the light of the Holy Spirit's continuing ministry of illuminating God's truth to his Church, and sometimes in the light of the pressures of the age to be less particularistic and more consensual in theological discourse and confession.

---

regard to this matter, it holds of them in the measure in which they are instructed and established in the knowledge of the Word that they are equally confident that the further light that is to break out will not cancel nor detract from the brightness with which the light of the Word already shines. What is new will only intensify what is old. It will not darken it or throw it in the shade' (*Scottish Theology in Relation to Church History* [reprinted Edinburgh: Banner of Truth, 1974], p. 239).

5. Packer, *op. cit.,* p. 4
6. Packer, *op. cit.,* p. 5

What follows is an attempt to sketch the developments in confession thinking in the post-Reformation Scottish Presbyterian Church, in particular how the church(es) developed and subsequently modified subscription to the Westminster Confession of Faith.

The contemporary relevance of this study is seen in the recent history of the Presbyterian Church in America (PCA). During the past twenty or so years, the PCA has been marked, if not dominated, by the question of confessional subscription.[7] 'Strict' subscriptionists and 'system' or 'good faith' subscriptionists have argued over what should be the PCA's position regarding ministerial and elder subscription to the WCF (the subordinate standard of faith for Presbyterian churches since 1729). This debate, however, has its origins in the earliest days of American Presbyterianism.[8] It is hoped that this present study will provide a case study of confessional subscription and better enable confessional churches to appreciate the inevitable loosening of bonds when subscription becomes a matter of 'good faith' and not of commitment to stated propositions.

Apart from the Bible, the Westminster Confession of Faith has had the greatest influence in moulding the life and doctrine of Scottish Presbyterianism. For the first two hundred years of its existence, the Westminster Confession of Faith exercised an historic role as the 'watchdog' of theological orthodoxy within the Scottish Presbyterian Churches. As the Subordinate Standard of Faith, held to, and subscribed by the various strands within Presbyterianism, the Confession occupied a position of the greatest importance. Indeed, so much was the Confession

---

7. See Morton H. Smith, *The Case for Full Subscription to the Westminster Standards in the Presbyterian Church in America*, Greenville, USA, 1992. Smith argues the case for 'strict' as against 'system' or 'good faith' subscription.

8. The standard modern text on confessional subscription in the USA is *The Practice of Confessional Subscription,* ed. David W. Hall (The Covenant Foundation, Oak Ridge, 1997). Hall provides a wide-ranging series of chapters analysing the development of confessional subscription since the Adopting Act of 1729. See also the brief overview in D.G. Hart and John R. Meuther, *Seeking A Better Country: 300 Years of American Presbyterianism* (P and R Publishing, New Jersey, 2007), pp. 40-49, 53-54, 57-58.

an integral part of the religious life in Scotland that it was considered by many to have an almost unimpeachable authority.

The particular aim of the present work is to trace and analyse the erosion of the Westminster Confession of Faith's status as *the* settled and constitutional symbol of Reformed theological orthodoxy among Scottish Seceders. The Scottish Secession Churches have remained something of a 'Cinderella' subject to students of Scottish Church history. Why this should be so remains a mystery. It was within the ranks of the Secession that Westminster Calvinism was first challenged and modified. It was a Secession Church, the United Presbyterian Church, which was the first Scottish Presbyterian denomination to qualify its official commitment to the Westminster Standards, in 1879. It has been the singular lack of historical and theological analysis of the Secession's position at the forefront of the movement for change within the Scottish Church that accounts for this present study.

The period covered has two termini, 1733 and 1892. That 1733 should be the *terminus a quo* is fairly obvious. In that year the Secession Church was born with the secession of Ebenezer Erskine and some others from the Church of Scotland. It may not be immediately obvious, however, why 1892 should be the *terminus ad quem* of the present work. In 1879, the Westminster Confession of Faith was relegated from its historic position as guardian of theological orthodoxy in the United Presbyterian Church. Although it was still retained as that Church's Subordinate Standard of Faith, subscription was no longer to the Westminster Confession of Faith as such, but to an undefined 'substance of the faith' contained within the Confession. In 1892, the Free Church Declaratory Act allowed liberty of opinion 'on such points in the Confession as do not enter into the substance of the Reformed Faith' (a substance that was nowhere defined or even sketched). Since that event, no significant advance has occurred in the relations of Scottish Presbyterianism to its Subordinate Standard of Faith.

A brief outline of the chapter divisions will indicate both the scope of the present work and the particular ways in which Westminster Calvinism was modified and eroded by Scottish Seceders.

*Chapter 2*: The relationship of the various branches of the Secession to the Formula of Subscription to the Westminster Confession of Faith will be examined. From a high point of unqualified subscription to the Confession of Faith in 1733, the various branches had all in some way or another qualified their Formulae of Subscription by the union of the main strands of the Secession in 1847.[9]

*Chapter 3*: In the second chapter focus is centred upon the much-neglected Atonement Controversy of 1841–1845. The argument of this chapter is central to the thesis. It will be argued that Professors Brown and Balmer qualified the teaching of the Westminster Standards on the Atonement, their Amyraldianism (or perhaps more accurately their 'hypothetical universalism') being supported by the United Secession Synod as not anti-confessional.

*Chapter 4*: In order to highlight the views of what other Presbyterians committed to the Westminster Standards' thought of the relationship of the United Presbyterian Church to the Confession of Faith, the Union Controversy of 1863–1873 is examined.

*Chapter 5*: Along with chapter 2, this chapter holds the key to the argument of this book. The heresy trials of the Rev. Fergus Ferguson revealed a deep-seated theological ambivalence in the United Presbyterian Church. Although holding views on soteriology and eschatology which were decidedly contrary to the teaching of the Westminster Standards, and to all the historic creeds of Christendom, Ferguson was allowed to remain a minister of the United Presbyterian Church. This case did more than any other to highlight the growing liberalising of Scottish

---

9. See J. Ligon Duncan, III, 'Owning the Confession: Subscription in the Scottish Presbyterian Tradition' in Hall *op. cit.*, pp. 77-91.

theological thinking, and its increasingly critical attitude to the Westminster Standards.

*Chapter 6*: The climax of the erosion of Westminster Calvinism among Scottish Seceders was reached with the passing of the 1879 United Presbyterian Church Declaratory Act. Due to the terms of the Declaratory legislation, subscription was no longer required to the Confession of Faith as such, but to an indeterminate 'substance of the faith' contained within the Confession.

The erosion of Westminster Calvinism among Scottish Seceders was part of a long historical process. A true appreciation of the erosion is only possible when the constituent elements which contributed to the process of erosion are examined in their historical setting.

*Chapter 7*: The Making of the Free Church Declaratory Act and the subsequent secession of 1893 which led to the forming of the Free Presbyterian Church. The 1892 Act brought the Free Church into line with the United Presbyterian Church and prepared the way for the union of 1900.

## Chronoligcal Outline for Chapter 2

*1711.* Act X of the General Assembly required all ministers to subscribe the Westminster Confession of Faith without qualification.

*1733.* The secession of Ebenezer Erskine, William Wilson, Alexander Moncrieff, and James Fisher from the Church of Scotland. The 'new' Church stressed its continued adherence to the doctrine and Standards of the Presbyterian Church in Scotland.

*1737.* The publication of the Secession's Formula.

*1752.* The deposition of Thomas Gillespie from the ministry. (The first Relief Presbytery was formed in 1761, and the forming of a Synod followed shortly thereafter.)

*1778.* The publication of *The Re-exhibition of the Secession's Testimony*, containing some criticism of the historic relationship between the Church and the civil magistrate.

*1796.* Thomas McCrie's refusal to subscribe the Confession unless allowed to state where he considered it to be defective in its teaching on the Civil Magistrate. The General Associate Synod, to which McCrie belonged (Anti-burgher), allowed him to qualify his subscription.

*1797.* Preamble of the Associate Synod (Burgher) qualifying the Confession's supposed commitment to the use of intolerant measures in religion.

*1804.* Thomas McCrie's opposition to the General Associate Synod's new *Testimony* which, he claimed, qualified its adherence to the *Confession*.

*1820.* The union of the major branches of the Secession into the United Secession Church. The union was characterised by a loosening of the new Church's attachment to the *Confession*, and the protest submitted by three future professors of the Church (Brown, Balmer, and Harper) concerning the inadequacy of the *Confession*, as it stood, as a suitable document for ministers to subscribe.

*1823.* The Relief Church set up their first theological hall, and draw up a Formula for ministers to subscribe.

*1847.* The union of the United Secession Church and the Relief Church to form the United Presbyterian Church. The Church introduced a new Formula which was a significant departure from the model Formula of 1711.

# 2

# The Secession and The Formula of Subscription

## 1. The Nature of Subscription to the Westminster Confession of Faith Prevailing at the Time of the Secession of 1733

The story of the erosion of Calvinist orthodoxy within the Scottish Church makes for sorry reading. On the one hand, the acrimony and invective that marked many of the debates and pamphlets was certainly sub-Christian. This is not to deny that truth must be contended for, and often vigorously. On the other hand, however, the spiritual declension that went hand in hand with the confessional decline was marked by, what John Owen called, 'The innate pride and vanity of the minds of men.'[1]

Tracing the history and pathology of confessional declension will give us a sense of how rapidly minor concessions to pressure can lead to doctrinal moderatism and even indifferentism.

Act X of the General Assembly of the Church of Scotland, May 22, 1711,[2] regulated its attitude to confessional subscription

---

1. John Owen, 'The Nature and Cause of Apostasy' in *The Works of John Owen* (The Banner of Truth Trust ed., London, 1965), Vol. VII, pp. 123.

2. *Acts of the General Assembly of the Church of Scotland 1638–1842* (Edinburgh, 1843), pp. 453-456.

at the time of the 1733 Secession. This Act introduced a stricter Formula than had previously held in the Church, and was probably intended as much as a protection against those outwith the Church, as a 'restraint on those within the Church'.[3] The Act related only to ministers and probationers. Two sets of questions were put to each respectively, and each was in turn required to subscribe the Formula. The second question put to ministers at their ordination revealed the extent of commitment required by the Church to the Westminster Confession, its Subordinate Standard of Faith:

> Do you sincerely own and believe the whole doctrine contained in the Confession of Faith…to be founded upon the Word of God; and do you acknowledge the same as the confession of your faith…?

To underline the minister's personal belief in, and commitment to, the Confession, he was required to sign the following Formula:

> I – do hereby declare, that I do sincerely own and believe the whole doctrine contained in the Confession of Faith…to be the truths of God; and I do own the same as the confession of my faith.[4]

It is interesting to note, in passing, that few historians have credited the Church with an increased desire for purity of doctrine in its passing of the 1711 Act. Innes suggested that the tightening of subscription was due largely to 'a vague but strong dread of heresy',[5] and a fear of Episcopalians entering the ministry,[6] while Cooper maintained that the whole legislation

---

3. A. T. Innes, *The Law of Creeds in Scotland* (1st ed.; Edinburgh and London, 1867), p. 88.

4. Acts, *op. cit.*, pp. 455-456. Cf. Innes, *op. cit.*, pp. 84-87; J. Cooper, *Confessions of Faith and Formulas of Subscription* (Glasgow, 1907), pp. 61-67.

5. Innes, *op. cit.*, p. 87.

6. *Ibid.* Cf. Cooper, *op. cit.*, p. 59.

of the period 1694–1711 was aimed 'not so much (at) the preservation of the Faith, as the protection of the party into whose hands the Revolution had placed ecclesiastical power in Scotland'.[7]

Whatever the precise reasons behind the adoption of the 1711 Formula, it seemed to impose on all ministers an absolute commitment to the doctrine of the Confession – a commitment, moreover, that allowed no reserve or qualification, written or mental. This understanding of the nature of confessional subscription imposed by the Act of 1711 was challenged by C. G. McCrie in his major work *The Confessions of the Church of Scotland*.[8] In this work, McCrie maintained that the Presbyterian Church in Scotland allowed ministers 'a certain measure of liberty to depart from the Confessional standard' during this period.[9] McCrie supplied two examples to support his contention. In as much as the Secession inherited its Confessional Standards from the Church of Scotland, it is important to know precisely in what light the established Church viewed its Standards, and what laxity, if any, it allowed its ministers in subscription.

### The Cases of James Wardlaw and Thomas Gillespie

McCrie maintained that when James Wardlaw – one of the twelve ministers who signed the *Representation* against the Act of Assembly condemning the *Marrow of Modern Divinity*[10] – was translated from Cruden to the charge of Dunfermline vacated by Ralph Erskine in 1718, he was allowed to renew his subscription to the Formula with an explanation regarding the extent of the atonement.[11]

The other example cited by McCrie was that of Thomas Gillespie. In 1741, the same Presbytery of Dunfermline met

---

7. Cooper, *op. cit.*, p. 67.

8. C.G. McCrie, *The Confessions of the Church of Scotland* (Edinburgh, 1907).

9. *Ibid.*, p. 232.

10. J. Brown, *Gospel Truth Accurately Stated and Illustrated* (Edinburgh, 1817), pp. 141ff.

11. McCrie, *Confessions, op. cit.*, p. 233.

to ordain Gillespie at the parish of Carnock. Having studied theology under the nonconformist Dr Philip Doddrige in England, Gillespie, so McCrie maintained,

> (formed) opinions respecting the province of magistracy which prevented him from giving an unqualified subscription to the Formula of 1711. He requested to be allowed to sign with an explanation. The court agreed to accept the qualified subscription, and his admission to the benefice was proceeded with.[12]

It is instructive to note the sources McCrie used to make his assertions. Of the three sources mentioned, John Brown's *Gospel Truth*,[13] Fraser's *Life and Diary of Ebenezer Erskine*,[14] and Struthers' *History of the Relief Church*,[15] not one belongs to the primary category, and none mention the Presbytery minutes which are supposed to contain the instances of qualified subscription.

A careful examination of the Dunfermline Presbytery Records for the dates under review reveals no mention of either Wardlaw or Gillespie qualifying their subscription to the

---

12. *Ibid.*, p. 234.

13. Brown states that of Wardlaw 'we know almost nothing', *op. cit.*, p. 136. The section in Brown's *Gospel Truth* on Wardlaw covers just three lines.

14. D. Fraser, *Life and Diary of Rev. Ebenezer Erskine* (Edinburgh, 1831). McCrie seems to have made a mistake in his source material at this point. Fraser's work on Ebenezer Erskine reveals no trace of any reference to Wardlaw's supposed qualification to the Formula of Subscription. However, in his companion work, *Life and Diary of Rev. Ralph Erskine*, published in Edinburgh in 1834, Fraser does make mention of the supposed qualification. Fraser does not, however, quote any primary sources. Quoting from Brown's *Gospel Truth*, p. 159, he writes: 'It appears from the Presbytery Records, that when called to renew his subscription to the Confession of Faith, he (Wardlaw) did it with an explanation regarding the extent of the death of Christ...' (p. 108). As will be shown, the Presbytery Records make no mention of any qualification.

15. G. Struthers, *History of the Relief Church*, Glasgow, 1843. Struthers helpfully surveys the Relief Church's attitude to subscription, but he also confuses 'hearsay' with fact when he states that Wardlaw and Gillespie certainly qualified their subscription to the Confession of Faith. No primary sources are adduced to substantiate the claim.

Formula.[16] On October 29, 1718, Wardlaw was accepted by the parish of Dunfermline as the minister they desired,[17] the Presbytery arranging to meet formally at a later date to ratify the call.[18] Wardlaw was officially admitted to the charge at the meeting of Presbytery on November 20, 1718.[19] Nowhere in the minutes is anything unusual mentioned about Wardlaw's subscription, and there is certainly no record in the minutes of Wardlaw qualifying his subscription to the Formula as McCrie maintained.

Brown's *Gospel Truth* does mention a controversy over subscription involving Ralph Erskine and James Wardlaw,[20] but it had nothing to do with Wardlaw's induction in 1718, or with his supposed inability to subscribe the Confession's teaching on the extent of the atonement.

The case of Gillespie is equally baffling. The minutes of the Presbytery concerning Gillespie's ordination at Carnock, August 19, 1741, read:

> Mr. Gillespie was called in and having declared his allegiance to the Doctrine worship and Government of this Church, and (sic.) judicially signed the Confession of Faith and Formula.[21]

---

16. *Register of the Actings and Proceedings of the Presbytery of Dunfermline* (n.d.). Vol. V September 24, 1717–April 4, 1729. Vol. VI April 23, 1729–October 9, 1745.

17. *Ibid.*, V, p. 29.

18. *Ibid.*, p. 30. It is interesting to note that the Presbytery on this occasion renewed their 'former Declaration against Patronage'.

19. *Ibid.*, p. 31.

20. Brown, *Gospel Truth*, *op. cit.*, p. 76-77. In 1729, the Synod of Fife sought to impose on all its members the General Assembly's ruling on the Marrow controversy. It resolved that all the ministers within its bounds should subscribe a revised Formula indicating agreement with the 1721 Act of Assembly. Erskine refused, along with Hog and Wardlaw, to sign this, and was allowed by his own Presbytery to subscribe the Confession in the following terms:

> I Ralph Erskine, minister at Dunfermline, do subscribe the above – written Confession of Faith, as the confession of my faith, according to the above-written formula, conform to the Acts of the General Assembly *allenarly* (*Register*, *op. cit.*, V, p. 76).

21. *Register*, *op. cit.*, VI, p. 359.

The actual ordination took place at Carnock on September 4, 1741.[22] Gillespie was admitted and ordained with no mention being made of any qualifications or explanations. A further examination of the Dunfermline Presbytery Records of *Subscription to the Confession of Faith and the Formula From 24 February 1697 to 23 April 1793*[23] reveals nothing but unqualified subscription by all those in the register.

McCrie's only written source for stating so categorically that Gillespie qualified his subscription was Struthers' *History of the Relief Church*. An examination of Struthers[24] shows that he gives no reference to the Presbytery minutes, but relies on the 'personal reminiscence'[25] of the Rev. Dr John Erskine, who wrote a memoir of Gillespie in 1774. In the memoir Erskine wrote:

> Before he (Gillespie) was admitted (to Carnock) he subscribed the Confession of Faith, and Formula, with a single explanation respecting the power of the civil magistrate.[26]

Struthers' comment that 'considering the intimacy which

---

22. *Ibid.*, p. 360.

23. *Subscription to the Confession of Faith and Formula. From February 1697 to 23 April 1793* (n.d.).

24. Struthers, *op. cit.*, pp. 8-9.

25. *Ibid.*, p. 9.

26. *Ibid.* Other sources and authorities make the same assertion. The *Fasti Ecclesiae Scoticanae* recounts that 'When signing the "Confession of Faith" he (Gillespie) took exception to Chapter xxiii, in which are defined the powers of the civil magistrate.' V, 'Synods of Fife, and of Angus and Mearns' (Edinburgh, 1925), p. 10.

Nathaniel Morren, in his *Annals of the General Assembly of the Church of Scotland, from the Final Secession in 1739 to the Origin of the Relief in 1752*, maintained that 'It is... rather a remarkable circumstance, and not generally known, that when he (Gillespie) signed the "Formula" and "Confession of Faith" at his admission at Carnock, it was with an explanation or reservation respecting "The power of the civil magistrate"' (I, Edinburgh, 1837, p. 276). Morren says in a footnote that his authority for the above statement was the 'Case for the Donors of his Church laid before the Assembly of 1774' (*Annals*, p. 276). Unfortunately, an extensive search of the Scottish Records Office failed to bring the 'Case for the Donors' to light. A. T. Innes also maintains that Gillespie signed with an 'explanation or modification' ( *Law of Creeds in Scotland*, 2nd ed.; Edinburgh, 1902, p. 213).

subsisted between them, he (Erskine) could not be mistaken',[27] places McCrie's assertions in their proper light! What we are left with is a 'personal intimacy' and not documented proof, to substantiate McCrie's contention that ministers were allowed a certain degree of laxity in subscribing the Confession. It is undeniable that Gillespie did hold views on the relation of the civil magistrate to the Church which seemed to clash with the Confession's teaching. Struthers gives ample evidence of this,[28] and few would deny that he had proved his case. However, the point at issue is McCrie's assertion that the *Presbytery*, an official church court, allowed Gillespie to qualify his subscription. This cannot be sustained. The complete lack of documentary evidence compelled Struthers to argue that the Presbytery allowed Gillespie to make a *verbal* qualification.[29] This conjecture virtually accuses the Presbytery of wearing two hats – allowing reserve and qualification in private, while maintaining a front of unqualified orthodoxy in public. As far as the documentary evidence goes, however, there is no evidence whatsoever that Gillespie was allowed to qualify his subscription to the Confession. Struthers' conclusion that ministers during this period were 'not understood to be bound by every iota which the Confession contained',[30] compounds his failure to check the requisite Presbyterial records, his only example being Wardlaw's supposed explanation regarding the extent of the atonement when admitted minister of Dunfermline in 1718!

The fact that ministers were required to subscribe the Confession without reserve or qualification did not mean that everyone agreed with all of the Confession's teachings. The rise of Moderatism, and the Church of Scotland's unwillingness to prosecute ministers who blatantly disregarded some of the Confession's fundamental doctrines, was an indication that 'orthodoxy' was something of an ambivalent concept to some in the Church.

---

27. Struthers, *op. cit.*, p. 9.
28. *Ibid.*
29. *Ibid.*, p. 10.
30. *Ibid.*

However, at the time of the Secession of 1733, there is no written evidence to suggest that ministers were allowed any laxity when subscribing the Confession of Faith.

## 2. The Secession Formula of 1737[31]

The Secession of 1733 was precipitated by the action of the General Assembly of the Church of Scotland in regard to a proposal which came before them at their meeting in May 1731. An overture was presented concerning the method of planting vacant churches. This overture sought to restrict the election of ministers to local heritors and the elders of the congregation, a proposal which rendered the Church's protests against the 1712 Patronage Act meaningless.[32] The overture was resisted by Ebenezer Erskine of Stirling. Erskine spoke out against the measure which the Assembly had approved.

> I can find no warrant from the word of God to confer the spiritual privileges of His house upon the rich beyond the poor; whereas by this Act, the man with the gold ring and gay clothing is preferred unto the man with the vile raiment and poor attire.[33]

Erskine was rebuked by his Synod for his outspoken criticism of the Assembly, and was later suspended by the General Assembly from his ministerial duties. The situation was brought to a crisis when Erskine and three others – William Wilson, Alexander Moncrieff, and James Fisher – met at Gairney Bridge near Kinross in December 1733, and constituted themselves into the Associate Presbytery.[34]

---

31. Contained in A. Gib, *The Present Truth: A Display of the Secession Testimony*, I (Edinburgh, 1774), pp. ixff.

Cf. *Proceedings of the United Presbyterian Synod*, VI (Glasgow, 1880), Report XXIII, Appendix A, pp. 899ff.

32. *Proceedings of the United Presbyterian Synod*, *op. cit.*, p. 891. A helpful summary of the controversy is found in W. Ferguson, *Scotland 1689 to the Present* (Edinburgh and London, 1968), pp. 121ff.

33. *The whole Works of the late Ebenezer Erskine*, ed. by James Fisher, I, p. 504, quoted by Ferguson, *op. cit.*, p. 123.

34. Gib, *op. cit.,* pp. 25-35.

Although reconciliation was attempted over the next few years, it became clear that the secession of Erskine, Wilson, Moncrieff, and Fisher was to be final and irrevocable. In 1737, the new denomination adopted a Formula of Questions to be put to those requesting licence as ministers of the Associate Presbytery. The Formula adopted indicated that the Associate Presbytery in no way thought of itself departing from the strict adherence to the Confession of Faith required by the Act of 1711.

Question 2 of the Formula, which all ministers, probationers, and elders had to sign, retained the distinctive wording of the 1711 Act.

> Do you sincerely own and believe the whole doctrine contained in the Confession of Faith…And do you acknowledge the same Confession as the Confession of your faith…?[35]

The only changes of any significance in the Formula from the model one of 1711 were the removal of the clause in the 1711 Act 'ratified by law in the year 1690', and the inserting into Question 2 of the requirement to 'own and believe…the whole doctrine contained in the Larger and Shorter Catechisms…'[36]

In the light of the early Seceders' commitment to the Standards of the Church of Scotland, Thomas McCrie considered that:

> Those ministers who left the communion of the established church…entertained no new or peculiar principles, different from those which were contained in the Standards of the Church of Scotland. With these they were fully satisfied…they composed no new standards… [They] approved of, adopted, and witnessed for them…as they had been received and owned by the reformed church in this land.[37]

---

35. *The Formula of Questions originally framed and settled by the Associate Presbytery*, Gib, *op. cit.*, p. ix.

36. *Ibid.*

37. T. McCrie, *Statement of the Difference Between the Profession of the Reformed Church of Scotland as Adopted by the Seceders, and the Profession Contained in the New Testimony and Other Acts* (Edinburgh, 1871 edition), p. 40.

## 3. The Dawning of a New Era[38]

The General Associate Synod[39] (Anti-burgher) entered the 1790s reviewing its relation to Chapter XXIII of the Confession of Faith. The Formula required that assent be given to the 'whole doctrine' of the Confession, and some in the Synod were beginning to question how possible such an assent was, given the terms of the controversial chapter.[40] The matter was

---

38. J. McKerrow, *History of the Secession Church*, II (Edinburgh, 1839), pp. 42-48, 301-328; *Proceedings of the United Presbyterian Synod, op. cit.*, p. 905.

39. The unity of the Secession Church was broken in 1747 by a dispute as to whether the Seceders should swear a certain clause in the oath taken by the free burgesses of a few Scottish towns. Due to the influence of Adam Gib, those who opposed the taking of the Burgess Oath (the Anit-Burghers) excommunicated their brethren who refused to take disciplinary measures over the matter (Burghers).

40. The most objectionable section of the controversial chapter was the third section: 'The civil magistrate... hath authority, and it is his duty, to take order, that unity and peace be preserved in the church, that the truth of God be kept pure and entire, that all blasphemies and heresies be suppressed, all corruptions and abuses in worship and discipline prevented or reformed...' ( *The Subordinate Standards and Other Authoritative Documents of the Free Church of Scotland*, Edinburgh, 1955, p. 36).

The role of the civil magistrate in relation to the Church as defined in the Westminster Confession of Faith has long been a matter for dispute. While many have argued that the sections in Chapters xx, xxiii, xxxi referring to the civil magistrate give him a degree of authority in the governing of the Church, and the power to 'use the sword' to suppress error, others have argued that such a view misinterprets the Confession's meaning.

James Bannerman asked the question: 'Is it true that the Westminster Confession of Faith arms the civil magistrate with a power to destroy the liberty of Christ's Church, giving to the state a proper jurisdiction in spiritual things?', and to his question he gave an unequivocal answer: 'The uniform and undeniable doctrine of the Confession of Faith...is a denial of the proper jurisdiction of the civil magistrate in spiritual and ecclesiastical matters' (*The Church of Christ*, I [first published 1869; references here to the Mack, ed., New Jersey, 1960], pp. 173, 176).

The whole chapter in Bannerman entitled 'The Doctrine of the Westminster Confession on Church and State' (pp. 171-185) is worthy of careful examination. He represents the views of the conservative wing of the Free Church during the troubled years of the 1860s on this subject. Cf. R. Shaw, *The Reformed Faith* (Inverness, 1974), pp. xx-xxiii.

The importance, however, of the Secession Churches' attitude to the role of the civil magistrate lies in what *they understood* the Confession to teach on this matter. It is also worth noting that the Secession Churches' 'qualification' of the Confession's teaching on the civil magistrate was not the first of its kind within Presbyterianism. In 1729, the Westminster Confession of Faith and the Larger and Shorter Catechisms

brought to a head by the refusal of two licentiates (Thomas McCrie was one) in 1796 to submit to ordination unless they were allowed to qualify their assent to the second question of the Formula.[41] The matter was brought before the Synod in May 1796, and a committee appointed to consider what could be done. The result was a declaration by the Synod to the effect that notwithstanding the Confession's teaching in Chapter XX section 4, and in Chapter XXIII,[43]

> … they approve of no other means of bringing men into the Church, or retaining them in it, than such as are spiritual… persuasion not force, the power of the gospel not the sword of the civil magistrate…[44]

This 'declaratory legislation' was constructed to enable those with scruples respecting the Confession's teaching on the role of the civil magistrate to sign the Formula. (McCrie subsequently changed his views, and seceded from the denomination.)

While this was taking place in the General Associate Synod, the Associate Synod (Burgher) was involved in a similar, though more acrimonious, debate. The outcome of the debate was the Synod's acceptance of a Preamble in 1797 which clearly qualified

---

were adopted by the original Synod in North America as its Confession of Faith. In the original Adopting Act, the Synod declared that it did not receive the Confession's views on the civil magistrate '… in any sense as to suppose the civil magistrate hath a controlling power over synods with respect to their ministerial authority; or power to persecute any for their religion…' (Quoted in A. A. Hodge, *Confession of Faith* [first published 1869, reference here is to the Banner of Truth, ed., London, 1958], p. 21). In 1787, the Synod altered the Confession by removing the offending clauses in Chapters xx, xxiii, xxxi. Cf. P. Schaff, *Creeds of Christendom*, III (New York, 1878), pp. 645, 653, 669.

41. McKerrow, *op. cit.*, p. 45.

42. *Acts and Proceedings of the General Associate Synod*, IV, 1795–1820 (Edinburgh?, n.d.), pp. 40ff.

43. In an age when 'liberty' was the watchword, and battle-cry, of many diverse movements, it is striking to find that the ecclesiastical scene in Scotland did not escape the influence of this phenomenon.

44. McKerrow, *op. cit.*, p. 46; *Acts and Proceedings of the General Associate Synod, op. cit.*, pp. 42-43.

the denomination's commitment to its Subordinate Standard. The Preamble declared:

> Whereas some parts of the Standard-books of this Synod have been interpreted as favouring compulsory measures in religion, the Synod hereby declares, That they do not require an approbation of any such principle from any candidate for license or ordination...[45]

The use of a Preamble to qualify the Church's understanding of the Confession's teaching on the role of the civil magistrate in relation to church affairs was devised only after a large number of petitions from sessions and congregations reached the Synod objecting to any alteration in the Church's historic relation to the Westminster Standards.[46]

McKerrow in his *History of the Secession* makes the observation that the terms of the Preamble reflected in substance part of the 1778 *Re-exhibition of the Testimony*.[47] The *Testimony* contained the following declaration:

> ... it must be acknowledged, that the enforcing of religious duties with civil penalties; and, in too many instances, blending the affairs of church and state with one another, is totally inconsistent with the spiritual nature of Christ's kingdom.[48]

In effect, the 1797 Preamble was a compromise measure. It was designed to alleviate the scruples of those who baulked at the Confession's teaching on the supposedly intolerant duties of the civil magistrate, and to pacify those who were against any

---

45. *Minutes of the Associate Synod, September 1787 to April 1806*, V (Edinburgh?, n.d.), p. 2245. Cf. McKerrow, *op. cit.*, p. 319.

46. McKerrow, *op. cit.*, p. 316; J. Gibson, *Free Churchism V Broad Churchism* (Edinburgh and Glasgow, 1870), p. 22. Of the forty-one petitions received by the Synod, twenty-seven were against any alteration in the Formula; nine were in favour of altering Question 2 of the Formula; and five were in favour of delaying any proposals for change.

47. *Re-Exhibition of the Testimony* (Glasgow, 1779), p. 321.

48. *Ibid.*, pp. 90-91.

tampering with the Formula itself. The measure led to a great deal of turmoil within the Church, but it was retained.

## 4. Thomas McCrie and the 1804 'Narrative and Testimony'

The relation of the Secession Churches to the Confession of Faith was further a cause for dispute at the turn of the nineteenth century. The publication of Thomas McCrie's *Statement of the Difference between the Profession of the Reformed Church of Scotland as adopted by the Seceders, and the Profession contained in the New Testimony and Other Acts, Lately adopted by the General Associate Synod…,*[49] in 1807, reflected his concern over certain new trends of thought which he believed were undermining the Church's historic relation to the Reformed faith.[50]

On May 1, 1804, the Synod approved the revision of their Testimony by adopting the following motion:

> The Synod agree to adopt the Introduction, Narrative, and Testimony, as now corrected and enlarged, as the term of admission for those who shall apply for joining in communion with us…[51]

The point at issue for McCrie was the alteration this made to the Church's Formula. Prior to 1804, the General Associate Synod required its ministers to subscribe the Formula's requirements without recourse to any qualifying factors (except, of course, for the declaration of 1796 regarding the civil magistrate). In that year, however, the Synod somewhat revised Question 2 of the Formula, approving the Westminster Confession of Faith and Larger and Shorter Catechisms only in so far as they were 'agreeable to the declaration in the Narrative and Testimony enacted by the General Associate Synod in the year 1804…'[52]

---

49. T. McCrie, *Statement, op. cit.*

50. *Ibid.*, pp. 40ff.

51. *Acts and Proceedings of the General Associate Synod, op. cit.*, p. 236 (1st May 1804). Also see McKerrow, *op. cit.*, pp. 121-122.

52. *Narrative and Testimony, agreed upon and enacted by the General Associate Synod* (Edinburgh, 1804), p. 249.

McCrie's main objection to the Synod's new *Narrative and Testimony* centred upon a statement found in the introduction:

> The foundation upon which we rest the whole of our Ecclesiastical Constitution is the testimony of God in his word... We acknowledge (the years 1638 to 1650) to have been a period of eminent ecclesiastical purity; but we call no man nor church Master. One is our Master, even Christ; and his word is our only un-erring rule...[53]

While McCrie did not in any way object to the sentiment of the above statement, he did object to what he considered the usurping of the time-honoured place given to the Confession in the Secession. He considered that the new *Testimony* by-passed the Church's theological heritage, establishing a precedent by examining doctrines in the light of Holy Scripture without recourse to the Church's doctrinal Standards.[54]

The point at issue is not to assess how right, or how wrong, the Synod was in adopting such an approach. Rather, it is to underline the fact that it was creating a precedent in so doing. McKerrow, while praising the Synod for adopting the new procedure in revising its *Narrative and Testimony*,[55] admits that it was creating a precedent by departing from the first *Testimony* of the Original Seceders.[56] Considering that McCrie himself had been partly responsible for the Synod qualifying its adherence to the Confession's teaching on the civil magistrate in 1796, it is quite ironic that a mere eight years later he renounced his former position and accused the Synod of changing the Confession's historic place in the life of the Church.

The General Associate Synod's willingness to examine critically the Westminster Standards is best seen in the following extract from the *Narrative and Testimony*:

---

53. *Ibid.*, p. 9 of Introduction.
54. T. McCrie, *Statement, op. cit.*, pp. 47-48.
55. McKerrow, *op. cit.*, p. 151.
56. *Ibid.*

That as no human composure, however excellent and well expressed, can be supposed to contain a full and comprehensive view of divine truth; so by this adherence (to the Westminster Confession of Faith), we are not precluded from embracing, upon due consideration, any further light which may afterward arise from the word of God, about any article of divine truth.[57]

Such a statement at first sight might seem fairly innocuous, as it merely elaborates the Confession's own teaching.[58] However, the Confession had stood as a well-nigh impregnable bulwark of orthodox theology and church polity since the 1690s, and the Synod's refusal to acknowledge it as a settled, unimpeachable reality in the life of the Church indicated, at least, a certain recasting of thought regarding the status of the Confession of Faith.[59] For one Church at least, the Confession of Faith was no longer considered the 'sacred cow' of orthodox Presbyterian theology.[60]

Due to these developments within the Secession, by the early years of the nineteenth century the Westminster Confession of Faith was no longer accepted *simpliciter* as their Subordinate Standard of Faith.[61] The nature of the change, however, in no way loosened the Secession's commitment to the Calvinistic theology of the Confession. Nowhere do we find the Secession

---

57. *Narrative and Testimony*, *op. cit.*, p. 13 of Introduction; cf, pp. 195-198. See also McKerrow, *op. cit.*, p. 125; A. C. Cheyne, 'The Westminster Standards: A Century of Re-appraisal', *Scottish Church History Society Records*, XIV (1963), p. 204.

58. 'All synods or councils since the apostles' times, whether general or particular, may err, and many have erred; therefore they are not to be made the rule of faith or practice…' (*Subordinate Standards*, *op. cit.*, Chapter xxxi, section iv, p. 46).

59. Cheyne, *op. cit.*, p. 204.

60. This attitude was seen in the Atonement Controversy in the 1840s. While the vast majority of the United Secession Church examined the teachings of professors Brown and Balmer in the light of Scripture first, and the Confession second, a small minority tenaciously clung to the Confession as the sole arbiter in theological debate.

61. The adoption of a new Testimony by the General Associate Synod led to another split in Scottish Presbyterianism. McCrie and Professor Bruce were responsible for forming a Constitutional Presbytery which sought to stand by the historic attachment of the Secession to the Confession of Faith. Cf. J. Macleod, *Scottish Theology* (Edinburgh, 1974), p. 236.

Churches granting any degree of liberty to those who could not *personally* own the doctrine of the Standards. Nonetheless, the slow process of erosion had begun – although on articles which were of relatively minor importance.[62] The initial breach had been made, and with gathering momentum the Standards were subjected to further, more detailed, and critical scrutiny.

## 5. The Union of the Secession in 1820

The union of 1820 brought together the major branches of the Secession excluding the Relief Church. The second article of the Basis of Union[63] practically canonised the Secession's criticism of the Confession's teaching on the civil magistrate, and established as a point of principle the new Church's attitude towards that problem issue. The Article maintained that:

> …we do not approve or require an approbation of any thing in those books (the Subordinate Standards) which teaches, or may be thought to teach, compulsory or persecuting and intolerant principles of religion.[64]

The chief significance of the Basis of Union lies, however, in other areas. In the second article of the Basis of Union, the United Secession Church introduced a new form of language to characterise its relation to the Westminster Confession. The article stated:

> We retain the Westminster Confession of Faith, with the Larger and Shorter Catechisms, as the confession of our faith, expressive of the sense in which we understand the Holy Scriptures…[65]

---

62. Cheyne, *op. cit.*, p. 203.
63. *Minutes of the United Associate Synod*, I, 1820-1836 (Glasgow, n.d.), pp. 1-2. McKerrow, *op cit.*, p. 402.
64. *Minutes of the United Associate Synod*, I, *op. cit.*, p. 1; McKerrow, *op. cit.*, p. 403.
65. *Minutes of the United Associate Synod*, I, *op. cit.*, p. 1. Agreed September 13, 1820.

The form of language used in the second article of the Basis of Union was incorporated into the new *Formula for the Ordination of Ministers.* Question 2 of the Formula asked:

> Do you acknowledge the Westminster Confession of Faith, with the Larger and Shorter Catechisms, as the confession of your faith, expressive of the sense in which you understand the Scriptures…?[66]

The significant phrase in each case is 'expressive of the sense'. Up until this point in time there had been little dubiety regarding the individual's commitment to the Confession, as he was required to subscribe its whole doctrine as the confession of his faith – except, of course, for the article on the civil magistrate. The form of language used in the new Formula introduced, however, a certain measure of ambiguity into the situation. The use of the new phraseology might well have passed without much discussion but for an incident which focused attention upon the Church's relation to the Confession of Faith.

During the 1820 Synod, three ministers – Brown, Balmer, and Harper (all future professors in the United Secession Church), along with some others – presented a document in which they criticised the nature of the Church's relation to the Confession. The statement read:

> The undersigned regret that they cannot express an unqualified approbation of the formula adopted by the United Synods of the Secession Church – and crave that it be marked in the records of the Synod – that without calling in question any doctrine contained in our subordinate standards, and even admitting that they do not contain a particle of error, they are yet so multifarious and extensive, that in their opinion, it must be very difficult for ministers, and still more for licentiates and elders to examine every proposition in these standards with such care, as to be qualified to give a rational assent to it with the solemnity of an oath. Besides, it will be universally admitted

---

66. *Ibid.*, pp. 23-24.

> that these standards contain some things, the knowledge and belief of which are not essential as qualifications for office in the Church of Christ.[67]

It was precisely this statement, allied to the 'novel' language used in the Formula, which precipitated yet another schism within the ranks of the Secession. Seven ministers and five elders seceded from the new united Church in 1821, unhappy with the 'new' theological emphases they believed to be displayed in the Basis of Union.[68] This small rump joined with the remnant of the Old Light Anti-Burghers, the new body calling itself the Associate Synod of Original Seceders.[69] It is difficult to assess how credible were the claims of those who saw the new Formula as a significant departure from the universally binding Formulae of past generations. Little has been written on this specific point apart from brief comments in the shorter writings of two very different commentators. From a more liberal perspective, George Pearson considered that the phrase 'expressive of the sense' put the Confession in its proper and 'inferior' place in the life of the Church. In his understanding, the phrase indicated that the minister was not obliged to believe the 'whole doctrine' of the Confession, but only regard it as 'an exhibition of the sense in which the Scriptures are to be understood'.[70] From a decidedly more conservative perspective, James Gibson, a prominent figure during the union controversy in the Free Church in the 1860s, concurred with Pearson's interpretation. However justified linguistically, he argued that theologically, the individual was no longer bound to subscribe the Confession in its entirety, but only as 'expressive' of his own sense of Scripture.[71]

---

67. *Ibid.*, p. 25-26. A paper given to the Synod on September 14, 1820, but dated September 13.

68. C. G. McCrie, *The Church of Scotland: Her Divisions and Reunions* (Edinburgh, 1901), p. 154.

69. *Ibid.*, p. 155.

70. G. Pearson, *The Principles of the United Presbyterian Church, wherein do they differ from other Presbyterian Churches?* (Glasgow, 1877), p. 2. A paper originally given at the Glasgow Association of United Presbyterian elders, January 18, 1877.

While it is open to doubt whether the offending phrase is linguistically chargeable with liberalising the terms of the Formula, the very fact that the phrase was considered ambiguous, to say the least, by some, and was prominent at a time when young ministers were openly criticising the *scope* of the Church's attachment to the Confession, gave it a notoriety that kindled the fires of theological debate. The chief significance of the whole controversy lies perhaps in the complete absence of criticism from the Synod regarding the document submitted by Brown, Balmer, and Harper. At least in this, something of a precedent had been set: ministers of a major Scottish Presbyterian Church had expressed publicly reservation over the nature of its attachment to the Confession of Faith, and the Synod concurred with their criticism.

### 6. The Relief Church and the Westminster Confession of Faith

Before advancing to the 1847 union of the Secession and the Relief, it will be necessary to outline the relation that existed between the Relief Church and the Westminster Confession of Faith. From its inception[72] the Relief Church held to a strict and total commitment to the 'whole doctrine' of the Confession. The measure of the Church's attachment to the Confession was illustrated in the Synod's prosecution of one of its members, the Rev. James Smith of Dunfermline.[73]

In 1789, Smith published two pamphlets, *An Essay on Confessing the Truth* and *A Discourse on the Necessity, Nature, and Design, of Christ's Sufferings*,[74] aimed at refuting some of the teaching of a Church of Scotland minister, the Rev. Dr. William McGill of Ayr.[75] In so doing, Smith commented that systems of theology

---

71. Gibson, *op. cit.*, pp. 22-23.

72. The Relief Church owed its origin to a dispute over the exercise of patronage in the parish of Inverkeithing in 1752.

73. See the whole section in Struthers, *op. cit.*, pp. 352-367.

74. J. Smith, *An Essay on Confessing the Truth* (Edinburgh, 1789); *A Discourse on the Necessity, Nature, and Design, of Christ's Sufferings* (Edinburgh, 1789).

75. McGill published in 1786 a treatise which reflected a Socinian interpretation of the atonement: *A Practical Essay on the Death of Christ* (Edinburgh, 1786). The

and creeds were too highly revered, and seemed also to stray into a Socinian interpretation of the atonement. The Relief Synod initiated a process of heresy against Smith, but before discipline could be applied he deserted to the established Church.[76] The reaction of the Synod to Smith's declared rejection of parts of the Confession, and his proposal to subscribe it only in so far as it agreed with Scripture, was swift and unequivocal. To prevent heretics gaining 'access to the denomination under the guise of subscribing the Confession of Faith, *so far as* it agrees with the Scripture',[77] the Synod passed the following overture:

> That the minister who presides in the Work of Ordination, or admission of any minister (not formerly ordained by any of the Presbyteries subject to this Synod) shall in the questions to be put to the person to be ordained or thus admitted keep precisely by the Act of Assembly relative to that affair and, in particular, shall not ask, 'Do you agree to the Confession of Faith, *in so far as agreeable to the Word of God*', but put the question in the identical words enjoined by the Assembly...[78]

In the light of the Synod's declaration as recorded in the *Minutes*, Struthers' wrote that:

> The meaning of this injunction was, that every person to be ordained should receive the Westminster Confession, *as the confession of his* faith. They wished it to be made a test of orthodoxy...[79]

---

Associate Synod published a pamphlet in 1788 warning against the Socinianism in McGill's treatise: *A Warning against Socinianism* (Falkirk, 1788). For an overview of the controversy, see A. McNair, *Scot's Theology in the Eighteenth Century* (London, 1928), pp. 10ff. The section in McNair dealing with the controversy reads at times more like an *apologia* for McGill and his views than sober history. In 1789, McGill was forced to apologise to the Synod of Glasgow and Ayr for his views.

76. *Minutes of the Relief Synod 1733-1829,* I (n.d.), p. 98. The Synod's case against Smith is given in good detail, pp. 91ff.

77. *Ibid.*

78. *Ibid.* The Synod unanimously adopted the overture. It is a little ambiguous, but the reference in the overture to the 'Act of Assembly' is most probably the regulative Act of 1711.

79. Struthers, *op. cit.*, p. 367.

It is undeniable that in passing such an overture, the Relief Church was expressing publicly a committed and unreserved attachment to the Confession of Faith.[80] It is difficult, therefore, to agree with John Macleod when he wrote of the Relief Church as 'always' professing itself less strict on doctrinal issues than the other branches of the Secession.[81] An examination of the *Minutes* of the Relief Synod from 1773 gives no indication that it treated doctrinal matters less strictly than the other Secession Churches.

Although formed in 1761, it was not until 1823, when the Church founded its own theological hall, that a Formula of Questions was drawn up to be put to licentiates and ministers at ordination.[82] Question 2 of the Formula asked:

> Do you own, and will you adhere to the doctrine of the Westminster Confession of Faith as founded on and consistent with the Word of God, except in so far as said Confession recognises the power of the civil magistrate to interfere in religious concerns?[83]

Two points should be noted here. First, the Relief explicitly considers the Confession to teach intolerant and persecuting principles as valid means to uphold true religion. Its disavowal of such principles in its Formula brought it into line with the other branches of the Secession. Secondly, the Formula was so constructed as to allow ministers a certain degree of laxity in subscription. With this in mind, Struthers argued that the new laxity reflected the liberality of spirit which had characterised the Relief during its existence. He maintained that

> The adoption of the stringent mode prescribed in later times by the Church of Scotland (the Act of 1711), and which was

---

80. This would mean that the Relief Church used the strictest Formula of subscription available to it.

81. Macleod, *op. cit.,* p. 244.

82. C.G. McCrie, *Confessions, op. cit.*, p. 238; Struthers, *op. cit.*, pp. 436-438.

83. Struthers, *op. cit.*, p. 438. There is no reference in the Minutes of the Relief Synod to the devising of a new Formula.

also enacted by the Relief Synod at the time of the McGill and
Smith heresies, was merely temporary, and was abrogated a few
years thereafter.[84]

However, Struthers' analysis reflects more wishful thinking, one
would suspect, than historical or theological fact. In the first
place, there is no evidence to suggest that the Synod's attitude
to Confessional laxity in the 1790s, and particularly its adopting
of a stringent mode to combat possible laxity, was merely an
act uncharacteristic of its 'normal', more liberal, attitude to the
Confession, as Struthers seems to suggest. In fact, the reverse is
the case, as the 1790 overture makes only too clear. The Synod's
commitment was to the verbal formulation of the 1711 Act of
Assembly!

In the second place, Struthers' claim that the Relief Church
considered the 1790 overture a 'temporary' expedient that was
'abrogated a few years thereafter', does not stand. There is no
evidence to suggest that the legislation was only a temporary
expedient, as a careful examination of the *Minutes* makes clear.
The Relief Church took no action towards changing its position
on subscription until nearly thirty-five years after the Smith case,
years during which the other branches of the Secession were
modifying their links with the Confession.

It is clear that the 1823 Formula marks a distinct change in
the Relief Church's attachment to the model Formula of 1711.
The new Formula patently allowed a degree of laxity hitherto
not enjoyed *de jure* in the Church. The very construction of the
Formula seemed fitted for those who baulked at subscribing
and owning the 'whole doctrine of the Confession', and
acknowledging it as the confession of *their own faith*.

## 7. The Union of 1847

The union of the United Secession Church and the Relief
Church in 1847 led to the drafting of a Basis of Union,[85] and the

---

84. *Ibid.*, p. 437.

drafting of a new Formula for ordination. The second article of the Basis and the second question of the revised Formula revealed a definite shift and readjustment in the Secession Church's relation to the Westminster Confession of Faith. C. G. McCrie has, however, maintained that:

> When the … Union of 1847 took place the article in the Basis on Union and the question in the Formula bearing upon the Westminster Standards were in substantial agreement with those of 1820.[86]

Such a judgment fails, however, to accommodate the facts. While it is true to say that there is a measure of agreement between the 1820 and 1847 documents, there is certainly no 'substantial agreement' as McCrie claimed. Article 2 of the Basis of Union confirmed that:

> …the Westminster Confession of Faith, and the Larger and Shorter Catechisms, are the confession and catechism of this Church, and contain the authorised exhibition of the sense in which we understand the Holy Scriptures,[87]

but removed the important phrase – 'and are the confession of our faith'.[88] A similar readjustment appeared in the second question of the revised Formula. We have seen that the 1820 Formula required candidates to acknowledge the Westminster Standards as the confession of *their* faith. In the revised Formula of 1847, however, candidates were no longer required to identify the Standards with their own personal confession of faith. They were asked:

---

85. *Proceedings of the Synod of the United Presbyterian Church 1847-1856* (Edinburgh, 1856), pp. 9-10, 64.

86. C. G. McCrie, *Confessions, op. cit.*, p. 240.

87. *Proceedings of the Synod of the United Presbyterian Church 1847-1856, op. cit.*, p. 64.

88. *Ibid.* p. 9.

> Do you acknowledge the Westminster Confession of Faith,
> and the Larger and Shorter Catechisms as an exhibition of the
> sense in which you understand the Holy Scriptures...?[89]

To suggest then, as McCrie does, that the Basis and Formula
of 1847 were substantially the same as the Basis and Formula
of 1820, is either to seek continuity where there is none, or to
fly in the face of historical fact. This same point was made in
the *Watchword Magazine* of January 1870.[90] After comparing the
United Presbyterian Church Formula of 1847 with that of the
Free Church of 1846, the magazine concluded that the 1847
Formula allowed a minister for the first time in the history
of the Secession the freedom not to own the Westminster
Confession as the confession of *his* faith.[91] A. T. Innes was of
the opinion that the United Presbyterian Church 'has wholly
abolished the Formula of Subscription...and has substituted...
the simple statement, that the Confession and Catechisms are
"an exhibition of the sense in which I understand the Holy
Scriptures"'.[92] The central element of the 1711 Formula had
finally been eroded. It was this very change which led the more
liberally minded George Pearson, as we have already noted, to
argue that his Church no longer held the Westminster Standards
on the same high level as the other Presbyterian Churches in
Scotland.

The Articles and Formula of 1847 did not conclude the new
Church's desire to provide its ministers with some measure of
laxity regarding their public and ecclesiastical attachment to
the Westminster Standards. The final step was not taken until
1879 when the United Presbyterian Church passed declaratory

---

89. *Ibid.*, p. 64.

90. The *Watchword* was the organ of the anti-union party in the Free Church
during the union talks of the 1860s and early 1870s between that Church and the
United Presbyterian Church.

91. *The Watchword Magazine*, IV (Edinburgh, Glasgow, London, 1870), pp. 444-
447.

92. Innes, *op. cit.* (1st ed., 1867), pp. 438-439.

legislation aimed at allowing its ministers personal liberty of opinion on matters which did not enter the 'substance of the faith'.

The 1840s were seminal years in other respects than witnessing the Church's changing attitude to its Subordinate Standards. From 1841 until 1845, the United Secession Church was embroiled in a theological controversy revolving around the extent of the atonement. In the Divinity Hall, two professors began to teach a scheme of doctrine which seemed to some to undermine the teaching of the Westminster Standards. As we will see, the Atonement Controversy afforded further evidence that the Secession was departing from its historic attachment to the Westminster Standards.

*1841*. Publication of Professor Brown's *Notes, Chiefly Historical* in the June issue of the US Church Magazine. James Morison suspended by Kilmarnock Presbytery. Morison appeals to the Synod, his appeal is dismissed and he is deposed from the ministry. Statement by the Synod on 'Doctrinal Errors Condemned By The United Secession Church'.

*1842*. Publication of Polhill's essay on the extent of the atonement, with a recommendatory preface by Professor Balmer. Marshall's *Death of Christ* published. A growing awareness in the Church of divergence of views over the extent of the atonement.

*1843*. Overtures at the Synod from the Presbytery of Paisley and Greenock, seeking clarification of the Church's stance on the atonement. Statement by Brown and Balmer to clarify their position. Committee considered the problem one of misunderstanding over 'ambiguous terms'. Synod advised that the phrases 'limited' and 'universal' atonement should not be used.

*1844*. Publication of Marshall's *Catholic Doctrine of Redemption* ... Brown and Balmer complain to Synod of defamatory remarks in the Appendix. Marshall agrees to suppress the Appendix, but is later accused of not doing so. Printing and publication of the professors' *Statements*.

*1845*. Marshall publishes *Remarks on the Statements of the Two Professors*. May Synod refuse to hear forty-seven Memorials on strife in the Church. Angry debates, and a large number dissent from the Synod's judgment. Marshall publicly censured by the Synod for his *Remarks*. Marshall 'forced' to take out a suit of Libel against Professor Brown. Five main charges to the Libel (signed by Marshall and Hay of Kinross). Brown exonerated on all counts. Long dispute over the supposed unconstitutional action of the Synod in refusing to examine the 'Relevancy' of the Libel as in normal procedure. Significant number of dissents over Brown's acquittal. Only four (?) left the Church, although Marshall refused to enter the union of 1847.

# 3

# The Atonement Controversy
# (1841–1845)

The decision of the General Associate Synod (Anti-Burgher) to qualify its commitment to the Westminster Confession of Faith's teaching on the role of the civil magistrate, and the decision of the Associate Synod (Burgher) to follow suit, involved, as we have seen, the first significant change in the attachment of Scottish Presbyterianism to the Westminster Standards. At a time when the Westminster Confession of Faith was considered by many as an unalterable rule and symbol of theological orthodoxy, the willingness of the Secession to modify its commitment to even *one* of the supposed teachings of its Subordinate Standard of Faith placed it in the forefront of theological change in the Scottish Church.

It was perhaps then to be expected that the Church which owed its existence to the Marrow Controversy in the early eighteenth century should be involved in the first *major* controversy in nineteenth-century Scotland over the Westminster Confession's teaching on the extent of Christ's atonement. (The 'Row Heresy' was not so much a 'controversy' in 1830 as a Church's near unanimous condemnation of teaching that contradicted that of its Subordinate Standard of Faith.)

Precisely what the Westminster Confession actually teaches on the extent of Christ's atonement has been a matter of debate over the past 350 years. While the language of the Confession, and in particular that of Chapter VIII, *Of Christ the Mediator*, appears absolutely to exclude an Amyraldian and a hypothetical universalist interpretation, it has been argued that the teaching of the Confession may not purposefully exclude such interpretations.[1] It is the contention of this chapter that the Westminster Confession's teaching on the extent of Christ's atonement clearly excludes a hypothetical universalist interpretation.

The Atonement Controversy in the United Secession Church occupied the years 1841 to 1845, although its genesis was to be found in the previous decade.[2] Although the Controversy excited a great deal of heated discussion and often acrimonious debate within the United Secession Church during those years, the ferment within the established Church due to its increasingly strained relations with the state ensured that the Controversy was carried on in a somewhat insular fashion.

The Controversy revolved around two schools of thought regarding the extent of Christ's atonement, both of which claimed to reflect the teaching of the Church's doctrinal Standards.

The antagonist in the Controversy was Dr Andrew Marshall of Kirkintilloch. He maintained that the teaching of the two senior professors in the Church, John Brown and Robert Balmer, was opposed to the clear teaching of the Westminster Standards. What Marshall objected to was the professors' teaching that Christ's atonement had a general and universal

---

1. Donald Macleod, *The Westminster Confession Today* in the Banner of Truth Magazine, February 1972, 18. See also the fine, if not wholly compelling, article by Lee Gattis: www.theologian.org.uk/gattisnet/documents/Shadesofopinionby LeeGattis.pdf.

2. Rev. A. Robertson, *History of the Atonement Controversy* (Edinburgh, 1846), is the only comprehensive history of the Controversy. It was written at the conclusion of the Controversy from a standpoint favourable to Brown and Balmer.

reference in addition to its particular and restricted reference. Marshall believed that the Westminster Confession of Faith related Christ's death only to the elect, and considered Brown and Balmer's emphasis upon a 'double-reference' to lie outside mainstream Westminster Calvinism.

Brown and Balmer's understanding of the extent of Christ's atonement has long been viewed as 'Amyraldian', holding to the theological emphases of Moises Amyraut, a seventeenth-century French (moderate) Calvinist. The recent study by Jonathan Moore, *English Hypothetical Universalism*,[3] provides us with a historically compelling analysis of the theological position held by men of similar convictions to those of Brown and Balmer. He shows clearly that while they (men like John Preston and John Davenant) were certainly hypothetical universalists they cannot rightly be called Amyraldians, as, not only did they precede Amyraut in their public teaching on redemption, but they also did not hold to the distinctive order of God's decrees that Amyraut was later to make central to his system, along with other modifications to Reformed doctrines.

What is unmistakably clear, however, is that Brown and Balmer believed that there was a divinely intended general or universal reference to Christ's atonement, teaching that went beyond the traditional Lombardian sufficiency-efficiency commonplace. They did not hold to the view that the death of Christ was solely and exclusively on behalf of God's elect.

## 1. The Course of the Controversy

The immediate cause of the Controversy was James Morison's suspension from ministerial duties by Kilmarnock Presbytery. Morison had been one of the more able students of Professor Brown in the Divinity Hall. When his Presbytery suspended him on eight counts of 'error taught and still maintained', some

---

3. Jonathan Moore, *English Hypothetical Universalism: John Preston and the Softening of Reformed Theology* (Eerdmans, Grand Rapids, 2007). I am grateful to Dr Moore for his help in appreciating the finer points of hypothetical universalism and its relationship to Amyraldianism.

began to trace the genesis of his teaching back to his time under Brown in the Divinity Hall. The main charge against Morison was the sixth in the list. This accused him of teaching that 'Election comes in the order of nature after the atonement'.[4] The implication of the Presbytery's charge was only too clear. To hold that atonement was prior to election in the order of God's decrees was to assert that Christ atoned for all men, election being a secondary consideration having reference to the application of the atonement and not to its provision.

Morison appealed to the 1841 Synod, which met in Glasgow against his suspension, but the appeal was dismissed.[5] The Synod appointed a committee to meet with Morison in order to discipline him, and, if possible, reclaim him to a right standing with the Church.[6] It was obvious, however, that Morison was in no mood to retract any of his firmly held convictions, or to equivocate in any way – he was too certain of his views and too honest to withhold them. The die was practically cast for his separation from the United Secession Church when he protested against the Synod's decision to suspend him from the ministry:

> Seeing the supreme court has given sentence against me, even my suspension from the Ministry, on most inadequate grounds, I hereby protest against the decision, and I shall hold myself at liberty to maintain and preach the same doctrines, as if no such decision had been come to.[7]

The Committee met with Morison for three hours with little success and adjourned to meet the following Monday.[8] However, in defiance of the Synod's suspension, Morison celebrated Communion in his Clerks Lane congregation in Kilmarnock

---

4. *Ibid.*, pp. 161-174. Cf. *Minutes of the United Associate Synod* (Glasgow, 1841), pp. 20-37; and W. Adamson, *Life of James Morison* (London, 1898), pp. 88ff. Morison was also accused of 'disingenuous conduct'.

5. *Minutes of the United Associate Synod* (1841), *op. cit.*, p. 20.

6. *Ibid.*, pp. 19, 27.

7. *Ibid.*, p. 28.

8. *Ibid.*, p. 36.

on the Sunday, thus virtually separating himself from the United Secession Church. When Morison failed to meet with the Committee on the Monday morning, the Synod officially removed him from its ministry.

The significance of Morison's deposition from the ministry and the circumstances surrounding it was twofold. First, although Professor Brown expressed his disapproval of some of Morison's views, he publicly dissented from the Synod's decision to reject Morison's appeal against his initial suspension from the ministry.[9] This action of Brown's was considered by Marshall and his supporters tantamount to giving a qualified approval to some of Morison's views. While Brown may very well be commended for his open support of his former student, it is possible that the Controversy might not have arisen had not Brown dissented from the Synod's decision. By so dissenting, the professor allowed the suspicions of his antagonism to gain a degree of credibility.[10] Secondly, it is significant that the main burden of Morison's father's dissent from the judgment of the Synod rested on his conviction that Holy Scripture was the only true judge in matters of doctrinal controversy. In recording his dissent he stated,

> … it is an unrighteous measure, sinfully disparaging to the holy oracles of God, and at once unscriptural and unprotestant in principle, to judge of the soundness of doctrine, or try alleged error *by any other standard* than the Holy Scriptures, and to acquit or condemn on the footing of any other authority than the Word of God alone.[11]

The point made by Mr Morison was one that Brown and Balmer used in their defence when their orthodoxy was challenged.

---

9. Brown's decision to dissent was only taken during the 15th Sederunt (Thursday), while Morison's appeal was overruled the previous Friday: *Ibid.*, p. 35.

10. It is interesting to note that the charges laid against Brown and Balmer by Marshall were very similar to those which resulted in Morison's deposition from the ministry.

11. *Minutes of the United Associate Synod* (1841), *op. cit.*, p. 29.

Whereas Marshall seemed to consider the Confession all but sacrosanct, and subscribed its teachings without any reservation, the two professors adopted a more lax position with regard to subscription, arguing the scripturalness of their views more than their compatibility with the Confession. (Although, it should be stressed that Brown and Balmer, on the whole, did attempt to show that their views were not in conflict with the teachings of the Confession.)[12]

The deposition of Morison brought the Controversy out into the open. During the following twelve months, 'battle-lines' for the conflict were all but drawn up with the publication of three works in particular: Brown's *Notes, Chiefly Historical, on the Question Respecting the Extent of the Reference of the Death of Christ*; Balmer's recommendatory preface to Edward Polhill's *Essay on the Extent of the Death of Christ*; and Marshall's *The Death of Christ*.[13]

While Marshall reiterated the 'orthodox' view of Christ's atonement as decreed for, purchased on behalf of, and applied to the elect alone, Balmer's preface and Polhill's essay emphasised that Christ's death had a universal as well as a particular reference. Balmer crystallised the 'general-reference theory' in the following way:

> ... so far as the requisitions of law and justice are required, he (Christ) has removed all the obstacles to the salvation of all; a principle which lies at the basis of the preaching probably of every evangelical minister in Scotland.[14]

---

12. J. Brown, *Hints to Divinity Students* (Edinburgh, 1841), pp. 29f.; J. Brown and R. Balmer, *Statements on Certain Doctrinal Points* (Edinburgh, Glasgow, Dublin, London, 1844), pp. 57-58.

13. This essay was taken from a larger work, *The Divine Will* (London, 1673). Edward Polhill was a professed hypothetical universalist in his understanding of the atonement.

J. Brown, *Notes, Chiefly Historical, on the Question Respecting the Extent of the Reference of the Death of Christ* (Edinburgh, 1841); the full text of this small work is also found in the *United Secession Magazine* for June 1841.

A. Marshall, *The Death of Christ the Redemption of His People; or the atonement regulated by the divine purpose* (Edinburgh, Glasgow, London, 1842).

14. E. Polhill, *Essay on the Extent of the Death of Christ* (Berwick, 1842), p. iv of Balmer's preface.

This preface, along with Brown's *Notes, Chiefly Historical*, sought to give an historical and Reformed lineage to the 'general-reference theory', and place it in the forefront of gospel preaching.[15]

In direct response to the publication of the above works with their divergence of thought on the precise extent of Christ's atonement, the Secession Presbytery of Paisley and Greenock initiated two overtures at the 1843 Synod aimed at clarifying the Church's relation to the 'new teaching'.[16] The overtures asked that:

> 1. The Synod examine an essay by Polhill on the extent of the death of Christ, lately published, with a recommendatory preface by Dr Balmer, and declare whether the sentiments contained in the said Essay and Preface are in accordance with the Word of God, as exhibited in the standards of this Church.[17]

> 2. That the Synod hold a Committee of the whole house, for conference on the divisions in sentiment on doctrinal points agited in our churches; and request the two senior Professors to express to the Synod their sentiments on these points.[18]

The Synod decided to take up the second overture first, and both Brown and Balmer indicated a willingness to explain their position. Balmer's statement in particular was of considerable length. While conceding that the Westminster Confession of Faith '...*prima facie* (seems)...to teach that Christ made atonement only for the elect',[19] Balmer nonetheless concluded that '...it is exceedingly problematical if the compilers of the Confession intended to deny a universal, and assert a limited

---

15. J. Brown, *Notes, op. cit.*, pp. 285ff.

16. *Minutes of the United Associate Synod* (Glasgow, 1843), pp. 22ff.; Robertson, *op. cit.*, pp. 176ff.; J. Cairns, *Memoir of John Brown D.D.* (Edinburgh, London, 1860), pp. 234ff.

17. *Minutes of the United Associate Synod* (1843), *op. cit.*, p. 22.

18. *Ibid.*

19. R. Balmer, J. Brown, *Statements, op. cit.*, p. 25.

atonement'.[20] Both professors stressed that they in no way denied the Westminster teaching on the particularity of Christ's death. The committee appointed by the Synod to examine the professors' statements arrived at the conclusion that the Controversy was in substance a misunderstanding over 'ambiguous language' such as 'universal atonement' and 'limited atonement'[21] and that scriptural harmony prevailed among the brethren.[22] That the committee could make such an assessment of the situation betrayed more their desire for ecclesiastical peace than for theological honesty. It was more than a little patronising of the committee to tell those who had questioned the orthodoxy of the professors' teaching on the atonement that their fears were groundless and that the problem was, in essence, no problem at all. It was not surprising that the committee's peace formula failed to achieve its purpose: ecclesiastical peace was not maintained and a new element in the Controversy appeared.

### The Professors' Statements

Contrary to the desire and expectation of the Synod that peace should prevail, the publication of the professors' *Statements* fuelled the Controversy considerably.[23] For Dr Marshall the teaching contained in the *Statements* seemed virtually to subvert the heart of the gospel as he understood it. In an appendix to his work *The Catholic Doctrine of Redemption Vindicated*,[24] Marshall insinuated that while the professors might not be teaching openly against the Confession, they were not expounding its theology in the natural, obvious, and received sense.[25] The controversialist

---

20. *Ibid.*

21. *Minutes of the United Associate Synod* (1843), *op. cit.*, p. 27.

22. *Ibid.*, p. 26.

23. The publication of the *Statements* forced Marshall to make his complaints more public, and set the whole dispute on a wider footing.

24. A. Marshall, *The Catholic Doctrine of Redemption Vindicated; or modern views of the atonement, particularly those of Dr. Wardlaw, Examined and Refuted. With an Appendix* (Glasgow, Edinburgh, London, 1844).

25. *Ibid.*, p. 250. Cf. Robertson, *op. cit.*, p. 190.

in Marshall was given full rein in the appendix. To claim, as he did, that:

> It may be found that a flood of Pelagianism has for years been issuing from our Divinity Halls ... (and) that missionaries tinctured with Pelagian and other kindred heresies have been going forth (from them),[26]

served only to escalate the Controversy. It is hardly to be wondered that the two professors lodged a complaint with the 1844 Synod against Marshall's insinuations.[27]

In response to the professors' complaint, the Synod appointed a committee to examine the defamatory statements in Marshall's work,[28] and instructed the same committee, at Marshall's request, to consider the professors' recently published *Statements*.[29] When the committee concluded its reports,[30] it seemed that the sting had been drawn from the dispute and that concord would once again reign in the Church respecting the doctrine of Christ's atonement. Marshall declared that he never intended to impute 'underhand' motives to Brown and Balmer (although this is quite impossible to square with many of the statements in the offending Appendix) and as a gesture of good faith 'spontaneously intimated his purpose to suppress the Appendix altogether'.[31] Marshall's virtual retraction satisfied the professors.[32] To remove any lingering doubts as to their orthodoxy, Brown and Balmer asserted that their teaching never countenanced Pelagianism in any form, and disassociated themselves from the Morisonian heresy of placing atonement prior to election in the order of God's decrees.[33] The seeming pre-empting of a widespread rift

---

26. A. Marshall, *The Catholic Doctrine, op. cit.*, p. 250.

27. *Minutes of the United Associate Synod* (Glasgow, 1844), p. 36; Robertson, *op. cit.*, p. 188; J. Cairns, *Memoir of John Brown D.D., op. cit.*, p. 239.

28. *Minutes of the United Associate Synod* (1844), *op. cit.*, p. 36.

29. *Ibid.*, p. 37.

30. *Ibid.*, p. 41.

31. *Ibid.*

32. *Ibid.*

33. For an historical examination and assessment of the Morisonian 'heresy', see

in the Church due to Marshall's conciliatory remarks before the Synodical committee was all but destroyed when he returned to his polemical stance in the publication of his *Remarks on the Pamphlet Intituled 'Statements on Certain Doctrinal Points, made October 5th 1843, Before the United Associate Synod'* in 1845.[34] This work of Marshall's heralded the final and most acrimonious stage in the Controversy. Up until this juncture a friendly, if somewhat strained, spirit had been maintained. However, the polemical, and at time virulent, nature of Marshall's pamphlet anticipated a sharper and more personalised emphasis in the dispute. In his *Remarks* Marshall accused Brown and Balmer of 'unsound doctrine and heresy',[35] the revived charge of Pelagianism,[36] of preaching 'a worthless gospel',[37] and of peddling 'the vulgar doctrine of the new theology'[38] which was nothing more than 'solemn mockery'.[39]

## The 1845 Synod

When the Synod met in May 1845, Brown registered his official complaint against Marshall's charge that he taught unsound doctrine.[40] It is not surprising that the Synod gave its 'undivided confidence'[41] to Brown, and simultaneously passed a motion condemning Marshall's views and the manner in which he publicised them.[42] Although he protested against the Synod's decision, Marshall was forced to endure the humiliation of a public censure from the Synod. It was obvious to Marshall

---

William Cunningham, *Historical Theology,* II (3rd ed.; Edinburgh, 1870), pp. 324ff.; James Orr, *Progress of Dogma* (London, 1901), pp. 297ff.

34. A. Marshall, *Remarks on the pamphlet Intituled 'Statements on Certain Doctrinal Points, made October 5th, 1843, Before the United Associate Synod'* (Glasgow, Edinburgh, Ayr, 1845).

35. *Ibid.,* p. 2.

36. *Ibid.,* p. 16.

37. *Ibid.,* p. 28.

38. *Ibid.,* p. 38.

39. *Ibid.,* p. 35.

40. *Minutes of the United Associate Synod* (Glasgow, May 1845), p. 31. Balmer had died earlier in the year.

41. *Ibid.,* p. 31.

42. *Ibid.,* p. 32. Thirty-four dissented from the Synod's decision.

that he would gain no satisfaction from a hostile Synod, and he set in motion the necessary steps which would enable him to initiate a process of libel against Professor Brown. Before Marshall presented his libel, however, the situation was further complicated by an unusual action on the part of the Synod.

During the May Synod, forty-seven Memorials were presented to the Synod on behalf of a number of Presbyteries and Sessions.[43] The Memorials reflected the concern of a section of the Church that 'the Synod had entered on a course of defection from the Word of God, as exhibited in our symbolical books'.[44]

The stated aim of the Memorials was to press the Synod to reopen the recent discussion on matters of doctrine, a course of action that some Presbyteries felt necessary due to their suspicion that a 'new theology' was indeed being tolerated within the Church. The reaction of the Synod to the Memorials was decisive. A motion was carried overwhelmingly condemning the Memorials, and recommending those behind them 'to abstain from unprofitable strife'.[45] The motion which was passed condemning the Memorials argued that due to

> … the criminatory spirit in which some of the papers now sent up have been composed, containing heavy charges not only against individuals, but inculpating the whole Church… (the Synod) agree to condemn such modes of procedure as unconstitutional, unjust and uncharitable.[46]

Such a high-handed action on the part of the Synod was bound to inflame the controversy. A total of sixty-nine dissented from the decision to disregard and condemn the Memorials, questioning the legality of the Synod's action.[47] The dissentients further remarked on the 'unprecedented number of dissents'[48]

43. *Ibid.*, p. 20.
44. *Ibid.*, p. 45.
45. *Ibid.*, p. 21.
46. *Ibid.*, p. 27.
47. *Ibid.*, p. 44.
48. *Ibid.*

and gave expression to their deeply held feelings by maintaining that 'Reiterated professions of adherence to our standards cannot be accepted as a satisfactory answer to reiterated complaints of departure from them.'[49]

The decision of the Synod to reject the Memorials widened the breach on the Church, and prepared the way for the concluding act in the Controversy – Marshall's libel against Brown.

### The July 1845 Synod

The ill feeling generated in the United Secession Church during the May Synod was compounded by the decision of the Synod when it met in July to refuse Marshall's request for an extension of time in which to prepare his libel against Brown.[50] Not only did the Synod refuse Marshall adequate time to prepare his libel, it also decided to by-pass the normal procedure of examining first the Relevancy of the libel, and proceeded to an examination of the libel's five charges of doctrinal error against Professor Brown.[51] By refusing to consider whether the stated doctrinal errors were in fact errors and contrary to the Church's Standards, the Synod gave the impression that it was determined at all costs to conclude the strife, exonerate Brown, and silence those who were disrupting the peace of the Church.

Marshall accused Brown of teaching five theological propositions contrary to the teaching of the Church's Standards, and, by implication, to Scripture. By far the most important was the third charge,

---

49. *Ibid.*, p. 45. When dissents came to be recorded only forty-six signed, far less than the earlier debates had anticipated.

50. Dr Hay signed the libel as he wanted some redress for the forty-seven Memorials rejected at a previous Synod. Cf. Robertson, *op. cit.*, p. 216.

51. *Minutes of the United Associate Synod* (Glasgow, July 1845), pp. 20ff.; Robertson, *op. cit.*, pp. 216-286. A libel consisted usually of three parts: First, the Relevancy, which was to consider whether the errors charged were contrary to Scripture and the Standards. Secondly, if the errors charged were indeed reckoned to be errors, they would be examined in the light of the defendant's teaching. Thirdly, the libel would be concluded either with an acquittal or with the Church exercising punitive discipline.

> … that Christ has not died for the elect only, or made satisfaction
> for their sins only, but that he has died for all men, and made
> atonement or satisfaction for the sins of all men…[52]

The doctrine of particular or limited atonement was considered
by many to be the *vox signata* of Westminster Calvinism[53] and
Marshall virtually accused Brown of teaching the Arminian
heresy on this important subject.

Marshall presented his evidence, and Brown replied stating
that he considered his teaching to be in no way contrary to that
of the Westminster Standards. Five motions were presented
at the end of the debate, all of them exonerating Brown from
Marshall's charge. The second motion by Rev. David Roberts of
Kilmaurs was the only one that even offered a hint of criticism.
He submitted that Professor Brown

> … repudiates the doctrine of a Universal atonement as held by
> the Arminians, but not in terms sufficiently definite to exhibit
> a proper statement of the truth upon this subject, as exhibited
> in the Scriptures and the Subordinate Standards of the United
> Secession Church.[54]

Brown was acquitted on every charge. At the conclusion of the
libel it was moved and seconded

> That the Synod on a review of its deliberations and decisions…
> in the case of libel against Dr. Brown, finds that all the charges
> made against Dr. Brown have been disposed of… (and) finds
> that there exists no ground even for suspicion, that he holds
> or has ever held, any opinion… inconsistent with the word of
> God or the Subordinate Standards of this Church;- the Synod
> therefore dismisses the Libel; and, while it sincerely sympathises
> with Dr. Brown in the unpleasant and painful circumstances
> in which he has been placed, it renews the expression of

---

52. *Minutes of the United Associate Synod* (July 1845), *op. cit.*, pp. 39ff.
53. J. Forsyth, *Remarks on Dr. Heugh's Irenicum* (Edinburgh, 1845), p. 5.
54. *Minutes of the United Associate Synod* (July 1845), op. cit., p. 39.

> confidence in him … And entertains the hope that the issue of this cause has been such as will, by the blessing of God, restore peace and confidence throughout this Church, and terminate the unhappy controversy which has so long agitated it.[55]

The decision of the Synod virtually concluded the Controversy. The immediate consequence of the Synod's decision was less than might have anticipated. Although the Synod had witnessed considerable in-fighting and heated debate, the unity of the Church was all but maintained. Two Secession ministers left the Synod and formed a Calvinistic Secession Presbytery[56] which quickly faded into near insignificance. The reasons given by the Rev. William Scott when presenting his declinature[57] crystallised the opposition of those who had supported Marshall's libel against Professor Brown. After arguing that the Synod occupied unconstitutional ground in rejecting the forty-seven Memorials, Scott spoke of the 'gross Arminian error' in the professors' published *Statements*, and concluded:

> I hereby conscientiously decline the authority of the United Secession Synod, now so manifestly and deeply divided in sentiment as to the fundamental doctrine of the atonement … (and) declare myself no longer a minister nor member of the United Secession Church.[58]

The conclusion of the Atonement Controversy in the United Secession Church opened up the way for the union of that Church with the other major branch of the Secession, the Relief Church, in 1847. 'Moderation' had won the day. It was not surprising, therefore, that when the union was formulated in 1847 the name of Dr Andrew Marshall was not found among those

---

55. *Ibid.*, p. 44. There was a substantial minority who voted against the proposed acquittal: the figures were 241–118 in favour of acquittal.

56. See Rev. R. Small, *History of the Congregations of the United Presbyterian Church 1733-1900*, I (Edinburgh, 1904), pp. 499-500.

57. *Minutes of the United Associate Synod* (May 1845), *op. cit.*, pp. 34-35.

58. *Ibid.*, p. 35.

who assented to the creation of the new United Presbyterian Church. Faced with a body he considered indefinite in its adherence to the Westminster teaching on Christ's atonement, Marshall resigned from the Church he had served for over forty years.

## 2. Brown and Balmer's Doctrine of the Atonement

The teaching of the professors on the subject of the atonement is found in a number of their written works.[59] The professors' main contention was that the death of Christ had a 'general' and 'universal' as well as a 'special' and 'particular' reference.[60] In his preface to Polhill's essay on the extent of Christ's death, Balmer wrote:

> The atonement is a means for the accomplishment of an end; and the ends which it was to accomplish were two-fold; one respecting mankind generally, one relating to a select and limited number.[61]

Polhill, in the extract taken from his larger work *The Divine Will*,[62] amplifies this emphasis:

> Christ's death was paid down by him, and accepted by God as a price, with a double respect. As for all men, it was paid and accepted as a price so far forth as to procure for them a ground for their faith, viz. that they might be saved on gospel terms; and as for the elect, it was further paid and accepted as a price, so far as to procure the very grace of faith for them.[63]

---

59. Brown, in particular, develops his understanding of the atonement in the works already cited. Unlike Balmer who wrote in a polemical fashion, it is clear from Brown's writings that he disliked controversy, and was reluctantly drawn into the dispute with Marshall.

60. Brown is credited with first using the phrase 'general reference'.

61. Polhill, *op. cit.*, p. VII.

62. The larger work was published, as we have seen in 1673, and was guaranteed a wide circulation due to a recommendatory preface written by John Owen, the most famous of the seventeenth-century Puritan divines.

63. Polhill, *op. cit.*, p. 10.

In his *Notes, Chiefly Historical* – written prior to the 1841 Synod in order to support the theory of a 'general reference' with an orthodox, historic lineage – Professor Brown specified in a fuller fashion what the general aspect of Christ's death actually accomplished. He wrote,

> Some hold that not only did Christ die with the intention of saving the elect, but that he died for all men *so as to lay a foundation for unlimited calls and invitations to mankind to accept salvation in the belief of the gospel; or so as to remove all the obstacles in the way of man's salvation except those which arise out of his indisposition to receive it.*[64]

The charge of 'unsound doctrine' made against the professors was not so much in respect to their using the phrase 'general or universal atonement' but in the content they attached to it. Reformation theology had been accustomed to expressing the nature and extent of Christ's death in universal as well as in particular categories, in a way similar to the Schoolmen.[65] The technical phrase often used to draw the universal and particular categories together, *sufficienter pro omnibus efficaciter pro electis,*[66] was considered by Brown and Balmer to exemplify the Reformed Church's awareness of the need for theological balance when dealing with the extent of Christ's atonement. In his *Notes, Chiefly Historical,* Brown seeks to show that this 'double-reference' theory was held by such Reformed worthies as Calvin, Melancthon, Bullinger, and even Zanchius.[67] Not content to claim a Reformation lineage for his teaching,[68] Brown endeavoured to expound the Westminster Confession of Faith to show that it also included a general or universal reference

---

64. Brown, *Notes, op. cit.,* p. 285.

65. *Ibid.,* p. 286.

66. The phrase itself is found in Lombard and Aquinas. Calvin uses the phrase in his commentary on 1 John 2:2, but qualifies his commitment to it. Cf. Cunningham, *op. cit.,* pp. 334-335.

67. Brown, *Notes, op. cit.,* p. 286.

68. *Ibid.,* pp. 287-289; Brown, *Hints, op. cit.,* Note B, pp. 83-85; Brown and Balmer, *Statements, op. cit.,* pp. 26, 73.

in its understanding of Christ's atonement. In his *Notes, Chiefly Historical*, Brown addressed himself to what he considered the main question in the debate:

> Is the doctrine of such a generality of reference of the death of Christ, as is maintained by some among us, consistent with the holy scriptures, *as their meaning is exhibited in our symbolical books?*[69]

Brown answers in the affirmative. Examining all the statements in the Westminster Confession of Faith which bear upon the death of Christ,[70] Brown concludes that it is unquestionable that the Confession allows for a universal reference to be included in the purpose of Christ's death.

Balmer, however, seemed less convinced that the Confession afforded any room for the 'general-reference theory' in its teaching. While arguing that the Subordinate Standard 'left room for some slight diversity' of thought on the subject of the atonement,[71] he considered that its teaching fell decidedly on the particular or limited reference. Although Brown and Balmer placed a different weight of emphasis on the Confession's actual doctrinal teaching, on one element they were in total agreement. Both stressed the argument that for the Westminster Confession of Faith (a document intended, among other things, for ministerial communion) to condemn out of hand the doctrine that Christ died in a particular respect for all men, would have meant the exclusion from ministerial communion of men like Usher, Davenant, Hall, and Baxter, who all held to the universal reference theory.[72] That these men were not excluded from ministerial communion was a powerful argument in the professors' favour.

In underlining the orthodoxy of their teaching Brown and Balmer drew attention to statements in the Secession *Testimony*

---

69. Brown, *Notes, op. cit.*, p. 287.
70. *Ibid*.
71. Polhill, *op. cit.*, p. IV.
72. Brown, *Notes, op. cit.*, p. 289. All of these men advocated a 'universal atonement' along the lines taught by Brown.

– documents which clarified the relation of the Secession to various theological areas of dispute. Balmer in his preface to Polhill's essay,[73] Brown in his *Notes, Chiefly Historical*,[74] and both in their *Statements*[75] make the point that the *Testimony* at various junctures emphasised the general as well as the particular reference in connection with Christ's atonement.[76] It is worth commenting that Professor Brown seemed to be somewhat aware of the ambiguity of this argument.[77]

*Pastoral Concern*

The stress which the professors placed on the death of Christ opening 'a door of mercy for all men'[78] and removing 'legal bars'[79] which once prevented God being gracious towards them was more than anything borne out of a desire to make 'credible' the universal gospel call. In reviewing the Controversy, Dr Robert S. Candlish made the same point:

> The reasons which, as it would appear, chiefly weigh with those who advocate the theory of a 'general reference', or 'general relations' in the atonement… are, on the one hand, a desire to explain and establish the consistency of God in the universal call of the gospel; and on the other, an extreme anxiety to facilitate the sinner's compliance with that call.[80]

There can be little doubt that Candlish assessed the situation correctly. One of Polhill's primary concerns was to ask the

---

73. Polhill, *op. cit.*, p. IV.

74. Brorn, *Notes, op. cit.*, pp. 290-291.

75. Brown and Balmer, *Statements, op. cit.*, p. 23.

76. Brown quotes from the 'Act of the Associate Presbytery concerning the Doctrine of Grace…' (1742), in the *Secession Testimony* (Edinburgh, 1828), section ii, article 1, p. 55; and from the 'Act Concerning Arminian Error', sections ii, iii, vii (1754), pp. 131-133.

77. See the *Testimony of the United Associate Synod* (Edinburgh, 1828), Part II, p. 132.

78. Brown and Balmer, *Statements, op. cit.*, pp. 8-9.

79. *Ibid.*, p. 68.

80. R.S. Candlish, 'On the Atonement Controversy – a Letter', *Free Church Magazine*, II (February 1845), p. 64. Cf. Marshall, *Catholic Doctrine, op. cit.*, p. 236.

question: 'But if Christ in no way died for all men, how came the minister's commission to be so large?'[81]

Balmer takes up the same point in his preface, arguing that if the Scriptures only teach particular atonement the universal call becomes an absurdity.

> ... if it be well-founded (that Christ made atonement only for the elect), the death of Christ cannot constitute an adequate basis for the universal overtures of the gospel.[82]

It would seem then, on reading the professors' *Statements* in particular, that an initial pastoral, rather than dogmatic, impulse led them to interpret Christ's death in universal as well as in particular categories.

If this was so, it is interesting to note the striking similarity, if not complete identity, between the concern of Brown and Balmer and that of John McLeod Campbell of Row.[83] More than anything else, McLeod Campbell was motivated in his rejection of Westminster Calvinism's teaching on the atonement by the pastoral needs of his parishioners. In this rejection McLeod Campbell was advocating a universal view of the atonement that was all but identical to that which caused the removal of James Morison from the Secession ministry. The similarity between Morison and McLeod Campbell is striking not only in their espousal of an atonement which preceded the decree of election. It would seem that Morison first began to question the traditional understanding of the atonement when he became involved in a 'revival ministry' in the middle and late 1830s. Confronted by individuals seeking the assurance of God's favour

---

81. Polhill, *op. cit.*, p. 6.

82. *Ibid.*, p. viii. Cf. Marshall, *Catholic Doctrine, op. cit.*, p. 209.

83. The details of the Row heresy are well known. McLeod Campbell ultimately rejected the Westminster teaching on the atonement because he considered preaching that Christ died only for the elect, and at the same time insisting that salvation was open to all and available to all was in effect meaningless. For the universal gospel offer to have any credibility it must be based on, and flow from, a universal atonement. On this point at least, McLeod Campbell, Morison, Brown, and Balmer were agreed.

and mercy, Morison sought to allay their fears by emphasising the universal nature of God's mercy in Christ.[84] The insistence upon dealing pastorally with people, and the desire to assure them of God's love in Christ, served as an unmistakeable link between the two 'heretics'. The fact that Morison's initial commitment to a universal atonement developed under Brown's teaching in the Divinity Hall[85] places the teaching of the professors in a somewhat clearer light.

### 3. The position of Dr. Marshall

The Controversy which arose over the senior professors' teaching on the atonement owed its origin to Dr. Andrew Marshall.[86] Marshall's view of the atonement, and his detailed objections to Brown and Balmer, are delineated in the three books he wrote during the period 1841–1845.[87] Ever since his *entrée* into the debate over Ecclesiastical Establishments in the late 1820s,[88] Marshall had acquired the reputation of being a polemical, theological *provocateur*.

The main thrust of Marshall's objections centred upon the use of the phrases 'general reference' and 'universal atonement'. It was not the terminology *per se* that Marshall objected to, but the content given to it by Brown and Balmer.[89] By conceiving of Christ's atonement in purely limited or particular categories, Marshall emphasised that he was in no way denying the implication

---

84. Adamson, *op. cit.*, pp. 80ff.

85. *Ibid.*, p. 88. Cf. D. Woodside, *The Soul of a Scottish Church* (Edinburgh, n.d.), p. 261.

86. Marshall was ordained in 1802, and was Moderator of the United Secession Synod in 1836. He resigned in 1847. See Small, *op. cit.*, pp. 328-329.

87. These three works exhibit a keen theological mind, but one which was happy to reproduce the learning and arguments of past generations.

88. *Ecclesiastical Establishments Considered* (Glasgow, 1829); and *Ecclesiastical Establisments Farther Considered* (Glasgow, 1831).

89. Marshall, *Death of Christ, op. cit.*, p. 69. Marshall was willing initially to admit a general, and even a universal, reference in the atonement. Later he regretted using such language in relation to the extent of Christ's atonement. Balmer, however, quotes Marshall in support of his own position: *Statements, op. cit.*, p. 16.

of the classical formulation, *sufficienter pro omnibus efficaciter pro electis*. It is undeniable, however, that Marshall understood this theological formulation in a different sense from that of the professors (the lack of precise theological definition, and the linguistic misconceptions and lack of uniformity greatly helped to complicate the Controversy). Marshall considered himself in the mainstream of Westminster and Calvinistic orthodoxy,[90] and his interpretation of the word *sufficienter* reflected, so he thought, the traditional interpretation. Marshall spoke of Christ's atonement as open to all, and sufficient for all, 'provided such had been agreeable to the Father's will'.[91] For Marshall, only the *elect* were included in the Father's decree to save sinners.[92] It was not therefore the *sufficiency* of the atonement that Marshall sought to limit, but its purpose and application. It was this which brought him into conflict with the professors who taught that all men were represented in Christ's death, and as such brought into a salvable state – 'sufficiency' being interpreted in terms of purpose if not in terms of application.[93]

The publication of the professors' *Statements* in 1844 provided the impulse Marshall needed to express openly his criticism of their teaching.

Up until this point, Marshall had understood the phrases in 'a harmless sense'.[94] The *Statements,* however, spelled out in detail

---

90. Marshall quotes throughout his works a plethora of Reformed theologians: Calvin, Witsius, Owen, Charnock, Hodge, and many more.

91. Marshall, *Death of Christ, op. cit.*, p. 88.

92. Marshall, *Catholic Doctrine, op. cit.*, pp. 82ff., pp. 145-183.

93. Brown and Balmer, *Statements, op. cit.*, p. 9. Cf. Rev. A. Robertson, *Second Letter to Rev. A. Marshall D.D., L.Ld., occasioned by his Overture to the Synod on the present state of doctrine in the United Secession Church* (Edinburgh and Glasgow, 1845), p. 5.

There is an interesting minute of the Westminster Assembly on the very point at issue. Commenting on the Synod of Dort's use of the word *sufficienter,* Edward Reynolds stated, 'The Synod intended no more than to declare the sufficiency of the death of Christ; it is *pretium in se*, of sufficient value to all, – nay ten thousand worlds' (Minute of October 21, 1645 in A.F. Mitchell and J. Struthers [eds.], *Minutes of the Sessions of the Westminster Assembly of Durnes* [Edinburgh and London, 1874], p. 153). Reynolds, as is clear from the context, understands the 'sufficiency' of Christ's atonement to lie within the Father's predestinating purpose to save the elect.

94. Marshall, *Remarks, op. cit.*, pp. 49-50.

what the professors meant by the terminology. 'Sufficient for all' was seen as meaning intrinsically made for all, with the purpose of appeasing God's wrath, and rendering satisfaction to his justice.[95] Marshall considered such an interpretation beyond the bounds of confessional orthodoxy, and contrary to the historical Testimonies of the Secession Church. When he came to draw up his libel against Professor Brown in the July 1845 Synod, Marshall charged him with,

1. Making the decree of God changeable.
2. Teaching that Christ made satisfaction for all men and not the elect only.
3. Teaching that Christ was the substitute for all men and bore the punishment for all men.[96]

(There were two other charges but they occupied little of the Synod's time, and were considered trifling in the extreme.)

It is unfortunate that the Synod did not adhere to normal procedure and judge the Relevancy of the charges in the light of the Church's Subordinate Standards,[97] as this would undoubtedly have clarified the Church's position vis-à-vis the controversial points at issue. It was left to men like Rev. A. Robertson to take issue with Marshall, challenge *his* orthodoxy, and accuse him of teaching 'unsound doctrine'.[98] Robertson stated unequivocally that it was an error, and contrary to the Church's Standards, to assert that Christ died to secure the salvation of the elect alone, and that a portion of the human race is not salvable.[99] Robertson

---

95. Polhill, *op. cit.*, p. IX; Brown and Balmer, *Statements, op. cit.*, p. 22.

96. *Minutes of the United Associate Synod* (July 1845), *op. cit.*, pp. 25-44. Cf. Robertson, *Atonement Controversy, op. cit.*, pp. 222-280.

97. Robertson, *Atonement Controversy, op. cit.*, p. 222; *Minutes of the United Associate Synod* (July 1845), *op. cit.*, p. 35. Thirty-nine dissented from the Synod's decision, considering it against the ordinary and constitutional form of procedure in the Church. Reasons for the dissents are given in the *Minutes*, pp. 47-50.

98. Rev. A. Robertson, *First Letter to the Rev. Andrew Marshall D.D., LL.D., Explaining and enforcing certain propositions embodied in a petition to be presented to the Synod, in condemnation of his views on the subject of the Atonement* (Glasgow, Edinburgh, London, Dublin, 1845), pp. 3ff.

99. *Ibid.*

perhaps spoke for the majority of the Synod when he accused Marshall of 'hyper-Calvinistic tenets', asserting that he 'would rather put (his) hand in the fire than subscribe them'.[100]

## 4. Historical Antecedents of Brown and Balmer's Teaching

Although maintaining that their views on the 'general reference theory' and universal atonement belonged to mainstream Calvinistic orthodoxy, the professors adopted a somewhat ambiguous relation to the Westminster Confession of Faith, the Subordinate Standard of their Church, and the rule of theological orthodoxy among Presbyterians in Scotland. While Professor Brown strove to demonstrate that the Confession in no way contradicted his position and in fact tacitly supported it, Professor Balmer considered that the Confession, barely, if at all, lent any support to their views. In his preface to Polhill's essay, Balmer recognised that:

> ... if they (Westminster Confession of Faith and the Catechisms) do not explicitly inculcate, (they) seem evidently to countenance the doctrine of a limited atonement, the doctrine that the Saviour died solely and exclusively for the elect.[101]

As we have already noted, Balmer was willing to admit that the doctrine of a universal atonement, in whatever form, was nowhere to be found in the Confession.[102] Brown, on the other hand, analysed all the sections in the Confession bearing on the nature and extent of the atonement. He concluded that there was nothing in the Westminster teaching which expressly contravened his understanding of a general reference or universal atonement. After a brief analysis of the Confession's teaching, Brown concludes:

---

100. Rev. A. Robertson, *Third Letter to the Rev. Andrew Marshall D.D., LL.D., in farther condemnation of his views on the Subject of the atonement; with proofs drawn from our standards and other official documents* (Edinburgh, Glasgow, 1845), p. 3.

101. Polhill, *op. cit.*, p. IV.

102. Brown and Balmer, *Statements, op. cit.*, p. 5.

> The doctrine of particular elections, and the doctrine of particular salvation, are very strongly asserted; but the doctrine of a certain generality of reference in the death of Christ, or the atonement made by it, is certainly not explicitly condemned.[103]

The almost ambivalent approach of Balmer to the teaching of the Confession was borne out of his particular relation to the Westminster Confession of Faith. On a number of occasions Balmer indicated that he did not consider himself bound to every aspect of the Confession's doctrine. In his *Statement*, Balmer declared at the outset that although he regarded the Westminster Confession of Faith and the Catechisms as the Church's Subordinate Standards, he readily dissented from some *expressions* in them.[104] (It is clear that by the word 'expressions' Balmer means not just words but doctrines.) Balmer further regarded the doctrinal statements (Testimonies) of the Secession as clarifying what is ambiguous and obscure in the Subordinate Standards.[105] It is also significant that Balmer introduces into his *Statement* a personal account of his attachment to the Standards. He writes that it was 'not until a year and a half after I had finished my theological course at the Hall, that I could make up my mind to assent to the formula...'[106]

The significance lies not so much in the delay in signing the Formula, but in the 'explanations' he appended to his signing – approving the Confession and Catechisms 'insofar as I had studied them'.[107] When the Formula was revised at the union of the two branches of the Secession in 1820, Balmer again made public his perplexity over the Confession's teaching on the extent of Christ's death, recognising what he thought to be 'an irreconcilable discrepancy between a limited remedy and an unlimited invitation'.[108] It is not surprising then to find that

---

103. Brown, *Notes, op. cit.*, p. 289.
104. Brown and Balmer, *Statements, op. cit.*, p. 4.
105. *Ibid.* Cf. Marshall's comment on this in *Remarks, op. cit.*, p. 56.
106. Brown and Balmer, *Statements, op. cit.*, p. 57.
107. *Ibid.*, p. 58.
108. *Ibid.*

Balmer was apparently not perturbed that the Confession seemed to lend no support to the general reference theory. He had not subscribed the Formula of Subscription without reservation and felt himself at 'liberty' to qualify his assent to its teaching on the atonement.[109] Professor Brown, on the other hand, was intent on maintaining a closer relation to the Confession's teaching than his colleague. This is seen in his constant desire to harmonise, or at least relate, his teaching to the Confession.[110] The crux of Brown's argument that the Confession did not condemn his position centred around the question of 'ministerial communion'. As we have seen, Brown maintained that it was impossible for the Westminster Confession of Faith, a document intended, among other things, for ministerial communion, to condemn out of hand the doctrine that Christ died for all men. To have done so would have meant excluding men like Usher, Davenant, Hall, and Baxter, all of whom held to the general reference theory as propounded by Brown.[111] Both Brown and Balmer made a great deal of this argument, and its force was something of a triumph for the professors in their claim that their teaching bore the stamp of Reformed orthodoxy. It is difficult, however, to determine exactly the amount of weight that should be given to Brown's claim that the Westminster Confession of Faith supported the position he was contending for.

The *Minutes* of the Westminster Assembly help to shed some light on the subject. The debate concerning 'the redemption of the elect only' in the Assembly Minutes[112] revealed that there were a

small body of men [in the Assembly] whose convictions lay in the direction of a modified Calvinism which had been lately

---

109. While Marshall subscribed the Confession with reservation, both Brown and Balmer approached subscription with certain reservations. Consequently, the disputants worked within different frameworks of reference.

110. Brown and Balmer, *Statements, op. cit.*, p. 73 (footnote).

111. Brown, *Notes, op. cit.*, p. 289. See also Note B in the Appendix to Brown's *Hints, op. cit.*, pp. 83-85, where Baxter elaborates on his relation to the Westminster Confession of Faith.

112. Mitchell and Struthers, *op. cit.,* p. 154, October 22, 1645.

promulgated by Cameron and Amyraut for the express purpose of finding a place for a universal redemption in the Calvinistic system.[113]

The principal proponent of this view was Edmund Calamy, whose views are almost identical to those of Brown and Balmer. Calamy spoke up for a universal redemption with limited application, not least because 'There is no verity in the universal offer except founded in the (universal redemption)!'[114]

> I am far from universal redemption on the Arminian sense, that that that I hold is in the sense of our divines in the Synod of Dort, that Christ did pay a price for all, – absolute intention for the elect, conditional intention for the reprobate in case they do believe – that all men should be *salvabiles non obstante lapsu Adami* ... That Jesus Christ did not only die sufficiently for all, but God did intend, in giving of Christ, and Christ in giving Himself, did intend to put all men in a state of salvation in case they do believe.[115]

Unfortunately, the Minutes of the Assembly have not survived intact and an incomplete picture is left with regard to the actual conclusion of this particular debate.

Warfield considers that the resulting expression of the Assembly's mind in the framing of the Confession rules out any idea that the Amyraldians, or 'hypothetical universalists', gained any support that allowed for their views to be countenanced. He summed up the debate thus:

> The result of the debate was a refusal to modify the Calvinistic statement in this direction – or perhaps we should say the definitive rejection of the Amyraldian views and the adoption of language which was openly framed to exclude them.[116]

---

113. B.B. Warfield, *The Westminster Assembly and its Work* (New Jersey, 1972 – Mack, ed.), p. 142. Warfield's work is one of the classic studies on the debates and formulations of the Westminster Assembly.

114. Mitchell and Struthers, *op. cit.*, p. 154, October 22, 1645.

115. Quoted in Warfield, *op. cit.*, pp. 138-139.

116. *Ibid.*, pp. 152-143; Cf. Cunningham, *op. cit.*, p. 327. Cunningham considered the Amyraldian scheme 'confusing and ambiguous' (p. 334). Many of the English

Although the language of the Confession, and the views of the greater majority of the Assembly, would seem to support Warfield's conclusion, those involved in the framing of the Confession's third chapter in particular might possibly have been willing to allow a degree of latitude on the subject. In the Minutes of October 20 1645, debating the question of the number and order of God's decrees (two days before the debate on universal atonement), Gillespie proposed that the chapter be framed with a certain degree of laxity 'so that every one may enjoy his own sense'.[117] It is impossible to be completely conclusive on the subject. However, it is undeniable that the language of the Westminster Confession of Faith, especially that of chapters 3 and 8, seems to preclude a universalistic interpretation of Christ's death, and decidedly rejects Balmer's 'double-atonement' theory.[118] The emphasis throughout the Confession upon the particular relation of Christ to the elect in his atonement is underscored in many places:

> … Wherefore they who are elected being fallen in Adam, are redeemed by Christ … Neither are any other redeemed by Christ … but the elect only.[119]

---

delegates at the Synod of Dort (1618-1619) advocated universal, if hypothetical, redemption. Bishop Davenant taught that 'Christ died for all on condition that they believe, and he will intercede for all if only they believe.' See Jonathan D Moore, *'Christ is Dead For Him': John Preston (1587-1628) and English Hypothetical Universalism* (Cambridge Phd, 2000; Eerdmans, Grand Rapids, 2007). See especially pp. 151-184 where Dr Moore helpfully and insightfully expounds the hypothetical universalism of Ussher and Davenant. It should be noted that Amyraldianism is not identical with hypothetical universalism. Hypothetical universalists such as Usher and Davenant, by and large held to the orthodox understanding of the order of the decrees, something Amyraut vigorously opposed, see Moore, *John Preston*, 59ff. The whole question of English Hypothetical Redemption has been carefully and fully discussed by Dr Moore in *John Preston*.

117. Mitchell and Struthers, *op. cit.*, p. 151.

118. Brown and Balmer, *Statements, op. cit.*, p. 20. John Macleod considered that Brown also taught a double-atonement theory: a general substitution, provisional and conditional, and a particular substitution, effective and redemptive: *Scottish Theology, op. cit.*, p. 243.

119. Subordinate Standards, *op. cit.*, Chapter 3, vi, pp. 8-9.

> To all those for whom Christ hath purchased redemption, he doth certainly and effectually apply and communicate the same...[120]

One of the most audacious pieces of theological defence used by Brown and Balmer was their attempt to enlist the support of John Owen, the greatest of the seventeenth century theologians. Both Brown and Balmer quote part of the preface that Owen wrote to Polhill's treatise. Owen wrote:

> ... where there is an agreement in the substance and design of any doctrine, as there is between my judgement and what is here solidly declared, it is our duty to bear with each other in things circumstantial, or different explanations of the same truth, when there is no incursions made upon the main principles we own.[121]

Owen was in fact the strongest opponent of any understanding of the atonement which sought to interpret it in terms of a general or universal reference. (As his massive treatise on Particular Atonement in Vol. 10 of his collected works clearly shows.)[122] It is significant that Owen's preface was to the complete work of Polhill's (*The Divine Will*) and not simply

---

120. *Ibid.*, Chapter 8, viii. The professors claimed that Dort's Canons expressed their distinctive views. But, Dort expressly condemns the Cameronian middle-scheme. Cf. J.L. Van Mosheim's assessment of the 'middle-way' theology of Cameron and Amyraut, and its relation to Dort. 'It is the opinion of many that this doctrine differs but little from that which was established by the Synod of Dort, but such do not seem to have attentively considered either the principles from whence it is derived, or the consequences to which it leads...' (Johan Lorenz Van Mosheim, *An Ecclesiastical History*, II [London, 1842], p. 428). First published in 1726, and translated by Archbishop Adams.

William Cunningham makes the same point more directly: 'It is a curious circumstance that the followers of Cameron maintained that the Synod of Dort did not condemn their views...', *op. cit.*, p. 329. Cf. J. Brown, *Opinions on Faith* (Edinburgh, 1841), pp. 63ff., Note D.

121. Polhill, *op. cit.*, p.XV; Brown, *Notes, op. cit.*, p. 287.

122. J. Owen, Collected Works, X (Banner of Truth, ed., London, 1967), pp. 222ff. First published London, 1850-1853.

to the extract devoted to the extent of Christ's death. Owen makes it clear that he in no way agreed with all that Polhill had written, and expresses his 'dissent from some of his [Polhill's] apprehensions, especially about the object and the extent of redemption…'[123] Although Brown and Balmer were aware of Owen's qualified approval of Polhill's work they still considered his preface of sufficient value to their cause to quote it, and give their teaching the seal of the greatest of seventeenth-century Calvinistic theologians. Audacious the professors' use of Owen may have been, but it is difficult to escape the conclusion that in this part of their defence at least Brown and Balmer were lacking in credibility, and straining to gather important support for their teaching. Although Brown sought to equate his emphasis with that of the Confession, he also did not give the total support to its teaching that Marshall and his supporters gave. Brown was aware that *prima facie* the Westminster Confession of Faith told against his emphasis upon universal atonement, and this may help explain why he also pleaded for a certain degree of 'latitude' in this area, emphasising that there is great danger in attempting to harmonise statements and ideas which seem to be contrary. (In this Brown was poles apart from Marshall who applied a rigorous logic to his analysis of the Confession.) The 'lower-ground' occupied by Brown vis-à-vis subscription to the Confession was clearly outlined in his *Hints to Students of Divinity*. Brown argued that subscription is:

> … something far above the dangerous laxness of a pledge to the *scope* (Morison's word) of a Confession, and something considerably below the impractical rigidity of a profession of adherence to every iota contained in it.[124]

In his attitude to subscription Brown was *possibly* reflecting the aim of the framers of the Westminster Confession of Faith, but

---

123. Polhill, *op. cit.*, p. XV.
124. Brown, *Hints, op. cit.*, p. 32.

he was not reflecting the idea of subscription prevailing in the Scottish churches as a result of the various acts passed during the period 1690 to 1711, which regulated the subscription principle in mainstream Scottish Presbyterianism.

### The Teaching of the Secession's Testimony

Brown and Balmer's conviction that the general or universal reference theory was integral to the Reformed scheme of doctrine did not rest solely upon the Westminster Confession of Faith giving its support. Both the professors considered that the Secession's Testimony lent support to their teaching.

In his preface to Polhill's essay, Balmer, while acknowledging that the Confession teaches a limited atonement, maintained that the Testimony upheld a general reference in the death of Christ.[125] Brown held the same conviction. In his *Notes, Chiefly Historical*, Brown quotes at length from various parts of the Testimony, acts which had been passed at different times to clarify the Secession's teaching on the elements of the faith.[126] While admitting (contrary to Balmer) that these acts do not have the same authority as the Westminster Confession of Faith and the Catechisms, Brown considered them worthy of consideration. Brown's conclusion is important:

> It is obvious that there is considerable diversity in these statements, and it would, perhaps, not be easy completely to reconcile them with each other, or with some of the statements in the symbolical books.[127]

For Brown then, the Testimony teaches both particular atonement and a general reference – an indication, Brown maintained, of the anxiety of the Secession to hold these emphases in tension. It is doubtful, however, if Brown clearly displays the Teaching of the Secession's Testimony on this subject. It is one thing to

---

125. Polhill, *op. cit.*, p. IV.
126. Brown, *Notes, op. cit.*, pp. 290-291.
127. *Ibid.*, pp. 291-292.

maintain that the Testimony holds to the universal gospel call, and quite another to assert that it holds to a universal atonement. (The strictest Calvinists in the Westminster Assembly held to the universal call while utterly rejecting any notion of a universal atonement – a point to which Marshall drew Brown's attention!)

A close examination of the *Testimony* of the Secession Church would seem to overrule Brown and Balmer's contention that the double-reference theory occupied a place in its teachings. The 'Act of the Associate Presbytery concerning the Doctrine of Grace' passed by the Presbytery in October 1742 clearly denies that the extent of Christ's atonement can be construed in other than particular or limited categories. In a section aimed at vindicating the orthodoxy of the *Marrow* theology condemned by the General Assembly in 1720, the above Act maintained,

> There is nothing in (the Marrow)… that in the least countenances *universal redemption as to purchase;* a doctrine which this Presbytery rejects and condemns, as contrary to the scriptures and places of our Confession…[128]

In the same section, the Presbytery contend that the author of the *Marrow* taught 'a *particular* redemption and representation … that Christ represented and suffered for none but the elect'.[129] The Associate Presbytery did not consider that the warrant for the universal gospel offer lay in the death of Christ having some universal implication as Brown and Balmer maintained:

> Although the purchase and application of redemption be peculiar to the elect; yet the warrant to receive Christ is common to all, as they are sinful men and women of Adam's family…[130]

The Secession's opposition to any form of universal redemption is further seen in the 'Act of the Associate Synod (commonly called Anti-Burgher) at Edinburgh, April 18th 1754; containing

---

128. Gib, I, *op. cit.*, p. 178.
129. *Ibid.*
130. *Ibid.*, p. 179.

an assertion of some Gospel-truths, in opposition to Arminian errors upon the head of Universal Redemption'. [131] The second article maintained:

> That our Lord Jesus Christ hath redeemed *none others* by his death, but the *elect only*: Because *for them only* he was made under the law, made sin and made a curse; being substituted only in their law-room, and stead... For *their sins* only he made satisfaction to divine Justice... and *for them* only he purchased redemption...[132]

The same doctrine is maintained with similar force in the third article:

> That there is *but one special redemption,* by the death of Christ, for all the objects thereof; as he died in *one and the same respect,* for all those for whom he in *any respect died....*[133]

In the years prior to 1830, the *Testimony* of the Secession Churches allowed no possibility of interpreting Christ's atonement in anything. In 1830 itself, the United Associate Synod passed an Act condemning the doctrine of a universal atonement. The opening paragraph is clear and precise in its refutation:

> ... the Synod enjoin all ministers and preachers to be on their guard against introducing discussions in their ministrations, or employing language, which may seem to oppose the doctrine of particular redemption, or that Christ in making atonement for sin was substituted in the room of the elect only...[134]

It is not without significance that Balmer makes little attempt to rake up support for his views from the history of the

---

131. Gib, II, *op. cit.*, pp. 138ff.

132. *Ibid.*, p. 139.

133. *Ibid.*

134. *Report of the Sub-Committee to bring up a Statement of the Various Doctrinal Findings by the Supreme Courts of the United Church In the Course of its History – October 1877* (Edinburgh? n.d.), p. 25, quoting from the 'Act of the United Associate Synod on the Extent of the Atonement passed at Glasgow 28 April 1830.'

Secession. Not that Balmer conceded that the Testimony gave him no support. He maintained that it did; but he nonetheless acknowledges the change that had taken place in the Synod over its commitment to the disputed doctrine. Writing in 1842 Balmer stated:

> Twelve years ago, the supreme court of the United Secession Church passed an act condemning the doctrine of a universal atonement, and forbidding the use of the phrase. But how great the change effected in the last two years … And although the expression (universal atonement) is not yet stamped by the seal of judicial approbation, the chief lets to the use of it are taken out of the way; and already it is sanctioned by such authority as will speedily ensure its all but universal adoption.[135]

Balmer was less intent than his colleague in marshalling the support of history to their 'cause', and consequently felt little need to demonstrate the existence of a link, however tenuous, with the theology of past generations.

It is difficult to concede that the Secession Testimony did offer any support to the professors' teaching. Rather, the change in the Secession's views were so great and clear that it caused Professor Balmer to declare:

> I am persuaded that within these few years there has been some change among us, some progress towards a clearer and more correct view of a very important subject.[136]

## 5. Linguistic and Doctrinal Confusion

One of the major problems of the Atonement Controversy was the ambivalent use of theological language, and lack of clarification, in works published during the course of the dispute. This is not to say that the Controversy was simply over 'ambiguous terms', as the Synod and Professor Balmer seemed

---

135. Polhill, *op. cit.*, p. XIII; cf. Brown and Balmer, *Statements, op. cit.*, p. 32.
136. Brown and Balmer, *Statements, op. cit.*, p. 34.

to think.[137] However, the Synod's assessment does point to an important factor in the debate. It is apparent throughout the course of the Controversy that crucial terms were not explained as clearly as they might have been. Marshall was left asking at the near conclusion of the dispute what the phrase 'legal bars' and their removal really meant.[138] His chief complaint is that Brown and Balmer never adequately explained what they meant by this term which was crucial to their theory.

Marshall was left to wonder how such a phrase could be equated with the work of Christ, and in what way it distinguished between the elect and the non-elect. It is not surprising to find Marshall imputing the worst possible construction to the 'legal bars theory', calling it a 'vulgar phrase'[139] and making theological capital out of his actions. Lack of clarification in this instance exacerbated the problem, and contributed to the frustration felt on both sides.

The ambivalent use of language was further demonstrated in Brown and Balmer's teaching on the order of God's decrees. The professors seemed to adopt a number of positions on the subject of the priority or posteriority of election to atonement. On occasions they assented to the orthodox formula,[140] at other times they said the subject was beyond human formulation and determination and should be the subject of toleration;[141] and all the while they quoted Cameron, Amyraut, and Baxter at such length that they seemed to adhere to their 'hypothetical universalism' which placed atonement prior to election in the order of the decrees.[142] Again it is not surprising to find Marshall

---

137. Robertson, *Atonement, op. cit.*, p. 182; Brown and Balmer, *Statements, op. cit.*, p. 5.

138. Marshall, *Catholic Doctrine, op. cit.*, p. 234; also see his *Remarks, op. cit.*, p. 23.

139. Marshall, *Remarks, op. cit.*, p. 28.

140. The traditional and orthodox understanding of God's decrees placed the decree to elect prior to the decree to atone. See the structure of Chapter III in the Westminster Confession of Faith, 'Of God's Eternal Decree' in *Subordinate Standards, op. cit.*, pp. 8-9; and the Larger Catechism, Questions 12, 13, 31, pp. 53, 57.

141. Brown and Balmer, *Statements, op. cit.*, p. 6; J. Cairns, *Memoir of John Brown, op. cit.*, p. 220; and Robertson, *Atonement, op. cit.*, p. 180.

putting the worst construction on the professors' statements, accusing them of subverting the Reformed *ordo salutis*, by teaching that atonement preceded election in the Father's eternal decree.[143]

The Controversy highlighted the different meanings placed by those involved in crucial theological terminology. Crucial terms such as 'atonement', 'sufficient', and 'substitution' were used by Brown and Balmer in particular in a most 'unusual' sense. Not that the constructions placed on these words defied understanding, but they seemed almost manufactured for the occasion, as if to lend support to their teaching of a general reference in the death of Christ. The *Statements* are littered with the professors' own understanding of these crucial terms, and it is difficult in the extreme to trace any sort of link or lineage with the theological constructions of Westminster.[144]

If Marshall was guilty of rushing in and failing to appreciate the teaching of Brown and Balmer, it must also be said that the professors gave him cause for so doing by their ambiguous use of language and doctrinal construction.

## 6. Results of the Controversy

The results of the Atonement Controversy are difficult to assess. On the one hand, Marshall and those who supported him considered the Synod's decision to clear Brown completely of all the charges a disaster for the Church and its commitment to Westminster theology. John MacLeod, surveying the dispute from a distance, summed up something of the 'conservative' attitude to the Synod's decision:

> To say the least, this decision left ambiguous the relation of the largest body in the Secession to the Confessional teaching

---

142. The 'hypothetical universalism' of Amyraut concentrated its main focus upon the unilateral love of God to all men in sending a Redeemer. Election was looked upon as an integral, though secondary, consideration.

143. Marshall, *Catholic Doctrine, op. cit.*, pp. 232-234.

144. Brown and Balmer, *Statements, op. cit.,* pp. 14, 20, 22, 74.

in regard to such a doctrine of a genuine Atonement as their previous Testimonies had helped to buttress. [145]

On the other hand, the more sympathetic figure of John Cairns, a personal friend of Brown, summed up the Controversy thus:

> Upon the whole it may be affirmed that the controversy... has, by its remote, as well as its direct impression, exerted a valuable influence in liberalising the tone of Scottish theology, while it has done nothing to derange its equilibrium or remove its landmarks.[146]

History surely shows that however positive and constructive Cairns intended to be by his analysis, MacLeod – although having the virtue of hindsight – proved the more correct.

Three definite results, however, can be clearly seen.

Firstly, the decision of the Synod in 1843 that the Church should avoid using the disputed expressions 'universal atonement' and 'limited atonement' indicated a significant departure from using language that had been current in Scottish theology since Westminster.[147] While it may be argued that there was no departure from the theology of Westminster – although that itself is doubtful – the significance of the Synod's decision to bar the use of the phrase 'limited atonement' was not lost on those who considered themselves defenders of orthodoxy.[148]

Secondly, Cairns made the point that the Synod's decision in favour of Brown provided a measure of relief to many minds 'hampered by an apparent inconsistency between the universal offer and limited atonement on which to rest it'.[149] It is abundantly clear that Brown and Balmer were motivated in their teaching of a universal atonement chiefly by the desire to render the universal offer meaningful, and give it a solid theological

---

145. MacLeod, *op. cit.*, pp. 244-245.

146. Cairns, *Memoir of John Brown, op. cit.*, p. 255.

147. Robertson, *Atonement, op. cit.*, p. 182; Minutes of the United Associate Synod (Glasgow, May 1843), p.

148. Forsyth, *op. cit.*, p. 5.

149. Cairns, *Memoir of John Brown, op. cit.*, p. 254.

basis on which to rest. Particular atonement was thought to be an inadequate, and even an impossible, basis on which to rest the universal gospel offer. There can be little doubt that Cairns points to an important result of the Controversy. However, the reason he gives for this relief afforded is to be doubted. Cairns said the relief given was:

> … an example afforded of Christian large-heartedness and charity, in giving to the terms of ministerial communion, and to the interpretation of symbolical books, the widest comprehension consistent with truth and sincerity.[150]

Such an analysis fails to account for the ill feeling and bitterness which attended the debates and the Synod's decision. Although only five men in all resigned, the upset in the Church was greater than the numbers might indicate. From even a cursory examination of the literature of the Controversy it is evident that 'Christian large-heartedness' had little to do with the Synod's eventual decision. The Synod was intent on dealing a blow to the 'extremists', and the 1843 decision to bar the use of 'limited atonement' in the Church was more a rebuke for Marshall and his supporters than an exercise in Christian charity, as Cairns seems to presume.[151]

Thirdly, there can be little doubt that an important result of the Controversy was the awareness in the Church that total subscription to the Westminster Confession of Faith was an unreasonable burden to impose on any of its ministers. Brown and Balmer occupied different ground from Marshall in their attitude towards subscription. While Marshall may have reflected the traditional attachment of unreserved subscription to the Confession, Brown and Balmer's more flexible approach reflected the change that was entering Scottish theological thought.[152]

---

150. *Ibid.*, p. 255.

151. Robertson's three public letters to Marshall clearly show the ill temper that was aroused by the Controversy.

152. Cf. whole section in MacLeod entitled 'The New Light', *op. cit.*, pp. 229-254.

The course of the Atonement Controversy reflected something of the characters of those who were most intimately involved. *Marshall*, for all his outbursts and provocative challenging of Brown and Balmer, considered that he was only contending for the truth as he believed it was taught in the Standards. He was something of an enigmatic figure, battling on in near isolation from the Church he had served for over forty years. MacLeod captures something of the pathos of Marshall when he describes 'The old warrior in his loneliness (as) a pathetic figure'.[153] Contrary to Brown and Balmer, Marshall was a logician, who saw theology in terms of black and white. For truth to be truth it had, for Marshall, to be logical and coherent. In this he differed from the senior professors who were willing to hold seeming irreconcilables in tension. This in itself was a significant factor in the debate. Both parties worked within a different theological framework, and it is not surprising that the difference between them should be so great.

John Brown (Tertius) was perhaps the leading biblical exegete of his day, noted for quiet, patient study, more than theological disputation. Of the two senior professors, Balmer stands out as the debater and more 'worldly-wise' of the two. Brown seemed almost remote at times from the cut and thrust of the Controversy, and was content to occupy a back seat for a large part of the time. It is noteworthy that while Balmer spends fifty-eight pages on his Statement, Brown spends less than nine pages – partly, it should be conceded, because he agrees entirely with Balmer's full exposition of his (Balmer's) teaching.

While Brown seemed intent on retaining the historical landmarks of the Secession Church, Balmer's concern was more to usher in a new era of theological change. Balmer was aware that a significant change had already occurred in the theological outlook of the Secession during the previous decade, and he eagerly anticipated the day when a universal conception of the extent of Christ's death would carry the honours in their branch of

---

153. *Ibid.*, p. 245.

Scottish Presbyterianism. Prognostication is in no real sense part of the historian's craft, but it is worth asking the question: 'Would Brown, in particular, have stood so closely beside his colleague, had he known where their teaching would lead to?' The question may very well be an academic one, but the gradual loosening of the United Presbyterian Church's commitment to the Westminster Standards from the 1847 Union was a development that Brown would almost certainly have protested against.

It is certainly questionable whether Marshall really understood just exactly what Brown was trying to say in his emphasis upon a general reference in the death of Christ. For this reason, Marshall was responsible for imputing crude theological interpretations to some of Brown's statements, even comparing him with Wardlaw – a comparison that does little justice to Brown's commitment to mainstream Calvinism.

It is undeniable that the chief result of the Controversy was to make a significant breach in the Westminster doctrine of Particular or Limited Atonement as it was understood, and held to, by many. The emphasis placed throughout the Controversy on the love of God to *all* men acted as something of a harbinger for *the* revolution in Scottish theology in the 1860s and 1870s, when the love of God to all became the trademark of those dissatisfied with what they considered the narrow exclusivism of the Westminster Standards.

It is, therefore, difficult to concur with the judgment of a 'recent' reviewer of the Westminster Standards who stated that 'The first half (of the nineteenth century) had not seen any great breach forced in the defences of Westminster Calvinism.'[154]

---

154. Cheyne, *op. cit.,* p. 207.

*1863*. The Free Church Assembly and the United Presbyterian Synod made overtures to each other respecting the desirability of union. Robert Buchanan proposed the motion in the Free Church to enter discussions with a prospect to union. The motion was passed unanimously after Professor Gibson withdrew an amendment aimed at safeguarding the 'principles of the Free Church'.

*1864*. First Report of the Joint-Committee. Julius Wood withdrew his motion aimed at replacing union with co-operation.

*1865*. Joint-Committee reported 'entire harmony' on discussions relating to the Confession's teaching on atonement. Wood asked for a clear declaration of the Free Church's views on the atonement in order to show how different it was from that of the United Presbyterians. Forbes withdraws from the Joint-Committee due to its unwillingness to investigate further the Churches' views of the relation of the civil magistrate to the Church.

*1866*. Buchanan proposed that the Churches press on to union as only minor 'subordinate' differences existed between them. Professor Gibson challenged the United Presbyterian views on the atonement and sought clarification of their attitude towards revision of the Confession. Debates become more heated.

*1867*. The crucial year. Presbyteries clearly unhappy with the Joint-Committee's Report on doctrinal agreement. Rainy's first major speech in the Assembly deputising for Candlish. Wood virtually accused Rainy of covering up the lack of harmony in the Joint-Committee's discussions on doctrine. James Begg delivered a 'Protest' to the Assembly on its decision to carry on with the union talks. Along with four others, including Wood, he resigned from the Joint-Committee.

*1868*. Committee reappointed with instructions to prosecute union. Wood again raised the issue of the United Presbyterian's 'unorthodox' view of the atonement.

*1869*. Joint-Committee reaffirmed that the two Churches were one in their views on the extent of the atonement.

*1870*. Joint-Committee proposed union on the basis of the Churches' common Standards. Increasing polarisation of views, and a growing fear of a disruption in the Free Church.

*1871*. United Presbyterians and the Reformed Presbyterians state they have no objection to union on the basis of the Westminster Standards. Due to the opposition of a substantial minority in the Free Church, Moncrieff proposed dropping the plans for union and proceeding with a plan of 'Mutual Eligibility'. Hugh Martin gave a long speech in the Free Church Assembly on the atonement, exposing the unorthodoxy of the United Presbyterian position.

*1872*. Mutual Eligibility opposed by a vocal minority in the Free Church. Safeguards guaranteed to preserve the 'distinct principles' of the Free Church.

*1873*. Candlish proposed the suspension of negotiations for union until 'God's time is clear'.

# 4

# The Union Controversy (1863–1873)

The middle decades of the nineteenth century were marked by a great degree of flux in almost every area in British society. Politics was increasingly losing its aristocratic and landed domination, with the wealthy *nouveaux riches* insisting on political power, and the labouring classes organising themselves (e.g. Chartism) to challenge the existing social order. The industrial revolution had all but transformed the nation's economy, the cities with their burgeoning industries replacing the country as the nation's workhouse. In order to keep up with the demands of an increasingly industrialised society, the transport system underwent its own revolution with a railway network that criss-crossed the land.

The rapid, even frantic, change that affected the 1840s, 1850s, and 1860s was no less felt in the institutional church. Church attendance rapidly declined, especially in the towns and cities. The Churches were slow to adapt to the changing circumstances of the new age and, apart from the notable exception of Thomas Chalmers' St John's experiment in Glasgow, little had been done to involve the Church in the squalor of urban life. The Churches in Scotland were faced with a society that was in many ways alienated from the life of the Church. This was seen most clearly perhaps in the growing conflict between the Churches' traditional stress on the sanctity of the Sabbath and the demands of society to work, travel, transport, and holiday on the holy day. Faced with such competition, it is not difficult to understand why thoughts of Church union should arise in two of the major denominations in Scotland. Other factors were involved, not least the desire to heal past differences, and present a unified front of free spiritual independence to the 'state encumbered' Church of Scotland. It is significant that when Robert Buchanan introduced the motion to seek union with the United Presbyterian Church at the Free Church Assembly in 1863, he argued that union would emphasise the Church's spiritual independence from the state, and better prosecute the evangelisation of Scotland.[1]

The purpose of this chapter is not to examine either the course of the 1863–1873 union controversy, or the nature of the debates for or against union. Rather, our purpose is to highlight the charge made throughout the ten years of debate, by a small but vocal minority in the Free Church, that the United Presbyterian Church did not exhibit Biblical or Confessional orthodoxy in its public testimony.

The previous two chapters have sought to show that there was a clear erosion of the Secession Churches' commitment to the Westminster Standards in the period up to 1847. However, it is one thing to claim that a Church was departing from its public Standards by analysing Acts, statements, and decisions, and another to compare it with a group who professed commitment to the same Standards without reservation or qualification. The object of such an exercise is neither to vindicate the claims of the minority in the Free Church who considered the United Presbyterians to have abandoned certain hallmarks of confessional orthodoxy, nor to

---

1. *Proceedings and Debates in the General Assembly of the Free Church of Scotland* (Edinburgh, 1863), pp. 183-188. See also Norman L. Walker's biography of Buchanan, *Robert Buchanan, an Ecclesiastical Biography* (London, New York, Edinburgh, 1877), pp. 407-408.

make theological pronouncements. The aim is simply to highlight the fact that there were Presbyterian churchmen in Scotland who believed that the United Presbyterian Church had departed substantially from the heritage of Westminster. As we shall see, those who opposed the union between the two Churches were so convinced of the 'unorthodoxy' of the United Presbyterian Church that they went so far as to contemplate, and even set in motion, the legal machinery for a disruption in the Free Church should the union become a reality.

The most cursory glance at the Proceedings and Debates in the General Assembly of the Free Church of Scotland[2] during the course of the controversy over the proposed union with the United Presbyterian Church reveals that the relationship between Church and State was by far the most debated and problematical issue.[3] While the vexed questions of establishment versus voluntaryism and the role of the civil magistrate in the Church occupied the forefront of the controversy, secondary, but nonetheless important, issues surfaced at frequent intervals. Of those opposed to union, a small number raised the issue of the United Presbyterians' supposed departure from certain elements of the Westminster Standards. This small number, of strong conservative bias, maintained that the United Presbyterians had departed from the Confession's teaching on the central doctrine of the atonement, and adopted an ambivalent stand over the question of subscription to the Confession – a stand characterised by a failure to discipline ministers who publicly opposed some of the Confession's teachings.

The chapter will in turn consider the claims of theological laxity and the problem over the nature of subscription to the Confession.[4]

---

2. The debates make fascinating reading over the years 1863–1873, though the speeches are at times interminable, and minutely detailed in their argument.

3. Although difficult to calculate, probably over 90 per cent of the speeches were taken up with the two Churches' attitude towards the State.

4. Later historical commentators who openly support the line taken by the anti-unionists seek to argue that one of the principle reasons for opposing union lay in the increasing approval that was being won for the introduction of non-inspired hymns into the worship of the Church. The debates do not bear out this contention. Only

## 1. The Union Debates and the Theological Laxity of the United Presbyterian Church

At regular intervals during the debates in the Free Church Assembly from 1863 to 1873, the charge was raised that the United Presbyterian Church had departed from the Confession's teachings on the extent, and even the nature, of Christ's atonement.[5] It needs to be stressed at the outset that the number of those who challenged the orthodoxy of the United Presbyterians rarely rose above one hundred, in an Assembly of more than six hundred. It is also difficult to ascertain exactly just how many considered the United Presbyterians to be theologically suspect. We have noted that the chief block to union was the differences between the Churches concerning the role of the civil magistrate, and the biblical basis of Church establishments. It is impossible, therefore, to determine with any real accuracy who voted against the union on account of the doctrinal laxity of the United Presbyterians. However, from the debates, and the apprehensions of many Presbyteries regarding the orthodoxy of the United Presbyterians,[6] it would seem that a sizeable proportion of those who opposed union did so, at least in part, due to their belief that the United Presbyterian Church had departed from some of the teachings of the Westminster Standards.

### 1. Old Wounds Disinterred

To the strongly conservative minority in the Free Church Assembly, the acquittal of Professors Brown and Balmer by the United Secession Church[7] indicated a less-than-committed attachment by the Church to the Westminster Standards.

At the 1865 Free Church Assembly, Dr Buchanan presented the Report of the Union Committee.[8] The Report stated that the

---

once is the subject raised in the debates in the Free Church Assembly, *Proceedings, op. cit.* (1865), pp. 128-129.

5. In particular the years 1865, 1867, and 1870.

6. See the 1867 *Report* No. XXXII, pp. 3-36, in *Proceedings* (1867), *op. cit.*

7. See the previous chapter.

8. *Proceedings* (1865), *op. cit.,* Appendix XII, pp. 4ff.

....Joint-Committee found, with lively satisfaction, that holding, as all the Churches in the Joint-Committee do, the Westminster Confession of Faith as their common standard, they were in entire harmony as to the views which that Confession gives of the teachings of the Word of God, on the following fundamental truths…[9]

The truths especially in view were: man's fallen estate; the nature, sufficiency, and extent of the atonement; and its application.[10]

Up until this juncture, discussions had been fairly low-key. The change came when Dr Julius Wood, a member of the Joint-Committee, disputed the truth of Buchanan's Report, considering it 'altogether inadequate'.[11] When the Report came to be debated,[12] Dr Wood proposed a motion aimed at clarifying the Free Church's views on the atonement.[13] He declared:

The present is an important crisis in the history of the Churches negotiating for union, and the doctrine of the Atonement is so important, and such diverse views are prevalent regarding it, even among those who have signed the Confession of Faith, that it seems absolutely necessary that, if we are to have union, we come to some common understanding as to what we hold on this vital point.[14]

In order to substantiate his argument Wood referred to the case of Brown and Balmer. Wood quoted from the professors'

---

9. *Ibid.*, p. 4.

10. *Ibid.*, pp. 4f.

11. *Ibid.*, p. 6.

12. See *Proceedings, op. cit.* (1865), pp. 86-133.

13. Wood was out to expose the unorthodoxy of the United Presbyterians. He was well aware that anyone could subscribe the Confession of Faith by putting his own construction on its teachings, and so he sought to have the areas of contention spelled out in unambiguous terms, thereby hoping to expose the United Presbyterians' 'novel' interpretation of some of the Confession's teachings.

14. *Proceedings, op. cit.* (1865), p. 107. This is the first mention of the atonement in the union debates.

writings[15] to the effect that 'the death of Christ is a satisfaction for all, that is a universal atonement, ransom or expiation'.[16] The point that Wood was making was the same one that Dr Marshall made during the Atonement Controversy in the 1840s.

> The gist of the mischief, in my judgment, lies in the doctrine of a double-reference of the atonement ... Drs. Balmer and Brown, and others who with them unmistakeably and tenaciously held this doctrine of a general and special reference of the atonement, were neither Arminians or Morisonions; but the doctrine held by them is logically, and at the present time *de facto*, the fruitful parent of both Armininism and Morisonianism.[17]

With the mood of the Assembly so bent on union, Wood only received 16 votes for his motion, 184 voting against him.[18]

Although Wood's motion was defeated heavily, the atonement question continued to occupy an important place in the arguments of the anti-unionists. The fact that John Brown represented something of a 'troubler in Israel' to the conservative wing in the Free Church was further seen in the comments of Moffat of Cairnie, who had seconded Wood's motion. Moffat complained that the United Presbyterians' *Summary of Principles*, which had been prepared largely by Brown,[19]

> In its general drift, as it appears to me... presents a somewhat serious modification or evasion of the high and definite teaching of our standards...[20]

---

15. The quotes seem to be from Brown and Balmer's *Statements*, although no reference is given.

16. *Proceedings, op. cit.* (1865), p. 108.

17. *Ibid.*, pp. 109-110.

18. *Ibid.*, p. 133. During the course of the debate Dr Forbes announced his withdrawal from the Joint-Committee. He did so because the Assembly refused to direct the Committee on Union to investigate further the views of the Churches on the relation of the civil magistrate to the Church (pp. 132-133).

19. *Summary of Principles* (Edinburgh, n.d.). See *Proceedings, op. cit.* (1865), pp. 118-120.

20. *Ibid.*, p. 120.

The 1865 Free Church Assembly represented something of a watershed in the union debates as it crystallised the opposition of those not in favour of a comprehensive Church union. Not only were the United Presbyterians suspect due to their voluntaryism, they were increasingly thought to have jettisoned one of the central dogmas of the faith.[21]

The tone of the debates from 1865 became more acrimonious. During the 1866 Assembly, John Forbes, one of the leading anti-unionists, accused the United Presbyterians of holding 'latitudinarian views' on the atonement.[22] The 1866 Assembly was also significant for the strongly anti-union speech of Professor James Gibson. Gibson again raised the Brown and Balmer trial verdict, and commented that the United Secession Synod did not unanimously acquit the professors.[23] The degree of opposition led Gibson to argue that 'These views (i.e. of a double-reference) the minority hold to be contrary to the Scriptures and to the standards…'[24]

What was remarkable about the debates over the question of union in the years up to 1866 is that none of the leading pro-unionists in any way commented upon the misgivings of the anti-unionists over the relation between the United Presbyterian Church and the Westminster Standards. Robert S. Candlish, at least, had gone on record as accusing Brown and Balmer of teaching a less than satisfactory doctrine of the atonement, and, moreover, one that was a variance with the Confession of Faith.[25]

The failure of the pro-unionists to even attempt to answer the anxieties of the anti-unionists only served to increase their

---

21. The anti-unionists became more convinced of the unorthodoxy of the United Presbyterians in areas of fundamental doctrine. The well-publicised 'unity' of the Joint-Committee was seen by them in terms of a theological 'cover-up', due mainly to them being aware of Wood's vociferous opposition to the position of the United Presbyterians on the subject of the atonement.

22. *Proceedings* (1866), *op. cit.*, p. 187.

23. The voting was in fact 241-118 in favour of their views being in accord with the Church's Standards, *Ibid.*, p. 200.

24. *Ibid.*

25. See previous chapter.

opposition to the whole scheme of union. It is also interesting to note that the years following 1866 marked a significant increase in support for the anti-unionists. Opposition to the union was brought to a head at the 1867 Assembly.

*2. The 1867 Report of the Joint-Committee on Union*[26]

The controversy surrounding the 1867 Report centred upon the statements that in matters of doctrine there was no bar to union between the Churches. The Report 'reflected' suggestions received from Presbyteries in response to the remit from the General Assembly.[27] Fifty-two Presbyteries submitted their suggestions regarding the area of doctrinal agreement (i.e. the Second Head of the Programme for Union).[28]

1. Twenty-four Presbyteries suggested the need for further discussion to remove any doubts over the measure of doctrinal agreement between the Free Church and the United Presbyterian Church.

2. Sixteen Presbyteries referred especially to the doctrine of the atonement and the need for further enquiry to be initiated.[29]

3. Twenty-four Presbyteries suggested that a simple and *bona fide* adherence to the Confession was a sufficient guarantee for union.

4. Fifteen Presbyteries enquired whether there was any intention to alter, modify, or abridge the Confession.[30]

It is interesting that the Presbytery of Meigle's submission observed that the 1866 Joint Statement of the Committee of Union[31] on which the Presbyteries made their observations, omitted an important part of the Confession's teaching on the atonement. The omission in the Statement of any reference to Chapter III, section 6, '... Neither are any other redeemed by

---

26. *Proceedings* (1867), *op. cit.,* Report XXXII.

27. *Ibid.,* 28, p. 2. *Ibid.,* pp. 3-6.

29. Apart from three Presbyteries (four if Islay is included), all the rest were north of the 'Highland Line'.

30. The number of Presbyteries is accounted for by the fact of overlapping.

31. *Proceedings* (1867), *op. cit.,* Report XXXII, p. 34. See also *Proceedings* (1866), *op. cit.,* Report XXVI, p. 14.

Christ… but the elect only',[32] seemed to indicate a desire to by-pass areas of possible controversy. The Presbytery therefore asked for further evidence of agreement between the two Churches on the nature and extent of the atonement.[33]

The reaction of the Presbyteries to the Committee's Joint-Statement on doctrine clearly reflected a certain degree of unhappiness with its conclusions. It was altogether striking then that Robert Rainy urged the reappointment of the Committee,[34] declaring that there was no obstacle to the accomplishment of union,[35] the view of the United Presbyterians on the atonement 'in its whole substance (being) identical with the doctrines of the Confession of Faith'.[36] The unwillingness of Rainy and Buchanan to take into consideration the less than unanimous observations of the Presbyteries led to a widening of the breach between the unionists and the anti-unionists in the Free Church.

Dr Wood virtually accused Rainy of covering up the facts.[37] He maintained that there was no 'entire harmony' in the Committee on the subject of doctrine as Rainy had suggested. In addition, he accused Rainy of neglecting the fact that thirty Presbyteries had expressed reservation over the Statement on Doctrine, wanting further clarification of the Church's views.[38] It is difficult to disagree with Wood's observations. The course of the *Proceedings and Debates* during 1867, in particular, give the impression of a 'conspiracy of silence'.

James MacGregor, the Professor of Systematic Theology at New College, added weight to the apprehensions of those unhappy with the course of the Union talks. In his important pamphlet *The Question of Principle now raised in the Free Church especially regarding the Atonement*, MacGregor echoed Wood's observations.

---

32. *Subordinate Standards of the Free Church, op. cit.,* p. 9.
33. *Proceedings* (1867), *op. cit.,* p. 34.
34. Due to Candlish being unwell, Rainy introduced his motion.
35. *Proceedings* (1867), *op. cit.,* p. 259.
36. *Ibid.,* p. 261.
37. *Ibid.,* p. 295.
38. *Ibid.*

I have often wondered why, when so large an amount of attention was given to the matter of the first 'head of programme', with reference to national obligation to serve Christ, so little, comparatively, was given to the far more important matter of the second head, with reference to the doctrine of Grace.[39]

Buchanan, who had the responsibility of being convener of the Committee, never mentions problems of doctrine. It is also significant that his biography fails to mention anything about the question of the United Presbyterians' supposed doctrinal laxity.[40] Wood, who served on the union Committee, maintained that the United Presbyterians on the Committee held to the view that Christ made satisfaction to the justice of God for all men's sins: such a view, he held, to be 'flatly contrary' to the Free Church understanding of the Confession's teaching on the extent of the atonement.[41] It should be said that Wood's assessment of the United Presbyterians was challenged by Sir Henry Moncreiff.

.... when they spoke of Christ satisfying divine justice for all men, I understand them to mean nothing contrary to this (that Christ was the substitute for the elect), but simply that the atonement was designed in the eternal counsel of God to be sufficient for all men, so that a free offer might be made to all on the ground of it.[42]

It is difficult, however, to accept Moncreiff's assessment in the light of our findings in the previous chapter.

39. James MacGregor, *The Question of Principle now raised in the Free Church specially regarding the Atonement* (Edinburgh, 1870), p. 42. MacGregor also virtually accuses the Joint-Committee of underplaying the Confession's teaching on the particularity of Christ's atonement. Cf. p. 64, pp. 68ff.

40. It is remarkable, given the text of the debates, that those in favour of union consistently failed to even attempt to answer the doctrinal fears of the anti-unionists. In eleven years as Convener of the Joint-Committee on Union, Buchanan never touches upon the claims of the anti-unionists that the United Presbyterians were doctrinally suspect.

41. *Proceedings* (1867), *op. cit.,* p. 297.

42. *Ibid.,* p. 316.

MacGregor was also of the opinion that 'There is some reason to suppose that Amyraldism, or un-Calvinistic universalism, with reference to the Atonement, *is tolerated* in her pulpit by the United Presbyterian Church.'[43] Although MacGregor admitted that he could not *prove* this to be the case, he argued that the 1845 Resolution clearing Brown and Balmer from holding unorthodox views on the atonement virtually tolerated 'un-Calvinistic universalism' in the United Secession Church – a decision which was not recalled at the Union of 1847. In addition, the Free Church Professor pointed to the series of public demonstrations by United Presbyterian ministers during the union discussions, at which 'un-Calvinistic universalism' was advocated.[44]

When it came to the vote, Rainy secured a large majority in favour of his motion.[45] Buchanan's biographer N.L. Walker dramatised the conclusion on the 1867 Assembly:

> Several members of it (the Committee) at once resigned; and thereafter began a war outside, which, like all civil, and especially like all religious wars, was far more bitter than those which take place between alien nations.[46]

The exaggeration of Walker's description was no doubt partly due to his antagonism to the anti-unionists. However, the campaign of the anti-unionists did become more pointed, especially with the setting up of a magazine to publicise their views. The *Watchword* sought to expose the unorthodoxy of the United

---

43. MacGregor, *op. cit.,* p. 59.

44. *Ibid.,* pp. 59-60. MacGregor was of the conviction that the Free Church did not tolerate such a position regarding the extent of Christ's atonement: 'There is much reason to believe that Amyradism is excluded from the pulpit of our Free Church by her law; or, in other words, that it is condemned, expressly and directly, by the Westminster Confession' (p. 60).

45. Rainy had a majority of over two hundred (346-120) for his motion urging the acceptance of the Committee's Report, the reappointment of the Committee, and the belief that there was no obstacle to the union going ahead. Begg and Wood immediately resigned from the Committee.

46. Walker, *Robert Buchanan, op. cit.,* p. 436.

Presbyterian Church and challenge the Free Church to hold fast
to its orthodox heritage.[47]

### 3. The Minority Triumph

The claims of Julius Wood that the unionists were trying to create
agreement with the United Presbyterian Church in matters of
doctrine where none existed were taken up by the *Watchword*. In
its editorial of May 1868, it stated:

> In the midst of the present keen discussions in regard to the civil
> magistrate, the views alleged to be maintained by many in the
> United Presbyterian Church on the subject of the Atonement
> have been a good deal overlooked. This is a matter, however, of
> paramount importance, and we do not see any attempt being
> made in the Union Committee … to have it cleared up.[48]

The same editorial in reviewing a recent work (*The Melchisidec of
the Scriptures*) by a United Presbyterian minister, the Rev. Andrew
Scott, commented that the doctrine of a universal atonement
was now conceded in that Church at large.[49]

The strange insistence of Buchanan that the two Churches
were at one in their understanding of the atonement was further
highlighted in the Committee's Report of the 1869 Assembly.
The Report declared:[50]

> … in regard to the extent of the atonement, after explanations
> given and received, it has been clearly ascertained, that the
> general expressions, *more or less* used on this subject in all the
> Churches, are simply different modes of stating the truth held
> by all the negotiating Churches, that the atonement is sufficient

---

47. The *Watchword* was a monthly magazine started by the anti-union party in May
1866, with Dr Begg as the editor. Dr Hugh Martin assisted Begg in the running of the
magazine, and was probably its leading contributor. Dr Rainy was the leading figure in
guiding the policy of the pro-union magazine, *The Presbyterian*.

48. The *Watchword* (*A Magazine for the defence of Bible Truth, and the advocacy of Free
Church Principles.*) II (Glasgow, Edinburgh, London, 1868), p. 53.

49. *Ibid.*

50. *Proceedings* (1869), *op. cit.*, Report XXIII, pp. 4ff.

for all and adapted to all, and that its benefits are freely offered to all to whom the Gospel comes.[51] [Italics mine]

Such a statement only served to increase the opposition of the anti-unionists. In a letter to the *Watchword*, Wood again maintained that a number of United Presbyterian men on the Committee believed that Jesus made satisfaction to the Father for the sins of all men without exception.[52] Later that same year, an editorial in the *Watchword* questioned the integrity of some of those on the Union Committee: If men on the Committee held different views, how could they be 'cordially at one'?[53] The language of the Committee's declaration concerning unanimity on doctrine also came under attack. Referring to the 1869 Report quoted above, the magazine commented:

> That the atonement is sufficient for all, and adapted to all, and that its benefits are freely offered to all, is the belief of the Arminian and Morisonian, as well as of the Calvinist.[54]

There can be no doubt that the anti-unionists believed that the Joint-Committee, and the leaders in the Free Church, were indulging in a form of 'theological cover-up', blurring differences in doctrine in order to pursue the aim of a comprehensive Church union. Professor George Smeaton, who opposed the union, expressed the fears of the minority that the desire for union was in the main due to a political, rather than a spiritual, impulse. At a speech in Glasgow in 1870 Smeaton remarked:

> Politics has much to do with it – I fear much more than religion. It has moved forward in an atmosphere of strong political partisanship, and seems destined to be a tool, and a willing tool, for the purposes of mere party politicians.[55]

---

51. *Ibid.*

52. *Watchword*, IV (1869), *op. cit.*, pp. 87f.

53. *Ibid.*, p. 351.

54. *Ibid.*, p. 352. The same point made by Candlish in his letters to the Free Church Magazine in May 1845, *op. cit.*

55. Quoted in A. Stewart and J. Kennedy Cameron, *The Free Church of Scotland. 1843-1910: A Vindication* (Edinburgh and Glasgow, 1910), p. 18.

The interest here is not to pronounce theological judgments, but to highlight the fact that the anti-unionists in the Free Church had at least grounds for suspecting that their objections to union, especially those regarding the United Presbyterian's views of the atonement, were almost summarily by-passed. The anti-unionists' feelings were so strong on this issue that they began to mention the possibility of seceding from the Free Church should it pursue union at all costs.[56]

The decision of the 1869 Assembly to press ahead with the union plans ushered in the final stage of the controversy. During the 1870 Assembly, Wood quoted Candlish's work on the atonement to the effect that the thought of a general reference in the atonement undermines the heart of the biblical teaching,[57] and fails to accord with the Confession.[58] At the same time, Professor Gibson attacked one of the United Presbyterian professors. In a pamphlet entitled *Free Churchism V Broad Churchism*,[59] Gibson accused Professor Eadie of unorthodox teaching on the atonement. After quoting Eadie, Gibson stated 'The rankest Arminian never said anything more offensive.'[60]

The Assembly of 1871 witnessed the appearance of Hugh Martin speaking on behalf of the anti-unionists.[61] Martin

---

56. See especially Professor Gibson's speech at the 1870 Assembly, *Proceedings* (1870), *op. cit.,* p. 159: '...in the event of any such motion or resolution being carried by a majority of the votes of this Assembly, and even with the ultimate consent of the presbyteries, we shall not be bound thereby, and shall be entitled to maintain all our rights and privileges, and adopt all competent means to obtain redress.' Dr Begg crystallised the anti-union position in his pamphlet, *Memorial, with the Opinions of Eminent Counsel in regard to the Constitution of the Free Church of Scotland; and Remarks on our Present State and Prospects* (Edinburgh, 1874).

57. R.S. Candlish, *The Atonement: Its Reality, Completeness and Extent* (London, New York, Edinburgh, 1861).

58. *Proceedings* (1870), *op. cit.,* pp. 211f.

59. James Gibson, *The Union Question: Re-Statement of the Difference. Free Churchism V Broad Churchism* (Edinburgh and Glasgow, 1870). The title of Gibson's pamphlet reveals how seriously he viewed the 'error' of the pro-unionists. Few epithets were more damning than 'Broad Churchism' with which to identify the position of Candlish, Buchanan, and Rainy.

60. *Ibid.,* p. 30.

61. Martin's speeches at the 1871 Assembly were closely argued, and theologically

considered that the Free Church must ascertain from the United Presbyterians their true position on the atonement. In particular, Martin was concerned to clarify whether the United Presbyterians understood the atonement first of all in the light of a general reference and then in a particular, or vice versa. The young theologian left no doubt regarding his intentions; if the atonement was to be understood first of all in the light of a general reference, then there could be no

> ... strict, proper, personal substitution; for that is eminently particularising... (and) without substitution you violate the essential postulate of a true, proper, perfect, and efficacious propitiation.[62]

The detail, length, and thoroughness of Martin's speech reflected something of the increasing opposition of the anti-unionists to the theological ambiguity of the United Presbyterian Church. The following two years saw the inevitable result of the Free Church Assembly's decision of 1871 to suspend negotiations for an incorporating union. The obdurate opposition of the anti-unionists over the years had made its mark.[63]

The opposition of the anti-unionists to the United Presbyterians was not restricted to their view of the atonement. The question of the relationship between the United Presbyterian Church and the Formula of Subscription to the Westminster Confession of Faith was also raised by those opposed to union.

---

oriented. Martin was a popular figure in the Free Church at large, and some have thought that his work on the Atonement was one of the finest of the nineteenth century – especially in its treatment of Robertson of Brighton's assessment of the nature of Christ's death. Martin was an 'old-school' Calvinist, and used his studies to defend the Reformed faith against what he considered perversions of its teaching.

62. *Proceedings* (1871), *op. cit.,* p. 145.

63. For fuller details, see C.G. McCrie, *The Church of Scotland: Her Divisions and Reunions, op. cit.,* pp. 255ff.

## 2. The Relationship of the United Presbyterian Church to the Formula of Subscription

What concerns us here is the claim by the anti-unionists that the United Presbyterian Church exhibited a different relationship to the Westminster Standards than the Free Church, and that its relationship to the Standards was characterised by looseness and ambiguity.

The debate over the United Presbyterian Church's relationship to the Standards only really came to life in 1870 when the Joint-Committee on Union proposed that union should be based upon the negotiating Churches' common Standards.[64] In proposing the adoption of the Committee's Report, Buchanan declared that 'on all matters of worship and doctrine, all the churches accept, *ex animo*, and without explanation or reservation, the same Confession of Faith, and by that Confession are ready and willing, in a united Church, to be tried'.[65]

The Union Committee of the United Presbyterian Church, in reviewing its work in 1873, concurred with Buchanan's understanding:

> It was found that all the Churches negotiating held the same confession in regard to doctrine – that by whatever form adherence to it was expressed, whether by signature or declaration, the extent of obligation in the acceptance of it was identical; that any variety in the phrases of the formula implied no diversity in the meaning conveyed or the obligation imposed.[66]

The United Presbyterian Church Report considered that apart from their stated views on the civil magistrate,[67] both Churches

---

64. *Proceedings* (1870), *op. cit.,* Report XXIII. See also Buchanan's speech, pp. 146ff.

65. *Ibid.,* p. 150.

66. *Report of the Committee on Union. United Presbyterian Church* (1873), p. 23. No other information.

67. The United Presbyterians, as we have seen, had long since qualified their commitment to chapter 23 of the Westminster Confession of Faith. The Free Church all but qualified their acceptance of the chapter in 1846. ('Act of the General

required subscription without 'qualification, reservation or explanation'.[68] However, the Report did recognise that it was one thing to use similar, even identical, language in stating what the Churches held, and another to agree over the *interpretation* of that language.[69]

During his last speech to the Free Church Assembly in 1861, the venerable Professor Cunningham declared:

> There is nothing in the Formula of the United Presbyterian Church to which I have any objection: I could sign it myself … they receive the Westminster Confession with just the same qualification and explanation which we have now embodied in our formula…[70]

Cunningham's view of the United Presbyterian Formula was that which held sway over the great majority on the Free Church Union Committee.

Dr Cairns, the 'Apostle of Union',[71] in a letter to a friend in 1864 discussed the Joint-Committee's debate on the Formula:

> We passed to a long and most valuable conversation on our several formulas of assent to the Confession. It came out that all meant the same thing, whether assent was, as in the Free Church, to the 'whole doctrine', or, as with us, to 'an

---

Assembly of the Free Church of Scotland Anent Questions and Formula', June 1846.) In this Act the Free Church disclaimed intolerant or persecuting principles in religion, and maintained that the Confession, when fairly interpreted, does not teach such principles. However, A.T. Innes surely points to the real purpose of the Act: 'the Act is seemingly intended to relieve those who would otherwise have scrupled to sign the Confession, by a declaration of the *animus impotentis*; … it seems…truly a qualification of the Confession, and therefore an addition to it…' (A.T. Innes, *Law of Creeds* [1st ed.], *op. cit.*, pp. 436f.).

68. *Report of the Committee on Union, op. cit.*, pp. 43ff.

69. *Ibid.* This perhaps helps us to understand why Wood earlier wanted clarification in language other than that of the Confessional statements.

70. Quoted in Drummond and Bulloch, *Church in Victorian Scotland 1843-1874, op. cit.*, p. 317. Cf. C.G. McCrie, *Confessions of the Church of Scotland, op. cit.*, pp. 230-233.

71. A.R. MacEwan, *Life and Letters of John Cairns* (London, 1898), p. 530.

authorised exhibition of the sense in which we understand the Scriptures...'[72]

The Joint-Committee's belief that the two Churches meant the same thing by their separate Formulas was challenged by some of the leading anti-unionists. Professor Gibson, who was characterised by Buchanan's biographer N.L. Walker as a 'traditional ecclesiastic',[73] published a pamphlet in 1870 which mainly dealt with the United Presbyterian Church and the Formula of Subscription.[74] Gibson maintained that it was 'bogus' to say that the United Presbyterians subscribed the Formula in the same way as the Free Church did.[75] In so doing, he challenged the public statement of Professor Harper of the United Presbyterian Church that the two Churches required the same approbation of the Westminster Confession of Faith from all candidates for the ministry.[76] One of the main thrusts of Gibson's pamphlet appears in his attempt to expose the difference between the statements of the United Presbyterian leaders and the actual position of 'many' parish ministers who sat loose to the teachings of the Confession. In the pamphlet he quoted a letter from a Mr George Bell of Newcastle, who, in supporting Gilfillan of Dundee's liberal stand on subscription, said:

> You (any United Presbyterian minister) are not required to approve of anything which teaches, or may be supposed to teach...*intolerant principles* in religion... And I have no hesitation in applying the word 'intolerant' to such doctrines as reprobation and infant damnation.[77]

---

72. *Ibid.*, p. 526.

73. Walker, *Robert Buchanan, op. cit.*, p. 446.

74. Gibson's pamphlet contained the substance of a speech he made to the Free Church Presbytery of Glasgow in November 1870, opposing Buchanan's motion that the Presbytery give no objection in principle to an incorporating union on the basis of the Church's present understanding of the Westminster Standards. See introduction, *op. cit.*

75. *Ibid.,* p. 16.

76. *Ibid.,* p. 17. Gibson quotes Harper in the *Daily Review*, October 6, 1870.

77. *Ibid.,* p. 20.

Both Bell and Gilfillan considered that the 'saving clause' in the Formula enabled them to subscribe the Confession while rejecting some of its central teachings.[78] Gibson had a willing supporter in the *Watchword* magazine. The magazine commented frequently upon the powerlessness of the United Presbyterian Formula to deal with heresy, and made a great deal of the 'Dalkeith Case' of 1871 involving Fergus Ferguson, a United Presbyterian minister.[79] Ferguson had been accused of heresy by certain members of the United Presbyterian Presbytery of Edinburgh, and although the case against him was considered proved he was subsequently acquitted. Commenting upon the acquittal, the *Watchword* declared:

> The loose formula of the United Presbyterian Church which we are called upon to approve has apparently smitten their Church with moral paralysis.[80]

In a later issue the magazine again challenged the meaningfulness of the United Presbyterian Formula describing it as an 'elastic formula'.[81] The *Watchword* played a strategic part in the campaign of the anti-unionists. It acted as a public platform for their opposition to the Joint-Committee's attempt to unite the Churches on the basis of their acceptance of the Westminster Standards. The Joint-Committee's declaration that there did not appear to be any difficulty to uniting on the basis of the Churches' common Formula[82] was challenged by the magazine: 'The statement and finding of the Committee on this....we pronounce, and engage to prove, to be utterly deceptive.'[83]

---

78. While it is possible to argue that the Confession in no way teaches what has been emotively termed 'infant damnation', it is surely impossible to relegate 'Reprobation', as it is expounded in the Confession, to the 'status' Gilfillan and Bell gave to it.

79. *Watchword,* V (1871), *op. cit.,* pp. 433ff.

80. *Ibid.,* p. 438.

81. *Ibid.,* p. 572.

82. *Watchword,* IV (1870), *op. cit.,* pp. 444.

83. *Ibid.*

The proof offered by the magazine was a close examination of the historical evolution of the Formula of Subscription in the Secession Churches from 1796 to 1847.[84] In particular, the *Watchword* examined the 1847 Formula and considered it to lack the definiteness and personal commitment required by the Free Church Formula.[85] The conclusion of the examination into the United Presbyterian Formula further revealed the anti-unionists' suspicion that the Free Church leadership were indulging in a 'theological cover-up':

> The question of the alteration of the formula, so much agitated in the Secession body, is one of the most serious with which the Free Church Committee has been called to deal, and yet they have evaded and staved it off.[86]

The anti-unionists' suspicion of the United Presbyterian Church's stand vis-à-vis the Confession of Faith was not limited to that Church's relation to the Formula. During the 1866 Free Church Assembly, Professor Gibson raised the question of the stated desire of the United Presbyterian Presbytery of Edinburgh to alter and abridge the Confession.[87] Although agreeing in principle that revision of the Confession was not unlawful, Gibson nonetheless maintained that 'this principle of revision was the small end of the wedge'.[88] As the content of his speech shows, the Professor questioned the United Presbyterian's relation to the Confession not so much because of his 'arch-conservatism' as because of his belief that the desire for change was motivated

---

84. The conclusions of the magazine are the same as those found in chapter one, i.e. that the Secession Churches had 'liberalised' their attachment to the Formula over the years.

85. *Watchword*, IV (1870), *op. cit.*, pp. 446ff.

86. *Ibid.*, p. 446. The magazine quotes at length the 1820 letter that Brown and Balmer submitted to the United Secession Synod as indicative of the differences in the Churches.

87. *Proceedings* (1866), *op. cit.*, pp. 200ff.

88. *Ibid.*, p. 201.

by that Church's lack of sympathy with fundamental elements in the Confession.[89]

## 3. Conclusion

The purpose of this chapter has been to highlight the fact that the United Presbyterian Church was considered less than orthodox in its relation to the Westminster Standards by a group of fellow Presbyterians. The fact that the anti-unionists in the Free Church only counted for a minority[90] could lead us to question the validity of using their opposition to the United Presbyterian Church as an indicator of its supposed defection from the Calvinism of the Confession. However, the circumstances of their opposition, and the nature of their arguments, make it impossible to discount the validity of their claims. It is difficult to read the *Proceedings of the Free Church Assembly* during the union controversy without concluding that the convenor of the Joint-Committee, Robert Buchanan, and the leading members of the Assembly,[91] seemed intent on by-passing the fears and suspicions of the anti-unionists. It would perhaps be more than invidious to subscribe to the view of the anti-unionists that there was an attempt to cover over

---

89. It needs to be remembered, in the light of the claims that Gibson was simply an obscurantist, that he was in effect seeking to expose what he believed to be the inconsistency between the Joint-Committee on Union's statements that the two Churches were at one in their relation to the Confession, and the actual situation of men in the United Presbyterian Church urging the necessity of altering and abridging the Confession. See *Ibid.,* p. 200. There is little doubt that Gibson thought the Confession all but sacrosanct, but he did throughout use detailed arguments, and rarely resorted to historical myopia and bare invective.

90. The highest number of votes gained by the anti-unionists was in the 1872 Assembly: 172 supporting the anti-unionists opposition to the proposed Mutual Eligibility Act, and 369 in favour of the proposed legislation. See *Proceedings* (1872), *op. cit.*, p. 196.

91. Although the great bulk of the debates centred upon the relation of the Church to that of the State, it is difficult to understand why there was no attempt to allay the fears of the anti-unionists concerning the doctrinal orthodoxy of the United Presbyterian Church. Only Moncrieff took up Wood's denunciation of the United Presbyterian's understanding of the general and special reference in Christ's atonement, cf. *Proceedings* (1867), *op. cit.,* p. 316, but that only accounted for a few paragraphs in ten years of debates.

the theological differences between the Churches in order to pursue the cause of union. However, analysis inevitably leads to conclusions; and it is difficult not at least to question why there seemed to be little attempt to answer the insistent suspicions of the anti-unionists regarding the unorthodoxy of the United Presbyterian Church's attachment to the Confession of Faith. To read the Proceedings of the Free Church Assembly, and then to read the majority of historical commentators on the union controversy, is to end up bemused. Few, if any, give consideration to the theological objections of the anti-unionists to the proposed union. McCrie suggested that the Disruption worthies who opposed union did so because they lagged behind progress,[92] considering 1843 as an ecclesiastical and theological *terminus ad quem*.[93] Candlish, on the other hand, was considered by McCrie to have had a 'breadth of vision',[94] something which was lacking in those who opposed the union. Such an analysis totally neglects the fact that the anti-unionists' opposition to union with the United Presbyterian Church was throughout ecclesiastical and theological. It was not 'new interpretations' of the Confession that the anti-unionists objected to (that never at any time entered the debate), but what they believed to be denials of its teaching, not least on the fundamental doctrine of the atonement. In almost fifty pages, McCrie gives no space to the claims of the anti-unionists that the United Presbyterian Church had departed from the Confession's teaching on the atonement.

The same sort of analysis is reflected by Buchanan's biographer, Norman Walker. In assessing the reasons for the outbreak of the

---

92. McCrie seems quite oblivious to the fact that there could have been any worthy motives in the objections of the anti-unionists. Again, it is revealing to discover how little the primary sources of the conflict were used as the basis of analysis and conclusion. See also J.R. Fleming *A History of the Church in Scotland 1843-74* (Edinburgh, 1927), where the same sort of attitude is graphically portrayed: Begg is thought of as 'champion of the obscurantist and ultra-conservative elements in the Church' (p. 180), and union is thwarted due to 'sectarian pride' (p. 187).

93. McCrie, *The Church of Scotland: Her Divisions and Reunions, op. cit.,* p. 270.

94. *Ibid.,* p. 272.

controversy, Walker placed the blame firmly upon those in the Free Church that he described as representing an 'ecclesiastico-traditional' strand within that Church.[95] Walker's thesis revolves around the belief that two strands of church development evolved within the Free Church in the years following the Disruption in 1843, 'one ecclesiastico-traditional, the other generously evangelical'.[96] The 'die-hard' traditionalism that Walker identified in the anti-union group was further characterised as being essentially Moderate in its ecclesiology and theology.[97] The Moderatism that Walker found in the anti-unionists consisted of their supposed lack of faith in Christian people, their 'low views of the Church', and the too great importance they attached to state patronage and endowments.[98] That Walker should analyse the Union Controversy in such terms is quite remarkable. No-one would deny Buchanan's noted biographer his right to categorise the anti-unionists in any way he chose to. However, it is one thing to append labels, and another to base one's analysis upon all the data that is to hand! Nowhere does Walker mention the claims of the anti-unionists that the United Presbyterians were departing from the Church's theological heritage. At least *they* seemed to consider that fundamental doctrines were at stake if the union was consummated. Walker may have profoundly disagreed with these beliefs, but surely he was under obligation at least to state accurately the anti-union position.

Perhaps the most surprising aspect of the Union Controversy has been its treatment at the hands of historians. Little attempt seems to have been made to assess the only real source of information available on this subject – the debates that took place within the Churches. Too often personalities are given the place that should be reserved for an analysis of the various arguments for and against union. Carnegie Simpson in his biography of

---

95. Walker, *op. cit.,* p. 447.
96. *Ibid.*
97. *Ibid.,* p. 451.
98. *Ibid.*

Rainy falls into such a trap. The nearest he comes to describing accurately the position of the anti-unionists who opposed Rainy is to accuse James Begg of 'poisoning the brotherhood of the Church'.[99] Rainy himself adopted a somewhat personality-centred approach to the controversy. In a private letter to Carnegie Simpson he maintained that:

> Begg was the evil genius of the Free Church. He introduced a policy of conspiracy and of attempting to carry points by threatening us with law. No man did more to lower the tone of the Church and to secularise it.[100]

Later commentators, supporting the policies of the anti-unionists, were no less guilty of failing to examine the issues on a dispassionate level. John MacLeod provides us with a good example of this. In assessing Candlish's part in the disputes over union he declared,

> In the features of his intellectual equipment we might say without invidiousness on the one side or on the other that in their respective spheres of statesmanship, he (Candlish) and David Lloyd George were very like each other.[101]

The aim of this chapter has not been to provide a detailed guide through the maze of arguments surrounding the Union Controversy of 1863–1873. That no-one has attempted a detailed study of these years is a fact that must be rectified. Notwithstanding the lack of historical analysis, the debates of the Free Church Assembly during these years clearly reveal that those who opposed the union did so, at least partly, because of their belief that the United Presbyterian Church had departed from the doctrinal Standards of the Church, the Westminster Confession of Faith. That these fears were not unfounded

---

99. P. Carnegie Simpson, *The Life of Principal Rainy*, I (London, 1909), p. 441.
100. Quoted in Cameron and Stewart, *op. cit.,* p. 37. No reference.
101. MacLeod, *op. cit.,* p. 275.

was suggested by the unwillingness of the United Presbyterian Church to discipline ministers who publicly dissented from some of the fundamental doctrines contained in the Confession of Faith – a fact that will be examined in the following chapter.

*1854*. Principal Tulloch's inaugural lecture at St Andrews on 'Theological Trends of the Age'.

*1860*. Publication in England of *Essays and Reviews*.

*1870*. Fergus Ferguson charged with teaching unsound doctrine by one of his elders.

*1871*. Ferguson examined by his Presbytery, and eventually agreed to support a modified representation of his doctrinal views. The Presbytery admonished him notwithstanding the opposition of sizeable minority.

*1877*. Ferguson proposed an overture in the Glasgow Presbytery of the United Presbyterian Church heavily criticising the content and status of the Confession of Faith. Ferguson's orthodoxy examined by a Committee of Presbytery.

*1878*. Presbytery initiated a process of Libel against Ferguson in order to determine precisely the extent and nature of his orthodoxy. Ferguson found guilty on five counts of holding unsound doctrine.

In May, Ferguson appealed to the Synod. While concurring in the judgment of the Glasgow Presbytery, the Synod admonished Ferguson with 'a brotherly admonition'.

# 5

# Theological Ambivalence in the United Presbyterian Church – The Trials of the Rev. Fergus Ferguson

The latter half of the nineteenth century witnessed a veritable revolution in every area of British society. While industrialisation was remoulding the face of the nation after its own image and destroying the rural heritage of the nation, other factors were at work challenging the framework of society's most enduring bastion – the Church. Although Darwin was not the first to postulate the evolutionary hypothesis, his publication of the *Origin of the Species*[1] in 1859 provided the opportunity for the dissemination and popularisation of the theory. Although it is probably true that the theory of evolution did not cause a great deal of panic in the Church at large,[2] it did seem to provide 'new

---

1. C. Darwin, *Origin of the Species* (London, 1859). Darwin, of course, was not the first scientist to postulate the theory of evolution. Sir Charles Lyell's *Principles of Geology*, published between 1830 and 1833, was based upon the principle of evolution. Darwin's 'achievement' was to give the theory a rationale in the form of 'natural selection', or the 'survival of the fittest' as Spencer popularised it.

2. This is no doubt partly to be explained by the absence of any large scale mass communication through which to disseminate news. Another factor, however, was probably more responsible for limiting the impact of Darwin's work – the religious revivals of 1859. Professor Kitson-Clark makes the point that '…it is necessary to think of the years which followed 1859 not as years of an acute crisis of the mind but rather as the years of the great religious revivals among people who were probably

and prestigious arguments' for those who claimed to be either atheists or agnostics.[3]

The challenge of the natural sciences to the Church had been preceded during the previous decade by those involved in the field of literature. The philosophical and theological scepticism of George Eliot, Francis Newman, and James Anthony Froude, and their questioning the morality of such orthodox Christian doctrines as vicarious atonement, and everlasting punishment, presented a challenge to traditional Christianity.[4] The great popularity of Thomas Carlyle during the middle decades of the century was, in itself, perhaps the most eloquent testimony to the challenge that faced the Church.[5]

If the institutional Church was faced with challenge from without, it was also confronted with a challenge from within. The dismissal of F.D. Maurice from the Chair of Theology at King's College, London, in 1853, proved to be almost prophetic of the theological currents that were arising within the Church of England.[6] The 'unacceptableness' of Maurice's views on eternal punishment to the Church establishment, and

little troubled by Darwinism and had actually never read *Essays and Reviews*' (*The Making of Victorian England*, London, 1962, p. 148).

3. A.L. Drummond and J. Bulloch, *The Church in Victorian Scotland 1843-1874* (Edinburgh and St Andrews, 1975), p. 215.

4. H.R. Murphy's interesting article, 'The Ethical Revolt Against Christian Orthodoxy in Early Victorian England', *American Historical Review*, LX, pp. 800ff., indicates something of the extent of the opposition to orthodox Christian doctrine. It is also worth mentioning that Eliot, Froude and Newman arrived at 'agnosticism' via, what was to all intents, orthodox Christianity.

5. Noel Annan's contribution to the *Ideas and Beliefs of the Victorians* (London, 1949), 'The Strands of Unbelief', outlined the step-by-step development of unbelief from the 1840s, concentrating upon three particular strands – the political, philosophical, and moral. Annan also shows something of Carlyle's influence on men like Huxley, who was given a sense of religion, without the trappings of theology, by reading *Sartor Resartus*; and J.A. Froude maintained that Carlyle saved him from Positivism, Romanism, and Atheism. Basil Willey is of the opinion that Carlyle was the 'most remarkable example of a phenomenon ... typical of the nineteenth century, that of the religious temperament severed from "religion"' (*Nineteenth Century Studies*, Middlesex, 1973 ed., p. 111).

6. Maurice was dismissed from King's College in 1853 after the publication of his *Theological Essays*, in which he attacked the popular biblical view of eternal punishment.

the stir they created, paled into near insignificance beside the furore which arose over the publication of *Essays and Reviews* in 1860.[7] The Essays varied in their unorthodoxy. Mark Pattison's contribution, 'Tendency of Religious Thought in England 1688-1750', and that of Baden-Powell, 'On the Study of the Evidences of Christianity', challenged the accepted notion that truth had been revealed once and for all in Scripture, stressing the importance of what was virtually historical criticism. Pattison's analysis of the development of religious ideas, and Baden-Powell's scepticism concerning the miraculous in Scripture, greatly disturbed the orthodox. However, the Essays of Rowland Williams and H.B. Wilson provoked the greatest controversy. A.P. Stanley thought their treatment of Scripture flippant and contemptuous, and considered the Essays offensive. Williams and Wilson were both tried by the Court of Arches for their views and found guilty. On appeal, however, the Privy Council reversed the decision of the lower court, and declared that the clergy were not obliged by the Church's formularies to believe or teach verbal inspiration, eternal punishment, or imputed righteousness.[8]

The effect of the Essays was, according to Bowen, to force upon an unwilling public open discussion of religious questions which it preferred to ignore.[9] Chadwick surely goes to the heart of the matter when he says that 'The unsettlement of faith about the Bible in 1861-5 was directly caused by historians … It was not caused by Darwin.'[10] The effect of historical criticism was to undermine the belief that truth was absolute and unchanging,

---

7. The *Essays* were condemned from almost every section of society. Frederick Harrison, who was a follower of Comte, condemned the essayists because he thought they should have the honesty to leave the Church and follow the religion of humanity (*Westminster Review*, October, 1860). From the other side of the spectrum, Wilberforce rushed to defend orthodoxy, and castigated the 'infidelity of the work'.

8. Cf. H.G. Wood, *Belief and Unbelief Since 1850* (Cambridge, 1955), pp. 63ff. D. Bowen, *The Idea of the Victorian Church* (Montreal, 1968), pp. 160ff.

9. Bowen, *op. cit.*, p. 169.

10. O. Chadwick, *The Victorian Church*, Part II (London, 1970), p. 3.

and to initiate the conviction that it was rather relative, genetic, and evolutionary.[11]

The challenge to the Church in its confessional conservatism was less dramatic, but nonetheless real, in Scotland. John Tulloch's inaugural lecture as Principal of St Mary's College, St Andrews University, in 1854 on the *Theological Trends of the Age*, heralded something of the dawning of a new era in Scottish Church life.[12] In assessing the force of 'Traditionalism' as a powerful factor in theological development,[13] Tulloch lays bare his challenge to the accepted order.

> The question, in short, is one between Tradition, in whatever shape, and Science. Is the truth to be held, unquestioned and unquestionable, in *any* outward formula, – at the simple dictation of any outward power? or is it ever only – for our time as for all time – the produce of two factors – of Scripture and Reason, of Revelation and free Inquiry? It is the implied principle of all genuine Protestantism that it is the latter.[14]

The approach to theology which all but deifies some historic formulation and elevates it above criticism is denounced by Tulloch:

> … we feel bound to protest against a system which… leaves us logically powerless, as Theologians, before the seductions of Popery and the assaults of Infidelity.[15]

Tulloch's approach combined restless enquiry and a commitment to Scripture as the Church's objective rule. He maintained that 'Infallible itself…[Scripture] lays no restraint on the freest Inquiry'.[16] The 'back to the Bible approach' advocated by Tulloch,

---

11. Cf. Annan, *op. cit.*
12. J. Tulloch, *Theological Tendencies of the Age* (Edinburgh, 1855).
13. *Ibid.*, p. 5ff.
14. *Ibid.*, p. 10.
15. *Ibid.*, p. 11f.
16. *Ibid.*, p. 31.

in effect, short-circuited the Church's doctrinal Standards as effective, or even desirable, formulations of the Christian faith.

Compared to Tulloch, John Caird represented a more disturbing challenge to the conservative orthodoxy of the Church. The genesis of Caird's thinking is not easy to determine. During the middle decades of the century, Ferrier was responsible for introducing the Hegelian idea of 'absolute idealism' into Scotland, and Fleming, for one, considered him 'the father of Hegelianism' in Scotland.[17] If Ferrier could be considered the father of Hegelianism in Scotland, then Caird could be considered its populariser. Through his preaching and writing, Caird popularised a new kind of theology, one that showed little sign of sympathy with the 'Puritans, Reformers and latter-day divines', and yielded much to German method, approach, and views.[18]

Professor Colin Brown crystallises what he considers to be the main thrust behind Idealism:

> The term Idealism is an elastic one. In its widest sense it denotes the view that the mind and spiritual values are more fundamental than material ones.[19]

Although Reardon considers that Caird kept Hegel's influence on him basically conservative,[20] it cannot be denied that Caird's

---

17. J.R. Fleming, *A History of the Church in Scotland 1843-1874* (Edinburgh, 1927), p. 110.

18. 'John Caird As A Thinker, Sermon-Writer and Divine.' *United Presbyterian Magazine* (August 1858, pp. 353ff.), p. 357. Author's name not given, only his initials, i.e. G.B.J. The influence of German philosophy on Caird increased as the years went by. Reviewing the publication in 1880 of Caird's *An Introduction to the Philosophy of Religion* (the substance of the 1878-1879 Croall Lectures), the *Bibliotheca Sacra* commented, 'The influence of German philosophy is now at its height in Scotland. The Westminster Confession is not more proof against it than is the unwritten creed of the Congregational churches. We find even the distinguished writer of the present volume acknowledging that to Hegel's "Philosophie der Religion', he has been more largely indebted than to any other book.' *Bibliotheca Sacra*, XXXVII (London, 1880), p. 577.

19. Colin Brown, *Philosophy and the Christian Faith* (London, 1969), p. 117.

20. B.M.G. Reardon, *From Coleridge to Gore. A Century of Religious Thought in Britain* (London, 1971), p. 417.

theology differed radically from that accepted by the Church as orthodox. Two particular elements marked out the 'novelty' of Caird's theological system. First, he utilised the evolutionary and developmental approach to theology initiated in Germany;[21] and secondly, he maintained that particular facts (of history) are of less importance than the underlying ideas which they represent. As he puts it in *The Fundamental Ideas of Christianity,* 'A true idea is true independently of the facts and events that first suggested it.'[22]

In his *Introduction to the Philosophy of Religion,* Caird elaborated upon the importance of the 'spiritual' as against the 'material':

> ... even in its most immature stage of spiritual culture, the religious mind passes beyond the anthropomorphic figures to seize, in an indefinite but not unreal way, the hidden spiritual meaning. The representation conveys a general impression which is of the nature of knowledge, though, literally conceived, it expresses what is untrue.[23]

Caird's stress on this subordinate, and subservient, role of the material as against that of the spiritual led him to conclude that even if scientific criticism shattered the biblical records, yet

> ... the ideas and doctrines concerning the nature of God and the hopes and destinies of humanity, which had their historic origin in that life, would be recognised as true in themselves, and as having an indestructible evidence in the reason and conscience of man.[24]

In a review of a book of his sermons, the *United Presbyterian Magazine* reflected something of the conservative reaction to the renowned preacher.[25] Caird is considered by the magazine to

---

21. J. Caird, *The Fundamental Ideas of Christianity,* I (Glasgow, 1899), p. 27.

22. *Ibid.,* II, p. 241, quoted in Reardon, op. cit., p. 419.

23. J. Caird, *An Introduction to the Philosophy of Religion* (Glasgow, 1920 edition), p. 174f.

24. Caird, *Fundamental Ideas, op. cit.,* p. 242, quoted in Reardon, *op. cit.,* p. 420.

25. J. Caird, *Book of Sermons* (Edinburgh and London 1858). The review in the magazine was also concerned to criticise Caird's famous Crathie sermon, which had been so highly praised in many quarters.

be less eminent than he is made out to be.[26] His thought and ideas are dismissed as being 'often vague and indistinct and shadowy…'[27] And his theology is thought of as conceding too much to reason, and essentially unbiblical.[28]

The traditional theological outlook of the Church in Scotland, as it was embodied in the Westminster Standards, was further challenged by those outwith the ecclesiastical spectrum. One of the most outspoken critics of Westminster Calvinism was George MacDonald.[29]

In one novel in particular, MacDonald attacks the rigid Calvinism which he considered to be stifling worship, and religion in general. In *David Elginbrod,* MacDonald uses the literary genre to castigate the theological orthodoxy of his day.[30] The scene is set when Hugh Sutherland, the young tutor, gives David Elginbrod's daughter Margaret a copy of Coleridge's poems.[31] The venerable Elginbrod is later heard ridiculing the Westminster Confession's doctrine of 'imputit richteousness' as a nonsense,[32] and Boston's famous *Fourfold State,* a pillar of Scottish Church piety, is dismissed as a 'fourfold fog' of God's ways with man.[33] At various points in the novel, MacDonald uses his characters to challenge the traditional theological views on the love of God,[34] election,[35] and salvation,[36] and highlights his belief in the universal Fatherhood of God, and universal salvation.[37]

In addition to the intellectual challenges facing the Church, the very fabric of the developing industrialised society acted as

---

26. *United Presbyterian Magazine, op. cit.,* p. 354.
27. *Ibid.*
28. *Ibid.,* p. 357.
29. Fleming, *op. cit.,* p. 169.
30. G. MacDonald, *David Elginbrod* (London, 1863).
31. *Ibid.,* p. 6.
32. *Ibid.,* p. 37.
33. *Ibid.,* p. 60.
34. *Ibid.,* pp. 66, 325.
35. *Ibid.,* p. 322.
36. *Ibid.,* p. 376.
37. Cf. A. Webster, *Theology in Scotland; Reviewed by a Heretic* (London, 1915), pp. 86ff. Webster considered MacDonald to have been the first 'distinctively Scottish

a force for change. The so-called 'Sabbath War' of the 1860s heralded a new era in the Church's relationship to society.[38] The increasing necessity to transport people and materials even on the Sabbath undermined the Westminster teaching on the sacrosanct nature of the day of rest.[39]

As the Scottish Church entered the 1870s, it was faced with a clamour from all sides to reassess its theological bearings, and come to terms with historical criticism, the rights of individuals to exercise a certain amount of personal discretion in their subscription to the Westminster Standards, and the virtual revolution affecting the social, economic, and political norms of the nation. In his Rectorial Address at St Andrews University in 1871, James Anthony Froude characterised the extent of the challenge facing those who were still committed to the theology of the Westminster Standards:

> Everyone here present must have become familiar in late years with the change of tone throughout Europe and America on the subject of Calvinism. After being accepted for two centuries in all Protestant countries as a final account of the relations between man and his Maker, it has come to be regarded by liberal thinkers as a system of belief incredible in itself, dishonouring in its object, and as intolerable as it has been intolerant.[40]

It was with such an intellectual climate as a backcloth that Scottish Presbyterianism witnessed the trials of the Rev. Fergus Ferguson for heresy.

---

writer to popularise the idea of God's Fatherhood' (p. 95). Such a statement reveals a great ignorance of Scottish theological writing! However, MacDonald did stress the idea of the 'universal' Fatherhood of God; and this theme underlines much of *David Elginbrod*. Cf. his novel *Robert Falconer*, London 1868, where he reduces the root of Calvinism to a belief in hell.

38. R.D. Brackenridge, 'The "Sabbath War" of 1865-66: The Shaking of the Foundations.' In *S.C.H.S. Records*, SVI (1969), pp. 22ff.

39. *Subordinate Standards, op. cit.*, Chapter XXI, p. 34. Sections VII and VIII identify the 'Lord's Day', when Christians meet for worship, with the Old Testament Sabbath, and consider the obligations for observing it to be identical with those pertaining to the fourth commandment.

40. W.A. Knight, *Rectorial Addresses at St. Andrews* (London, 1894), p. 112.

With the collapse of the union talks in 1873, the idea of a comprehensive Church union within Scottish Presbyterianism was postponed for nearly thirty years. The 1870s were not only notable for the failure of the union fostered by the Free and United Presbyterian Churches, but also for the climax of the erosion of Westminster Calvinism in the Church of the Secession. While the United Presbyterian Church Declaratory Act of 1879 introduced into the idea of Confessional subscription what has come to be thought of as 'the conscience clause', the Declaratory legislation itself developed out of circumstances which all but intimated the United Presbyterian Church's departure from the doctrinal Standards of Westminster. The circumstances in question revolved around the Rev. Fergus Ferguson. On two occasions during the 1870s, Ferguson was tried for holding opinions contrary to the Scriptures and the Westminster Standards. Although a number of his views were finally condemned by the Church's highest court, the Synod, the unwillingness of the Church to do other than give a 'brotherly admonition' to Ferguson reflected to a considerable degree its toleration of doctrines and attitudes which flatly contradicted those in the Westminster Standards.

The trials of Fergus Ferguson for heresy illustrated the United Presbyterian Church's unwillingness to remove from its ministry one who had been convicted of holding certain heretical opinions, and provided the necessary impetus towards Confessional revision within Scottish Presbyterianism.

## 1. The Dalkeith Case of 1871

At a Presbytery meeting in November 1870, an elder in Ferguson's Church at Dalkeith, Mr Richard Dodds, gave notice of a complaint he wished to register against some aspects of his minister's teaching.[41] In particular, Dodds charged Ferguson with teaching: first, that in the intermediate, or middle, state, infants and heathen will have the gospel preached to them, thus

---

41. *Edinburgh Presbytery of the United Presbyterian Church. Minute Book 1868-1874.*

allowing for the possibility of salvation beyond the grave; and secondly, that the death of Christ was sufficient for the salvation of Satan, even though he subsequently refused God's offer of pardon.[42]

In response to these charges, the Presbytery appointed a committee comprising of the Rev. Drs Peddie, Thomson, and Gemmell to talk with Ferguson and ascertain the validity or otherwise of the charges.[43] The Report of the Committee was quite favourable to Ferguson. They felt that he had been largely misunderstood, but added the warning that Scripture gave no warrant to suppose that those who died without hearing the gospel will hear it after death.[44] The matter might have rested there but for a speech Ferguson made in the Presbytery. The contents of the speech proved so upsetting to some, and the report of it in the *Dalkeith Herald* gave it such wide publicity[45] that the above committee were requested to examine it, and report upon it.[46]

This time the committee exposed what it considered the 'unorthodoxy' of a number of Ferguson's views. They stated in their report that the speech as reported was 'ambiguous, confused and inconsistent',[47] and that the errant minister spoke of the intermediate state as a 'dispensation of mercy', a period when an increase in knowledge could lead to salvation.[48] The Committee concluded 'That there can be no question that he (Ferguson) holds –

(1) That there is for men who have not embraced the Gospel here a dispensation of mercy after death; and

(2) That there is a place or state for departed souls beside heaven and hell in the interval between death and judgment.'[49]

---

(Scottish Records Office). No other information. Minutes, 1 November 1870, p. 140.

42. *Ibid.*

43. *Ibid.*, 6 December 1870, p. 147.

44. *Ibid.*, p. 149.

45. The Dalkeith Herald of 14 December 1870, reported Ferguson's speech in full.

46. *Minutes, op. cit.*, 7 March 1871, pp. 167f.

47. *Ibid.*, p. 168.

48. *Ibid.*, p. 170.

The Committee's indictment of Ferguson's views was straight to the point; they were 'very erroneous, Contrary to the doctrines of the Scriptures and the Subordinate Standards'.[50]

Considering the nature of the Committee's report, it is surprising to find that it was rejected by thirty-one to eighteen by the Presbytery.[51] In response to the Presbytery's decision, Peddie, Professor Harper, and five others entered their dissent. The Presbytery minutes record Peddie's dissent in full, and in so doing reflected the extent and seriousness of the opposition to Ferguson's theological opinions.

Peddie gave four reasons for his dissent. First, he believed that the Presbytery's decision left the case in an unsatisfactory situation. Secondly, he considered Ferguson's doctrines 'gravely dangerous'. Thirdly, Peddie maintained that:

> ... in the opinion of the Protesters it is deeply prejudicial to the interests of truth and most painfully wounding to the character of this Presbytery that after having had these matters under consideration for weeks past they should by their decision dismiss the whole case without any remark or animadversion whatsoever, thereby conniving at, and directly giving sanction to views opposed to the teaching of Scripture as understood in this Church and exhibited in our Subordinate Standards.[52]

Fourthly, Peddie underlined the fact that Ferguson had made no recantation of these views.

The opposition of the 'Protesters' proved so adamant that the Synod appointed a committee to meet with Ferguson. At first Ferguson refused to meet with the Committee, but after John Cairns and John Eadie had counselled him, Ferguson returned with them to Edinburgh. (The appearance of Cairns and Eadie revealed the unwillingness of even the most conservative to expel Ferguson from the ministry.) The case was to all intents

---

49. *Ibid.*, p. 170.
50. *Ibid.*
51. *Ibid.*, 20 March 1871, p. 175.
52. *Ibid.*, pp. 177f.

concluded when the Committee asked Ferguson to subscribe four propositions, designed to satisfy his opponents as to his orthodoxy.[53] The propositions were:

First, that all those eventually saved were chosen in Christ before the foundation of the world.

Secondly, that all those eventually saved are accepted by God only by grace through the redemption of Christ, at or before the time of death; and that none dying unsaved will after death have the opportunity of obtaining salvation.

Thirdly, that any new revelations after death, of Christ or truth, are not to free from sin, but to increase the blessing and knowledge of the saved.

Fourthly, that unbelievers are fully answerable to God for their rejection of the gospel.[54]

The fact that Ferguson 'intimated his unqualified assent' to the propositions is difficult to understand.[55] J.H. Leckie, Ferguson's great admirer and biographer, recognised the ambiguity. He wrote with a certain degree of embarrassment, 'These propositions certainly do…appear to be inconsistent with some of Ferguson's contentions.'[56] The desire of the Presbytery to bring the issue to a peaceful conclusion was fulfilled when Ferguson accepted the propositions. That the issue was not fully resolved was evident from a letter that Ferguson sent to the Synodical Committee prior to his acquittal.

> I still hold all the interpretations of Scripture given by me from the pulpit, and understand that my liberty as a Minister of the Gospel, to speak according to my own light, conscience and sense of responsibility, remains unimpaired.[57]

Whether Ferguson acceded to the Committee's propositions either out of weakness or a desire for peace[58] is impossible to

---

53. *Ibid.*, 6 June 1871, p. 195.
54. *Ibid.*
55. *Ibid.*, p. 196.
56. J.D. Leckie, *Fergus Ferguson, his Theology and Heresy Trial* (Edinburgh, 1923), p. 78.
57. *Minutes, op. cit.*, 6 June 1871, p. 195.

determine. That he later regretted ever having given his assent to them precludes us from the option that he subscribed the propositions out of a wholehearted agreement with them.[59]

The main point to arise from the Dalkeith trial was Ferguson's refusal to recant any of his views pertaining to the possibility of salvation after death, and the willingness of the Synod to construct a formula that would save Ferguson for the Church and remove any disunity. That the United Presbyterian Church did not require exact, unqualified assent from its ministers to the Westminster Confession no-one would deny. However, that the Church should seem to tolerate views which undermined not only the traditional eschatology of the Church, but which cut at the very heart of the Confession's teaching on the work of Christ, marks a new departure from the Confessional Calvinism that had characterised the Secession's public testimony. It was the unwillingness of the United Presbyterian Church to discipline Ferguson that led the *Watchword* to question the morality of its use of the Formula of Subscription.[60]

Leckie makes the important point that the Dalkeith Case marked the first appearance of eschatological problems in Scottish ecclesiastical life.[61] Up until this juncture, the teaching of the Westminster Confession was considered to be a faithful summary of the Scriptures' teaching concerning those who die without faith in Christ. That such a cornerstone of the Confession's teaching should be challenged and pass without real censure indicated that Confessional revision would not be long in coming.

---

58. Leckie, *op. cit.*, p. 79.

59. *Ibid.*

60. See the previous chapter.

61. Leckie, *op. cit.*, p. 81. Already in England the Privy Council decision concerning Wilson and Williams' views on eternal punishment had all but made the orthodox teaching an open question, and not one that carried official sanction. The 1870s in England witnessed a number of works specifically dealing with the question of eternal punishment, e.g. Farrar's *Eternal Hope*, 1879; Cox's *Salvator Mundi*, 1878; and E.B. Pusey's *What is of Faith as to Everlasting Punishment*, 1879. *The Westminster Confession of Faith*, which had governed the views of all the Presbyterian Churches in Scotland

## 2. Accusation of Heresy – Act II

At a meeting of the Glasgow Presbytery of the United Presbyterian Church on March 13 1877, Fergus Ferguson, who was now minister in Queen's Park, intimated that he would propose the following overture at the next Presbytery meeting:

> … whereas…the existing Subordinate doctrinal Standards of this Church…are not in …perfect harmony with the Supreme Standards, being not only in respect of their logical form badly constructed and also in respect of their literary style unhappily expressed, but above all in respect of their subject matter giving an inadequate exhibition of the truth; first of all as regards the three fundamental topics of natural religion VIZ. the truth concerning God, the Universe and Man, and in the Second place as regards the fundamental topics of revealed religion, VIZ. the truth concerning Christ, the Church and the Bible; The Synod…is hereby humbly and respectfully overtured (to consider)…the rectification of an anomaly so painful and injurious to the highest interests of the Church and the world, and for the purpose also of contributing thereby to the reconstruction of the creed of Christendom, and the consequent unification of the Church throughout the world.[62]

It is doubtful if any Presbyterian minister in Scotland had ever approached the extent and thoroughness of Ferguson's attack on the Westminster Standards. At the next two meetings of the Presbytery, a number of motions were tabled reflecting on Ferguson's motion.[63] After a long debate, the Presbytery

---

on the subject, unequivocally maintained the reality, and eternity, of the punishment inflicted by God upon the wicked and disobedient. See in particular Chapters XXXII, and XXXIII sections I and II.

62. *Glasgow Presbytery of the United Presbyterian Church. Minutes 1875-1878*, VI, (Scottish Records Office.) No Other Information. *Minutes*, 13 March 1877, pp. 219f. The whole speech is found in Ferguson's pamphlet, *Reconstruction of the Creed* (Glasgow 1877), pp. 13ff. This pamphlet reveals the extent and bitterness of Ferguson's condemnation of the Westminster Standards.

63. *Minutes of Glasgow Presbytery, op. cit.*, 10 and 17 April 1877, pp. 231-240.

favoured the 'moderate' motion of Dr Brown. Brown's motion called for the rejecting of Ferguson's motion, but added the rider that the Presbytery should approach the Synod with a view towards the revision of the Church's Standards.[64] The furore that arose over Ferguson's overture resulted in an elder, Mr Robert Wilson, threatening to draw up a libel against Ferguson for heresy, unless the Presbytery agreed to appoint a committee to investigate the situation.[65] Wilson was so committed to the expulsion of Ferguson from the ministry that he later reserved the right of further action if the Committee's report proved unsatisfactory to him.[66]

## 1. The Examination

Dr Young was appointed Convener of the Committee to examine Ferguson's statements in Presbytery, and to comment upon an article he had written in the *Young Men's Christian Magazine*.[67] In his report to Presbytery, Young quoted Ferguson at length on the teaching of certain elements in the Confession.[68]

The view of the Confession reduces man to the level of a beast.[69]

The Confession teaches a Salvation out of harmony with what we know of God himself.[70]

The whole conception of the two Covenants – a Covenant of works and a Covenant of grace is merely a piece of theological mechanism dead and wooden to the core.[71]

---

64. *Ibid.*, 17 April 1877, p. 240.
65. *Ibid.*, 1 May 1877, p. 249.
66. *Ibid.*, 12 June 1877, p.
67. *Ibid.*, 14 August 1877, p. 283. Ferguson, *Reconstruction of the Creed, op. cit.*, Appendix, pp. 60f.
68. *Minutes of Glasgow Presbytery, op. cit.*, 14 August 1877, pp. 283ff.
69. *Ibid.*, p. 284. (Also in Ferguson, *Reconstruction of the Creed, op. cit.*, p. 26.)
70. *Ibid.*
71. *Ibid.*, p. 285.

It does not consist with the divine absoluteness to provide a Salvation only for a limited number of men. The whole conception of such a salvation involves a violation of the righteousness of God.[72]

...the three-fold decree of predestination, foreordination and election degenerates in the Confession into a compound of fatalism and favouritism.[73]

The harshness of Ferguson's condemnation of certain parts of the Confession, as outlined in the Committee's report, induced the Presbytery to draw up questions to put to him. In particular, the Presbytery asked Ferguson to clarify his views on the Trinity, man's sinfulness, the Covenants, and the nature of Christ's propitiation.[74]

Ferguson refused to meet with the Committee because he considered the situation to be at an impasse: How could the Confession, which he thought to be suspect on a number of issues, and which he was in revolt against, be used as a test of his, or anyone's orthodoxy?[75] However, Ferguson did provide the Presbytery with a statement clarifying his views, but this was regarded by the court as 'unsatisfactory'.[76]

The 'deep regret' felt by the Presbytery over Ferguson's unwillingness to meet with its appointed Committee left it with little alternative but to initiate a process of libel against the recalcitrant minister.[77] Due to the Synod's decision the previous year to set up a Committee to enquire into the Church's relationship with its Subordinate Standards,[78] and the fact that Ferguson had been appointed to that Committee, some of the

---

72. *Ibid.*

73. *Ibid.*, pp. 285f.

74. *Ibid.*, pp. 286ff.

75. Leckie, *op. cit.*, p. 170.

76. *Minutes of the Glasgow Presbytery, op. cit.*, 9 October 1877, p. 300.

77. *Ibid.*, 12 February 1878, p. 328.

78. *Proceedings of the Synod of the United Presbyterian Church. Vol. VI 1877–1879* (Glasgow 1880), p. 50.

Presbytery thought it would be best to defer prosecution until the Church's relationship to the Westminster Standards had been clarified.[79] It was possible that such a course of action might have been adopted but for the publishing in February 1878 by Ferguson of his *Additional Statements In Defence of my Doctrinal Position.*[80] The conservative members of the Presbytery considered the publication final proof of Ferguson's heresy, and any possibility of compromise was dismissed when the clerk, Dr George Jeffrey, was instructed to prepare the libel.[81] Ferguson was suspended from his ministerial duties until the libel was concluded.

In his pamphlet, Ferguson attempted to clarify those of his beliefs which were considered erroneous and suspect, and to establish them as eminently scriptural. The publication of the *Statements* only served, however, to intensify the opposition of the conservative members of Presbytery. It is not difficult to understand why any form of compromise was rejected when the contents of the *Statements* are examined.

On the question of human depravity, Ferguson maintained that Man

> has fallen beyond the power of self recovery, without the help of God; but not beyond the power of self-recovery with the help of God. The way of salvation is just the divine method of helping man to attain his true and ultimate position.[82]

When Ferguson turns to discussing the 'Ultimate Ground of Human Condemnation',[83] he endeavours to establish his conviction that the 'so-called orthodox view',[84] what he calls 'isolation', the final separation of the wicked from God and the blessed, is completely wrong:

---

79. Leckie, *op. cit.*, pp. 185f.

80. Fergus Ferguson, *Additional Statements In Defence of my Doctrinal Position* (Glasgow, 1878).

81. *Minutes of the Glasgow Presbytery, op. cit.*, 12 February 1878, p. 339.

82. Ferguson, *Additional Statements, op. cit.*, p. 26.

83. *Ibid.*, p. 51.

84. *Ibid.*, p. 65.

Separation from God, in every form, must be abolished. But before it can be abolished, the whole matter must be thought out to its ground, and the universe as a whole, burned white and clean. Every soul must be brought face to face with the uttermost truth of things and must stand before that truth until it is, in some shape or form, reconciled therewith.[85]

Those who sin outwith the 'light of Christendom', and are therefore not deliberately refusing Christ, '…may be forgiven, not only in this world, but also in that which is to come'.[86]

According to Ferguson, there are only four possible theories about the destination of the wicked: Annihilation, Isolation, Restoration, and Restitution, and with great conviction he asserted that 'We are in a position absolutely to disprove the first three, and equally to establish the fourth'.[87] The apex of Ferguson's unorthodoxy in this area of doctrine is exhibited in his utter rejection of the traditional view of eternal separation and punishment. He argued that such a view

… is irreconcilable with the GOODNESS of God… If such suffering is to exist for ever, God must be under the necessity of inflicting it. He cannot inflict it as a pure act of will, and yet retain his character as goodness itself.[88]

Ferguson's own convictions on this subject reflect a universalism of thought quite foreign to the prevailing Confessional orthodoxy of his day.

Every man is already saved from the doom of sin, as annihilation, and must ultimately be brought into a definite position in relation to God. There are only two such positions – that of a servant, and that of a son: a position on earth, as God's footstool; and a position in heaven, as God's throne.[89]

---

85. *Ibid.*, p. 59.
86. *Ibid.*, p. 60.
87. *Ibid.*, p. 63.
88. *Ibid.*, p. 66.
89. *Ibid.*, p. 70.

## 2. The Libel Drafted

Ferguson's biographer, Leckie, considered that the libel process against him was essentially irrelevant and weighted towards his conviction. Leckie's objection to the libel, however, centred upon his belief that in any Presbytery there are elders, and many ministers, who do not deserve to judge 'profound metaphysical questions and intricate problems of Scriptural criticism and interpretation'.[90] In addition to questioning the competence of the Presbytery, Leckie cast doubt upon the competence of the libel process to unravel and assess Ferguson's thought:

> Now a libel… is theoretically a magnificent instrument of justice and well designed to secure a fair and thorough trial. But… it is unfitted to deal with teaching so subtle and speculative, so systematic and coherent as Ferguson's.[91]

The section in the biography dealing with the trial and subsequent conviction almost seems like an attempt to pre-empt and undermine the Presbytery's decision concerning Ferguson's guilt. Leckie's concern over the competence of the Presbytery to judge Ferguson's opinions gives the impression of lame pleading. Nowhere does Ferguson accuse any member of Presbytery of misunderstanding his views. It is difficult, therefore, to give any sort of credibility to Leckie's claim of incompetence. It is also difficult to comprehend what Leckie means when he says that the libel process was punctuated by 'occasional paroxysms of wrathful energy'.[92]

The Presbytery minutes reveal the Presbytery bending over backwards to accommodate Ferguson and give him a fair hearing. Even the most praiseworthy biographies must guard against failing to apply the most basic rules of historical investigation viz. the careful use of primary sources, and the objective assessment of those sources. When the libel was drafted,[93] it had six counts.

---

90. Leckie, *op. cit.*, p. 194.
91. *Ibid.*, p. 201.
92. *Ibid.*, p. 204.
93. The full extent of the libel is found in the *Minutes of the Glasgow Presbytery, op. cit., 26 February 1878*, pp. 343ff., *12 March 1878*, pp. 365f.

First, that Ferguson taught that Christ delivered all men from the penalty of sin as the annihilation of the creature, and ultimately from death to the body and darkness of soul.[94]

Secondly, that to be justified means that we are one with God in the spirit and purpose of our lives.[95]

Thirdly, that God has only one Covenant with man, 'Be true to thyself and thou art true to God.'[96]

Fourthly, that man by the Fall has not lost all ability to will any good accompanying salvation.[97]

Fifthly, that there are no grounds of condemnation apart from rejecting Christ in the sight of God; and that men are purified in the intermediate state.[98]

Sixthly, that the ultimate distinction in human destiny is that of Son and servant; the loss of sonship not necessarily meaning the loss of a tolerable and useful existence. The final part of the sixth count accused Ferguson of teaching that those who die in unbelief depart from the immediate presence of Christ, but do not suffer eternally thereby as the penalty of sin cannot be eternal suffering.[99]

At a special meeting of Presbytery in March 1878, Rev. Drs Black and Buchanan were appointed to prosecute the libel.[100] The first step in the libel process was to consider the relevance of the six counts. Ferguson objected to the libel proceeding,[101]

---

94. *Minutes of the Glasgow Presbytery, op. cit., 26 February 1878*, pp. 349f.

95. *Ibid.*, p. 350.

96. *Ibid.*, p. 352.

97. *Ibid.*, p. 354.

98. *Ibid.*, p. 355.

99. *Minutes of the Glasgow Presbytery, op. cit., 12 March 1878*, pp. 365f.

100. Black and Buchanan were known to be men who stood by the Westminster Standards in their entirety. Leckie considered it amazing that Black 'taught the Confession of Faith to his Bible class!' (Leckie, *op. cit.*, p. 206). The whole section in Leckie's biography dealing with the libel seems like an attempt to highlight the theological narrowness of Ferguson's accusers, and to question whether in fact he got a fair trial. Dr Joseph Brown championed Ferguson's cause in the Presbytery – not because he supported all of his views, but because he believed the views to be in general harmony with Christian thought, and wanted to save him for the Church (Cf. Leckie, *op. cit.*, 209).

101. *Minutes of the Glasgow Presbytery, op. cit., 8 April 1878*, p. 379.

and in his speech again clearly displayed his antagonism to the Confession's teachings:

> … the (theological) system in the Confession is a little dark and morbid arrangement, narrow and exclusive… unworthy of God, unsuited to man, and for all practical purposes a dead letter in the living world, save as it is used as a fetter to thought and an engine of spiritual oppression, in the way of crushing out the best life of the Church.[102]

The Relevancy was considered over three meetings of Presbytery,[103] and all six counts were judged to be relevant.[104]

### 3. The Probation of the Libel

Having considered the Relevancy of the libel, the Presbytery turned its attention to whether Ferguson was personally guilty of the charges.[105] Apart from the fourth count of the libel, all charges were found proven.[106] The next step would have been to remove Ferguson from the ministry, but due to Ferguson's supporters intimating that they were going to appeal to Synod, the Presbytery agreed to

> …continue Mr. Ferguson's suspension from the exercise of his office, declare that the errors found proven cannot be tolerated in this Church, but in view of the Appeals to Synod delay to issue the case finally till the Synod has given judgment.[107]

---

102. Quoted in Leckie, *op. cit.*, p. 217.

103. *Minutes of the Glasgow Presbytery, op. cit., 17 April 1878,* pp. 402ff., *22 April 1878*, pp. 404ff., *29 April 1878*, pp. 411ff.

104. D. Woodside, *Soul of a Scottish Church* (Edinburgh, n.d.), p. 273. Leckie, *op. cit.,* pp. 221f. A minority objected to the findings of the Court in terms of the Relevancy, and reserved the right to appeal to the Synod for a reversal of the decisions. (Between 12 and 21 objected to the decision on each count of the Relevancy.)

105. *Minutes of the Glasgow Presbytery, op. cit., 30 April 1878*, pp. 417ff., *1 May 1878*, pp. 420ff., *2 May 1878*, pp. 425ff.

106. *Ibid., 2 May 1878*, p. 426.

107. *Ibid.*, p. 429.

## 4. The Appeal to Synod, May 1878

The course and conclusion of Ferguson's 'Protest and Appeals against the Deeds of the Presbytery of Glasgow',[108] highlighted not only the doctrinal ambiguity within the United Presbyterian Church, but the willingness to tolerate theological opinions that challenged not the 'mere outworks'[109] of Confessional Calvinism, but its 'inner defences'.[110]

The case itself covered almost the whole duration of the Synod. Having sustained the Presbytery of Glasgow's decisions on the five counts of the libel, and having also sustained the appeal of Black and Buchanan on the fourth count found not proven by the Presbytery, the Synod adopted an unusual procedure. Instead of disciplining Ferguson, the Church's highest court appointed a Committee under Professor Calderwood to 'confer' with him.[111] It is clear that the Synod were unwilling, in view of the Declaratory legislation in the process of being sent down to Presbyteries for their consideration, to discipline a man, who, according to the proposed legislation would be in little danger of being removed from the Church.

However, the fact that 106 people dissented from the decision to postpone judgment on Ferguson until the Committee had conferred with him, indicated the sizeable opposition to the Synod's determination to keep Ferguson in the Church.[112]

The Report of the Committee is difficult to understand.[113] The Committee questioned Ferguson on each of the counts

---

108. *Proceedings, 1877-1879, op. cit., 16 May 1878*, p. 344.

109. Cheyne, *op. cit.*, p. 203.

110. *Ibid.*

111. *Proceedings, 1877–1879, op. cit., 16 May 1878*, p. 351. Professor Calderwood's role in the Ferguson affair is both interesting and mystifying. It was through the conciliation of Calderwood, and his willingness to find a way whereby Ferguson might be saved from the prospect of dismissal from the ministry, that the Queen's Park minister was eventually saved for the Church. However, Calderwood was equally adamant that David Macrae should be removed from the ministry, although the Greenock minister said nothing that Ferguson had not already stated to be his own convictions. See *Life of Henry Calderwood*, by his son and the Rev. D. Woodside (London 1900), pp. 261ff. Cf. Leckie, *op. cit.*, pp. 229ff.

112. *Proceedings 1877-1879, op. cit., 16 May 1878*, p. 348.

113. *Ibid.*, Appendix C, pp. 420-425.

of libel, asking him for further clarification of his views. Even Leckie has to admit that Ferguson seemed to 'climb down' from his previous answers when explaining his views.[114] However, it would be wrong to consider Ferguson alone culpable for such an action. Both James Orr who questioned Ferguson in the Synod, and Professor Calderwood who questioned him in the Committee, did so in language that was aimed at securing favourable answers.[115] Considering the fact that both the Presbytery and the Synod had found Ferguson guilty of holding heretical opinions, it is difficult to understand Calderwood's position. In the Report he stated,

> [Ferguson]…Further stated it to be his deep conscientious conviction, that while in some things he may go beyond the positions formulated in the Confession, he is in fundamental harmony with the essential doctrines of it, and that while he claims no liberty to contravene the Confession, he claims the liberty of holding, on the basis of the Scriptures, views of truth that may go beyond it.[116]

The above statement all but mirrored the seventh clause in the proposed Declaratory legislation, and probably saved Ferguson from being removed from the Church. Although the Committee was not unanimous in accepting Ferguson's answers, a majority considered them acceptable.[117]

---

114. Leckie, *op. cit.*, pp. 234f.

115. *Ibid.*, p. 238.

116. *Proceedings 1877-1879, op. cit.*, Appendix C, p. 422.

117. Only on the sixth count were a majority unsatisfied with Ferguson's answer: five were unsatisfied, two were satisfied, and three declined to vote. (*Ibid.*, p. 424.) It is significant, though not in terms of the eventual result of the appeal, that the unhappiness of the Committee regarding the sixth count should be so clear. The gist of the sixth count accused Ferguson of virtually teaching that men do not suffer an eternal penalty for their sin (see p. 16). That Ferguson should have been subsequently saved for the Church, and Macrae lost from it, perhaps points to the theological ambiguity that prevailed in the Church immediately prior to the passing of the Declaratory legislation in 1879.

Although the Committee's Report spoke of their deep regret at 'the novelty and ambiguity' of Ferguson's language as tending to mislead, it upheld Ferguson's essential orthodoxy. Calderwood recommended that the Synod satisfy itself with the Committee's findings, regret Ferguson's speculations, especially on the ultimate penalty of sin, restore him to the ministry, and give him 'an affectionate and solemn admonition'. [118] The motion was passed by fifty-two votes, and effectively brought the case to a conclusion. [119]

## 3. Conclusion

Leckie sums up the patent ambiguity of the Synod's decision to allow Ferguson to continue in the ministry after having condemned a number of his theological opinions:

> Let it be agreed... that the Synod did an amazing thing when it condemned a man for heresy, did not withdraw that condemnation, and yet refused to punish him! And let it, finally, be conceded that motives of ecclesiastical policy had a share in directing this eccentric, inconsistent line of action. [120]

It must be conceded that the Synod were faced with a difficult situation. The Declaratory legislation was all but certain to become law within the year, and it seemed invidious to some not to take such into account in dealing with Ferguson. In addition to this, Ferguson did tone down his antagonism to the Confession. In a letter to the Synod, Ferguson wrote:

> ... I feel thankful to God... that the Synod has been able to satisfy itself as to my soundness in the faith as regards the fundamental doctrines of the Church. I have not been conscious of any departure from those doctrines, nor have I

---

118. *Ibid., 22 May 1878*, p. 381.

119. *Ibid.*, pp. 381f. The Minutes record that fifty-eight entered their dissent at the findings of the Synod.

120. Leckie, *op. cit.*, p. 274.

121. *Proceedings 1877-1879, op. cit., 23 May 1878*, p. 385.

been able to discover any discrepancy between what I hold, in respect of that which is central and vital, and that which is more remote and subordinate.[121]

Ferguson's letter to the Synod illustrates the ambiguity that existed concerning the exact implications of the proposed seventh article in the Declaratory legislation. The proposed article read, 'That in accordance with the practice hitherto observed in this Church, liberty of opinion is allowed on such points in the Standards, not entering the substance of the faith...'[122] Considering that Ferguson had criticised, and challenged the Confession's teaching on the decrees, the nature and extent of the atonement, and its soteriology and eschatology, it is remarkable that he could place these in the category of belonging to the 'remote and subordinate' doctrines of the Church,[123] and that the Synod could consider them outwith those points in the Standards centring on the 'substance of the faith'.

It may be argued that the case of the Rev. David Macrae more than shows that the United Presbyterian Church was concerned to deal summarily with views which transgressed the bounds of reasonable freedom.[124] Macrae was accused of holding views on future punishment opposed to scriptural truth, thereby fomenting disunity in the Church.[125] At the 1879 Synod, Macrae tried to move the adoption of an eighth article in the Declaratory Statement, viz. 'That in regard to

---

122. *Ibid., 17 May 1878*, p. 352.

123. To some in the Church, at least, Ferguson's views were considered sub-Christian. Rev. David Young, commenting on Ferguson's speech delivered in the Presbytery on 9 October 1877, considered his view of the atonement 'utterly subversive of the idea of an Atonement proper in any sense at all...(and) utterly subversive of any theory of Atonement which has ever been held by evangelical Christians' (Rev. David Young, *Speech on the Case of the Rev. Fergus Ferguson*, Glasgow, 1877, p. 10).

124. *Proceedings 1877-1879, op. cit., 6 May 1879*, pp. 625ff.

125. See especially the *United Presbyterian Magazine's* account of the Synodical Committee's meeting with Macrae. 11 June 1879, p. 330, and 22 July 1879, XXIII (Edinburgh, London, Glagow, 1879), p. 416.

the ultimate penalty of sin, the Church does not hold herself bound to the Westminster interpretation of what the Scriptures say on the subject.'[126] In response to Macrae's attack on the Confession's teaching on eternal punishment, the Synod appointed a Committee to confer with him.[127] The Committee's Report showed that Macrae refused to moderate his views: views which the Committee considered irreconcilable with Scripture as exhibited in the Church's Standards, 'and with any reasonable amount of liberty that can be allowed to ministers of…(the) Church in relation to these Standards'.[128] Dr Duff's speech persuaded the Synod to suspend Macrae from the ministry, and set up a Committee with powers 'to issue the case as they shall see cause'.[129] The basis of the case against Macrae rested on his belief that it was 'inconsistent with the justice of God to permit a human being to continue for ever in a state of sin, or of moral and spiritual separation from God'.[130] The Committee which met with Macrae under the convenership of John Cairns recommended that he be suspended from the ministry *sine die*.[131] In no respects did Macrae say anything that had not already been said by Ferguson. The deposition of Macrae from the ministry seemed like a sacrifice to the conservative members of the Church, worried that the 'conscience clause' would open the floodgates of unorthodoxy within the denomination. Perhaps Macrae's only 'mistake' was to speak to the Committee

---

126. *Proceedings 1877-1879, op. cit., 6 May 1879*, p. 624.

127. *Ibid.*, p. 625.

128. Report of the Committee set up to confer with Macrae; *Ibid., 8 May 1879*, p. 643.

129. *Ibid.*

130. *Ibid., 9 May 1879*, p. 650. It was Dr Duff who actually spoke these words.

131. The actual voting was 228 to 29 to remove Macrae from the ministry. See A.R. MacEwan, *Life and Letters of John Cairns* (London, 1898), p. 677. Macrae's claim to hold the doctrine of universal salvation within the Church was dismissed by Cairns. Cairns' speech on the debate is full of interest. While recognising that Churches which do hold to a universal restoration 'are portions of the Church of Christ, if they hold nothing worse…it is better, more in harmony with the history of our Scottish Presbyterianism, that, if we differ with regard to these matters, we should differ with peaceful separation'.

in a 'frank and kindly spirit',[132] whereas Ferguson allowed his views to be moderated and expressed in Confessional language.

The trials of Fergus Ferguson, and the subsequent toleration of his views, all but signalled the final stage in the erosion of Westminster Calvinism within the United Presbyterian Church. Dr Leckie made the same point:

> He [Ferguson] had secured in a measure every one of the ends for which he had fought; increase of liberty, a loosening of ancient bonds, an opening of the doors of an olden prison-house, a step towards a wider comprehension… In fine, he had achieved the explicit toleration of anti-Calvinistic beliefs within the walls of a Calvinistic Communion.[133]

The only amendment that might be made to the above statement is perhaps to question whether the United Presbyterian Church could still be termed a 'Calvinistic Communion' by 1878. Certainly John Cairns protested that the Church still held to its Confessional heritage. However, in the light of the acquittal of Fergus Ferguson, and the passing of the Declaratory Act the following year, it is at least questionable whether the denomination could justly be considered Calvinistic in its theological orientation.

It would be more than unjust not to mention Ferguson's claimed motive in challenging many of the teachings in the Westminster Standards. In the Appendix to his pamphlet, *Reconstruction of the Creed*, Ferguson asks a question concerning the role of the minister:

> Is he not a minister of the Word before he is a minister of the Confession? If a man loves God more than he loves the Westminster divines, is that the man who ought to be banished from the house of God?[134]

---

132. *Proceedings 1877–1879, op. cit., 8 May 1879*, p. 643. The same point is made by Drummond and Bulloch in their latest volume on Scottish Church history, *The Church in Late Victorian Scotland* (Edinburgh, 1978), pp. 33ff. See also MacEwen, *op. cit.*, p. 666, for a slightly different view.

133. Leckie, *op. cit.*, p. 262.

134. Ferguson, *Reconstruction of the Creed, op. cit.*, Appendix, p. 61.

Here Ferguson is all but challenging the historic function of a Confession of Faith. Ferguson's question was answered within two years. The Declaratory legislation of 1879 removed the Confession from its place as the 'watchdog of orthodoxy', and substituted the individual conscience. Ambiguity, not definition, was the rule of the day.

*Chronological Outline for Chapter 6*

*1877*. Overture presented by David Macrae at the United Presbyterian Church Synod urging the Church to re-examine radically its relation to the Westminster Standards. The Synod rejected his overture and reaffirmed its 'steadfast adherence to the Westminster Confession of Faith...'

John Cairns' speech on the Subordinate Standards.

A Committee formed, including Fergus Ferguson, to examine the Church's relation to the Westminster Standards.

*1878*. A proposed Declaratory Statement submitted by the Committee for the Synod to discuss.

*1879*. The United Presbyterian Church Declaratory Act passed unanimously in the Synod. 'Liberty of opinion' given to ministers in subscribing the Confession on doctrines not entering the 'substance of the faith'.

# 6

# The 1879 United Presbyterian Church Declaratory Act

## 1. The Movement for Change: The 1877 Synod

The 1877 Synod of the United Presbyterian Church opened in Glasgow with an air of expectation. It was common knowledge that a number of overtures were to be submitted with a view to urging the Synod to re-examine its relation to the Westminster Standards. One of the overtures was presented by the Rev. David Macrae on behalf of the Session of Gourock where he was the minister.[1] It is instructive to note the definiteness of the Synod's dismissal of Macrae's radical overture, and the qualifications under which the supreme court sanctioned the setting up of a Committee to examine the Church's relation to its Subordinate Standards.

(1) The Synod dismisses the Overture from Gourock, and declares its steadfast adherence to the Westminster Confession of Faith and Catechisms as containing the system of doctrine taught in the Holy Scriptures.

(2) The Synod strongly disapproves of and condemns the

---

1. *Proceedings of the United Presbyterian Synod, op. cit.*, May 17, 1877, p. 42.

conduct of those persons who, having solemnly professed to give their assent to these standards, do notwithstanding indulge in denouncing them as erroneous and unscriptural...

(3) In particular the Synod cannot tolerate the denial or disparagement of those doctrines commonly called the doctrines of grace, which it has been the distinguishing glory of this Church in every period of its history to maintain and preach.

(4) ...however...the Synod appoints a Committee to consider the whole subject...and report to the Synod in May 1878.[2]

The Committee that was set up had Principal Harper and Professor Cairns as Joint-Conveners, and contained most of the leading minds in the Church.[3] Considering the Synod's strong disapproval of those ministers who paid lip service to the Church's Confession, it is interesting to find that a motion was passed proposing Fergus Ferguson as a member of the Committee.[4]

Apart from the radical views of men like Ferguson, Macrae, and Gilfillan of Dundee, who wanted an 'entire re-statement of the creed',[5] the general mood of the majority of ministers favoured some degree of relaxation in the terms of subscription to the Confession. From the outset, the name of John Cairns dominated the scene.

Cairns was one of the leading conservatives in the United Presbyterian Church, but had a reputation for open-mindedness and fairness. When still a probationer, Cairns applied himself to

---

2. *Ibid.*, p. 43. The recognition of the Synod that there were ministers who professed commitment to the Standards but publicly denounced them, would have seemed to indicate an awareness for the need of ministerial discipline. It is difficult, however, to understand the strongly conservative tone of the Synod's statement in the light of its subsequent decision to retain Fergus Ferguson in the Church's ministry.

3. *Ibid.*, May 18, 1877, p. 50.

4. *Ibid.* It was also moved that David Macrae be included in the Revision Committee. The motion was ruled incompetent by the Moderator as Macrae had earlier dissented from the proposal to set up a Committee to examine the Church's relation to the Standards (p. 51).

5. Leckie, *op. cit.*, p. 99.

a rigorous examination of the Confession.[6] The well-travelled student makes it clear in his notes that his subscription was no unthinking acceptance of the Westminster teaching. MacEwen gives the impression that Cairns threw aside a substantial portion of the Confessional teaching, but much of his argument with the Confession seems to be linguistic: he considered the article on the internal evidence of inspiration of the Scriptures (Westminster Confession of Faith, Chapter 1, sec. V.) to be 'very confusedly and imperfectly stated';[7] and the definition of the Godhead is considered 'very irregularly arranged and far inferior to the Shorter Catechism'.[8] In addition to disputing the form and arrangement of some articles, MacEwen states that Cairns also discarded 'entirely the teaching of the Confession as to the Civil Magistrate, and almost entirely its teaching with regard to Providence and the Freedom of the Will'.[9]

Although Cairns remained 'a fixed Calvinist'[10] to the end of his days, his refusal to accept traditional beliefs unthinkingly, his early travels as a student in Germany, and his voracious capacity for reading literature from all points of the spectrum fitted him admirably to lead the Church during a period of change.[11]

Cairns' speech during the 1877 Synod highlighted both the conservatism of the Professor and his opposition to radical change, and also his determination to proceed with change at a measured pace. It is interesting to note that Cairns went out of his way during his speech to make public his inability to understand Ferguson's complaints against the Confession.[12]

---

6. A.R. MacEwen, *The Life and Letters of John Cairns* (London 1898), pp. 212-213.

7. *Ibid.*, p. 212.

8. *Ibid.*

9. *Ibid.* See also p. 226.

10. *Ibid.*, p. 779.

11. Cairns travelled widely in Germany, and continued to apply himself to German and the German authors after he returned home. Writing to a friend in 1844, Cairns says, 'I have been…reading a good deal of Hegel, Schleiemacher, Neander, De Wette and old friends… The influence of Germany and travel is still deeply felt…' (*Ibid.*, p. 255).

12. *Ibid.*, p. 667.

Focusing his attention on the Confession's teaching on eternal punishment, Cairns offered a direct rebuff to Ferguson and Macrae's challenge to this element of the Westminster teaching.

> However mysterious and awful the doctrine of future punishment as we have hitherto held it, we should, in breaking with it, cast away one of the mightiest instruments in dealing with the souls of men, and we should substitute an arbitrary conclusion for the revealed Word of Him who knows, as we know it not, the harmony of the whole dark mystery of evil, in its entrance and continuance, with His own eternal love.[13]

The approach of Cairns to the revision of the Standards is well illustrated in his speech:

> I contend for true liberty and improvement where these can make good their claim; and I trust that the spirit of the reformers and martyrs of our country would inspire us to rise above themselves, if in anything they should have been in error.[14]

As if to check any suggestion that he was abandoning the theological heritage of the Church, Cairns proceeded to give what amounted to an *apologia* for the Calvinism of the Confession, urging the Church not to be ashamed of a system which is identified with men like Knox, Melville, Henderson, Chalmers, and Edwards, and with groups like the Puritans.[15] Perhaps the most revealing part of Cairns' speech, however, is the conclusion. While recognising the 'blasts' that are threatening the Church, Cairns declared, 'I am willing, if need be, to cast out the tackling of the ship, but I will not throw the wheat into the sea.'[16]

---

13. *Ibid.*, p. 668.
14. *Ibid.*, p. 670.
15. *Ibid.*
16. *Ibid.*, p. 671.

The 'wheat' is the 'solid cargo' of the doctrines of grace, and for the Church to survive the storm it must hold fast to its basic, and precious, cargo.[17]

We have quoted much from the speech because it outlines what Cairns thought about revision, and the limits that should be imposed on it. The speech also reveals a man struggling to keep his Church from the influence of more extreme spirits. While caution and conservatism marked Cairns' whole approach, it is difficult not to detect a certain tentativeness that failed to grasp the nettle of theological reality. While it may just be the perfect vision of hindsight that sees Cairns as tentative, it cannot be denied that in opening the door to a measure of liberty regarding the teachings of the Confession, he failed to appreciate the extent of the liberty that some were claiming. This is a theme that we will return to at a later juncture.

The Committee of which Cairns was the Joint-Convener included a wide cross-section of views. In his biography of Cairns, MacEwen includes comments by Professor Orr on the composition of the Committee. First, 'There was a staunchly conservative phalanx of seniors, who proposed no change, and held the reins tightly when changes were proposed by others.'[18] Secondly, 'a smaller, and more radical section, generally in favour of a shortening and simplification of the Creed'.[19] Thirdly, a group of a 'mediating tendency', to which Cairns belonged.[20]

It would seem that the principle of a Declaratory Act was quickly agreed on, although the Committee's discussions are not available for analysis.[21]

---

17. *Ibid.*

18. Dr Marshall was one of the leaders in this group. *Ibid.*

19. Dr James Brown, Dr Leckie, Fergus Ferguson, and Professor Orr himself, 'belonged to this more active and aggressive party'. *Ibid.*

20. *Ibid.*, pp. 671-672.

21. Orr's comments on the composition of the Committee are revealing. He also makes it clear that 'battles' were fought within the Committee, but that Cairns acted as a wise mediator. This seems to be the only source of information which undermines (in part) the picture of unanimity presented in the *Proceedings*.

## 2. 1878 Synod. Proposed Declaratory Statement Submitted[22] (See Appendix A)

The discussions on the Committee's proposed means of meeting the need for a measure of relaxation for ministers in their relation to the Church's Subordinate Standards were straight-forward and relatively uncomplicated.[23] In his speech proposing the Committee's Report, Professor Cairns spoke of the 'virtually unanimous approval' of the Committee.[24] According to Cairns, the Committee

> propose nothing in the way of repeal or abrogation or recall of the Standards. We only propose what, I trust, will explain them and free them from difficulty, and also put them in such a position as, when looked upon in connection with the explanation, will have the effect of granting liberty *here and there* which was not formally allowed, although generally believed to be acted upon[25] [italics mine].

Taken at face value, the above statement would indicate that the conservatives on the Committee had won the day. The general thrust of Cairns' speech centred upon his contention that the proposed legislation was in no way anti-Confessional. Rather, the proposed Statement was an 'explanatory' device aimed at highlighting elements that had not received the attention they deserved in the Standards. With regard to the question of ministerial liberty, the most important article in the Statement was the seventh.

> That, in accordance with the practice hitherto observed in this Church, liberty of opinion is allowed on such points in the Standards not entering the substance of the faith, as the interpretation of the 'six days' in the Mosaic account of the

---

22. *Proceedings, op. cit.*, May 1878, Appendix D, pp. 425f.

23. *Ibid.*, pp. 333ff.

24. J. Cairns, *Speech on the Subordinate Standards (With the Report of the Committee and Declaratory Statement)* (Edinburgh 1878), p. 3.

25. *Ibid.*, p. 6.

creation: the Church guarding against the abuse of this liberty to the injury of its unity and peace.[26]

Cairns admitted that he was not altogether happy with the article, but indicated a willingness to give it a trial in the hope that it would not be abused.[27] The guarded acceptance by Cairns of the article arose out of his awareness that unlimited liberty of opinion could render the purpose and function of the article meaningless. Although he was open in his reservations, Cairns declared that he was prepared to trust the integrity and honour of the Synod, and the Church's future ministry:

> ...I humbly trust that, with this qualification allowing liberty, this Church will sacredly and zealously guard this liberty from destroying the very faith it is brought in to strengthen and uphold.[28]

That Cairns could speak with such passion against the dangers of misusing the liberty granted by the seventh article, when Fergus Ferguson was being saved for the Church after being found guilty on six counts of heresy, is difficult to comprehend. The 'here and there' liberty envisaged by Cairns could by no stretch of the imagination cover the case of Ferguson, who challenged the very fundamentals of the Confession's teachings – especially, as we have seen, its soteriology and eschatology.

The discussion on the proposed Declaratory Statement provoked little in the way of controversy. Dr Marshall proposed the insertion of a further article aimed at clarifying the Church's opposition to the state establishment of religion:

> ... all compulsory taxation for religious purposes is ... a violation of liberty of conscience, while it is contrary to the law of Christ, Who has forbidden the exercise of force in the affairs of His Kingdom.[29]

---

26. *Proceedings, op. cit.*, Appendix D, p. 426.
27. Cairns, *Speech, op. cit.*, p. 15.
28. *Ibid.*
29. *Proceedings, op. cit.*, May 17, 1878, p. 352.

*The Proposal Was Decisively Defeated.*
It is significant that whereas a sizeable minority opposed almost identical Declaratory legislation with great passion and threats of secession when it was introduced in the Free Church a little over ten years later, the Proceedings of the United Presbyterian Church reveal no evidence of disagreement. As far as the records are trustworthy guides, almost complete harmony reigned in the Synod regarding the proposed Declaratory Statement. The Synod agreed to send the Statement down to the Presbyteries and sessions for their consideration, with instructions to forward any suggestions to the Committee before 1st October 1878.[30]

### 3. 1879 Synod. The Passing of the Declaratory Act[31] (See Appendix B)

The Proceedings fail to give any indication of the attitude of the Presbyteries to the Declaratory Statement, but the lack of any disagreement during the debates at the 1879 Synod would seem to indicate that no significant proposals were made.

The seven articles were debated one by one,[32] and within the compass of one evening the Synod, with minor linguistic alterations, gave its assent to the Statement. The only ripple of dissent came from the Rev. David Macrae who attempted to introduce an eighth article dealing with the ultimate penalty for sin. It was moved and seconded that

> … whereas the proposed Declaratory Act seems to leave the Church bound to identify the Scriptural doctrine of future punishment with the Westminster doctrine of everlasting and unspeakable torment, that the following Article be introduced as number VIII, namely: 'That in regard to the ultimate penalty of sin, the Church does not hold herself bound to the Westminster interpretation of what the Scriptures say on the subject.'[33]

---

30. *Ibid.*, p. 353.
31. *Proceedings, op. cit.*, May 8, 1879, pp. 637f.
32. *Ibid.*, May 6, 1879, pp. 623ff.
33. *Ibid.*, p. 624.

After a brief discussion the seconder of Macrae's motion withdrew his support, and the proposed amendment was dropped.[34]

Macrae's open condemnation of the Westminster teaching on future punishment not only made public his heterodoxy, but initiated the process that culminated in his deposition from the ministry of the United Presbyterian Church. At the very time when Fergus Ferguson was being saved for the Church, Macrae, due to his frank and open criticism of the Standards, all but signed his own warrant of deposition.[35]

The Act that was eventually passed differed from the proposed Statement of 1878 only in some minor verbal corrections.[36] Due to the Act's contents, the Synod recognised the need to change the second question of the Formula used at ordination. The new Formula asked the question:

Do you acknowledge the Westminster Confession of Faith and the Larger and Shorter Catechisms as an exhibition of the sense in which you understand the Holy Scriptures, this acknowledgment being made in view of the explanations contained in the Declaratory Act of Synod thereanent?[37]

No sooner had the Declaratory Act been given Synodical authority when it was proposed that the

Declaratory Act is not to be held as superseding the needs of new Standards within the United Presbyterian Church; and ...

---

34. *Ibid.*, p. 625. Macrae used the word 'Jesuitical' with reference to the Synod's procedure in the preparation of the Declaratory Statement, and a Committee was appointed to 'confer' with him.

35. Macrae almost seemed to invite the Synod to examine him for holding heterodox views, and he refused either to back down or equivocate over his convictions. While holding an almost identical view of 'eternal punishment' as Fergus Ferguson, Macrae maintained a position of confrontation with the Synod, while Ferguson allowed his views to be cast in an 'orthodox mould', saving himself from the threat of deposition.

36. The corrections did nothing to alter the meaning of any of the articles.

37. *Proceedings, op. cit.*, May 8, 1879, p. 638.

> That failing the early combination of the Churches in preparing new Standards, the United Presbyterian Church would not be justified in declining by its own action to supply the want within its own borders.[38]

It was not surprising, however, considering the momentous step involved in passing the Declaratory Act, that the Synod rejected the appeal, maintaining that 'it is not expedient at present to travel further in the matters contained in the motion'.[39] Two points should be noted with regard to the desire of those who sought a complete revision of the Westminster Standards. First, the Declaratory Act was not considered the *terminus ad quem* that Cairns anticipated. The desire of some for a less comprehensive and defined Confession pointed to the problems that lay ahead for the Church as it entered a new era. Secondly, it should be noted that the Synod did not reject the appeal for new Standards, but only deemed the timing of the request 'inexpedient'

## 4. The Significance of the Declaratory Legislation

It is a remarkable fact that the passing of the United Presbyterian Declaratory Act at the Church's Synod in May 1879 went almost unnoticed by the media of the day and the historians of the period. That a major Scottish Presbyterian Church should publicly and officially qualify its historic relation to its Subordinate Standard of Faith, the Westminster Confession of Faith, was surely an event worthy of comment and analysis. Yet, it remains the case that the event, epoch-making though it may have been, passed into the history of the Church in Scotland unheralded and scarcely noticed. Commenting on the passing of the Declaratory Act, the *United Presbyterian Magazine* stated in an editorial,

> (The Declaratory Act) is not, indeed, reckoned final in the direction in which it travels. All parties were agreed on this; but

---

38. *Ibid.*, p. 639.
39. *Ibid.*

the large majority which voted in favour of its being allowed now time to prove itself, shows that the Church is not disposed in the meantime to begin afresh the supremely important and arduous work of formulating a new creed.[40]

Considering the importance of the Act, not least in an age when the old symbols of orthodoxy were being challenged at every turn, it is striking that this is the only comment made in the magazine concerning the significance of the new legislation.

A similar paucity of comment is found in the *Scotsman* newspaper's accounts of the 1879 Synod. While the newspaper devotes space each day to covering the Synod's discussions, it passes over the Synod's acceptance of the Declaratory legislation with barely a comment.[41] An examination of the leading periodicals of the day reveals a similar picture. Either no-one appreciated the importance of the Declaratory Act as an instrument of change in Scottish Presbyterianism's relation to the Westminster Standards, or they simply chose to ignore the event altogether.

The main interest concerning the silence of comment on the Declaratory Act lies, however, not in the silence of contemporary sources, but in the virtual silence of historical comment during the past one hundred years. Apart from some brief comments in A. R. MacEwen's biography of John Cairns,[42] and a cursory analysis in C.G. McCrie's *The Confessions of the Church of Scotland*,[43] the United Presbyterian Declaratory Act has been accorded little in the way of analysis or comment. It is also worth noting that a recent general history of the Scottish Church during the last quarter of the nineteenth century barely stops to pass comment on the Act.[44]

---

40. *United Presbyterian Magazine*, XXIII (Edinburgh 1879), p. 266.

41. *Scotsman*, May 9, 1879, p. 3; May 10, p. 8; May 12, p. 4.

42. MacEwen, *op. cit.*, pp. 662ff. MacEwen mostly outlines the attitude of John Cairns towards the Declaratory legislation. Analysis of the Act is conspicuous by its absence.

43. McCrie, *Confessions, op. cit.*, pp. 279ff.

44. A.L. Drummond & J. Bulloch, *The Church in Late Victorian Scotland 1874-1900* (Edinburgh 1978).

Although it is difficult to explain why there should have been so little in the way of open comment on the nature and importance of the Declaratory legislation, at least two points might be made to attempt a partial explanation.

First, the Declaratory legislation was debated in the Synod at the same time as the Ferguson and Macrae cases. The Minutes and Proceedings of the Synod during the years 1878 and 1879, in particular, devote a far greater proportion of time and debate to the heresy trial of Fergus Ferguson, and the examination of David Macrae, than they do to the proposed Declaratory legislation. Although the cases of Ferguson and Macrae were bound up with the proposals to redefine the Church's relation to the Westminster Standards, both the 1878 and the 1879 Synods are dominated by the figures of these men. It is perhaps understandable, therefore, that the *Scotsman* should devote more space and comment to the heresy trials than to the passing of Church legislation.

Secondly, it is a remarkable fact that a close examination of the Synod's Proceedings during the years 1877 to 1879 reveals no trace of any dissent over the proposals to qualify the Church's historic relation to the Westminster Standards. Even when the proposed legislation was sent down to Presbyteries for comment, the Synod's Proceedings indicate no evidence of dissent at any point. The picture of complete unanimity presented in the Proceedings is all the more striking when compared with the internal turmoil created in the Free Church during the years 1889 to 1893 over almost identical proposals to introduce a Declaratory Act to qualify that Church's relation to the Westminster Standards.[45] Unless the Synod's Proceedings have failed to give an accurate account of the debates,[46] the available evidence points to a Church completely at one in its desire to alter its relation to the Westminster Standards.

---

45. *Proceedings and Debates of the General Assembly of the Free Church of Scotland*, ed. T. Crerar (Edinburgh 1889, 1890, 1891, 1892, 1893, 1894).

46. If there had been any dissent, the *United Presbyterian Magazine* would surely have commented on it.

*a. Contemporary Assessments of the Declaratory Act*

Whereas John Cairns made much of the fact that the Declaratory legislation was not intended to repeal or abrogate the Confession's teaching at any point, the few individuals who did comment on the Act regarded it as a liberalising device, created to qualify the Confession's teaching at particular points.

In his pamphlet on *The Relations of the Presbyterian Churches to the Confession of Faith*,[47] James S. Candlish of the Free Church maintained that the United Presbyterian Declaratory Act

> is of importance, as making it plain that the Calvinism to which some subscribers adhere is not the extreme doctrine that some have held, but moderate evangelistic Calvinism; and that they are not held to signify agreement with every proposition in the Confession, but only with its essential substance.[48]

Candlish, for one, seems at least to consider the Declaratory Act as marking a significant turning point in Scottish Presbyterianism's relation to the Calvinistic theology of the Westminster Confession (a turning point that he supported). By using the words 'moderate evangelistic' to qualify Calvinism, Candlish introduced the idea that the Declaratory Act was responsible for qualifying some of the Confession's teachings. Unfortunately, Candlish does not define what he means by 'moderate evangelistic Calvinism'. However, his comments appear in a section of his pamphlet designated 'The Doctrine of Grace'.[49] In this section, Candlish concentrates

---

47. J.S. Candlish, *The Relations of the Presbyterian Churches to the Confession of Faith* (Glasgow 1886).

48. *Ibid.*, p. 18. J.R. Fleming, *Scotland...1875-1929, op. cit.*, goes much further than Candlish. He maintained that the Declaratory Act was the 'first formulation of the points on which liberal Scottish Presbyterianism was prepared to modify the traditional Calvinism' (p. 18). However, Fleming does not stop to explain what exactly he means, and where the Act specifically modified the traditional Calvinism. Leckie also agreed with Fleming's view. He wrote in his *Secession Memories*, 'By a curious irony of fate, a Church which had begun in a passionate revolt against all theological liberalism...had been constrained by circumstances to figure as a pioneer of the modern movement out of Calvinistic bondage...' (p. 219).

49. Candlish, *op. cit.*, pp. 16ff.

his attention on the ways in which the Presbyterian Churches have qualified – so he argues – the Confession's teaching on the extent of the atonement, and the free offer of the gospel.[50] In this respect, the 1879 Declaratory Act illustrated, for Candlish, at least a move away from the well-defined, theologically exact statements of the Confession.

A similar, though more dogmatic, assessment of the Act was given by Oswald Dykes a few years later. In his paper 'Recent Action by British Churches in Relations to the Westminster Confession of Faith', given at the Eighth General Council of the Alliance of Reformed Churches,[51] Dykes maintained that the United Presbyterian Declaratory Act was constructed to disown certain extreme or erroneous statements in the Confession of Faith. Among these he included the teaching about total depravity, predestination to life and foreordination to death, elect infants, and the extent of the atonement.[52]

The view that the Declaratory Act undermined the specifically Calvinistic teaching of the Westminster Standards was the opinion of Professor Smeaton of the Free Church. In a letter to a friend, Smeaton wrote:

> There are good Calvinists in the United Presbyterian Synod; but I should not find it difficult to prove that in its Declaratory Statement the Synod has taken up Arminian ground.[53]

There can be little doubt that Smeaton had in mind the first two articles of the Declaratory legislation in particular. These two articles emphasise the *universality* of God's love and grace and redemptive provision in Christ. They speak of 'the love of God

---

50. *Ibid.*, p. 4.

51. O. Dykes, 'Recent Action by British Churches in Relations to the Westminster Confession of Faith', *Proceedings of the Eighth General Council of the Alliance of Reformed Churches Holding the Presbyterian System* (London 1904), pp. 105ff. The Council was held in Liverpool that year.

52. *Ibid.*, p. 108.

53. Macleod, *op. cit.*, p. 307.

to all mankind';[54] the gift of Christ to be the propitiation for the sins 'of the whole world';[55] and the provision of a salvation 'sufficient for all, adapted to all, and offered to all in the Gospel ...'[56] It is also possible that Smeaton considered the third article of the legislation, on man's total depravity, as conceding too much to an Arminian anthropology.[57] Although Smeaton must have been aware that the Articles were held to be consistent with the Confession's teaching in these areas, he nonetheless was persuaded that no such consistency existed.

The comments of Candlish, Dykes, and Smeaton illustrate a fundamental problem in historical interpretation. Cairns, the guiding light and architect of the legislation, argued forcibly that the terms of the Declaratory articles in no way contradicted the teaching of the Confession. At most, Cairns considered the articles as supplements and explanations of the Confession's teaching in the light of the teaching of Holy Scripture.

That Cairns was not isolated in his understanding of the function of the Act is readily seen in the Synod's public commitment to the Westminster Standards as containing the system of doctrine taught in the Holy Scriptures. The question must then be asked: What has led those who have commented on the Act, almost without exception, to see it as conflicting with the Confession's teaching at particular points?

*b. The Declaratory Act and the Westminster Confession of Faith*
As the Declaratory Act stands, it should be conceded that it is difficult, if not impossible, to charge it with departing from the teaching of the Confession. As a study in linguistics, the Declaratory legislation neither expressly contradicts the Confession's teaching, nor uses language that cannot be interpreted in a 'Confessional sense'. However, the Declaratory

---

54. *Proceedings, op. cit.*, May 8, 1879, p. 637.
55. *Ibid.*
56. *Ibid.*
57. *Ibid.*, pp. 637f.

Act must not be judged solely in terms of what it actually says. The Act was the product of a particular historical and theological milieu, and must be assessed in that light. It is only with this in view that it is possible to understand the comments of Candlish, Dykes, and Smeaton.

If the Act had nothing in the way of historical antecedents, it would be difficult to charge it with departing from Westminster Orthodoxy. But, as was noted in an earlier chapter,[58] the Atonement Controversy of the 1840s resulted in the sanctioning of Amyraldianism, or hypothetical universalism, in the Secession Church. It is almost certain that individuals who have commented on the Declaratory Act since its enactment in 1879 have interpreted its contents, at least the contents of the first two articles, in the light of the theological framework espoused by Brown and Balmer.

Brown and Balmer refused to accept that the atonement could only be thought of in terms of Christ's relationship to his elect. Although they did not deny in any way the effectiveness of Christ's redemption of the elect, they cast their whole understanding of the atonement into a 'universalistic mould', and spoke in terms of a universal redemption.

Professor Balmer, and it must be remembered that his teaching was sanctioned by the United Secession Synod, clearly evinced the scheme of universal redemption:

> If without a satisfaction, God cannot pardon the sins of any man ... It follows, as an obvious and necessary consequence, that the death of Christ is a satisfaction or atonement for all; that is, a universal atonement, ransom, or expiation.[59]

If the teaching of Brown and Balmer underlies the Declaratory articles, and provides the key with which to understand the

---

58. See Chapter 2 on the Atonement Controversy. See also A.N. Fairbairn, 'The Westminster Confession of Faith and Scotch Theology', *Contemporary Review*, XXI, (Dec. 1872-May 1873), p. 80.

59. Brown and Balmer, *Statement, op. cit.*, p. 22.

language of them, it would be difficult to reconcile them with the teaching of the Confession. In contrast to the 'universalism' of the professors, the Confession is unequivocal in its stress on the limited extent of Christ's atonement. The redemptive scheme as detailed in the Confession is precise and unambiguous: those whom the Father 'gave' to Christ are redeemed by him, and have that redemption applied to them by the ministry of the Holy Spirit:

> they who are elected being fallen in Adam, are redeemed by Christ; are effectually called unto faith in Christ by his Spirit working in due season...neither are any other redeemed by Christ but the elect only.[60]

It will be obvious, however, that the language of the Declaratory Act precludes any dogmatic conclusion as to its relation to the Confession of Faith in this particular area.

It has been suggested that in at least one other area the Declaratory Act contradicts the teaching of the Subordinate Standards. The fourth article of the Act stated,

> ...in accepting the Standards, it is not required to be held that any who die in infancy are lost, or that God may not extend His grace to any who are outwith the pale of ordinary means, as it may seem good in His sight.[61]

The view of Oswald Dykes that the Declaratory Act challenged the Confession of Faith's teaching on 'elect infants' is difficult

---

60. *Westminster Confession of Faith, op. cit.*, Chapter III, 6 pp. 8f. See also Chapter VIII, 8 pp. 16f., Chapter X, 1 p. 18.

61. *Proceedings, op. cit.*, May 8, 1879, p. 638. The corresponding section in the Confession reads: 'Elect infants, dying in infancy, are regenerated and saved by Christ through the Spirit, who worketh when, and where, and how he pleaseth. So also are other elect persons, who are incapable of being outwardly called by the ministry of the word' (Chapter X, 3. p. 18). It is unfortunate that the Minutes of the Westminster Assembly are not complete. The debates on this section of the Confession have not survived.

to sustain. It is true that the above article goes further than the Confession in seeking to identify 'elect infants' with all children who die in infancy. However, it must be stressed that the Confession does not rule out the possibility of equating 'elect infants' with all children who die in infancy. In his exposition of the Confession of Faith, A.A. Hodge makes the same point:

> The phrase 'elect infants' is precise and fit for its purpose. It is not intended to suggest that there are any infants not elect … It is not positively revealed that all infants are elect, but we are left, for many reasons, to indulge a highly probable hope that such is the fact. The Confession affirms what is certainly revealed, and leaves that which revelation has not decided to remain, with the suggestion of a positive opinion upon one side or the other.[62]

A more difficult problem occurs in the interpretation of the second half of the fourth article in the Declaratory Act. The problem may be posed in terms of a question: Who are those referred to as being 'outwith the pale of ordinary means'? MacEwen, in his biography of John Cairns, seems inclined to identify this group with the heathen who have never heard the gospel. Sketching in the background to the passing of the Declaratory Act, MacEwen observed,

> Among the beneficial influences of foreign missions upon the faith of the Church, one of the most important…is that they open the eyes to the vastness of the world, and, except in the crudest minds, undermine the belief that those who have never heard the Gospel are doomed to eternal punishment. This influence combined with an appreciation of the more scientific knowledge of non-Christian religions to create a rebellion against the dogmas of the Confession on the subject.[63]

---

62. A.A. Hodge, *The Confession of Faith*, Banner of Truth Trust edition (London, 1958), pp. 174f. See also B.B. Warfield's study on 'Infant Salvation' in *Studies in Theology* (New York, 1932), pp. 411ff.

63. MacEwen, *op. cit.*, p. 665. Woodside, *op. cit.*, p. 278, is of the same opinion.

While the language of the fourth article of the Declaratory Act is open to different interpretations, the most straightforward interpretation does identify those incapable of being called to Christ through the preaching of the gospel – those outwith the ordinary means – with the heathen.[64] The Confession of Faith treats of this subject in the tenth chapter, 'Of Effectual Calling'. Two points need to be made regarding the Confession's teaching. First, when the Confession speaks of 'those incapable of being outwardly called by the ministry of the word'[65] being 'regenerated and saved by Christ through the Spirit',[66] it has been commonly understood as referring to imbeciles who have no capacity for reason. Commenting on this section in the Confession, Robert Shaw quotes Dick's *Lectures on Theology*:

> There are adult persons, too, to whom the use of reason has been denied. It would be harsh and unwarrantable to suppose that they are, on this account excluded from salvation...[67]

A.A. Hodge makes the same point in a more positive manner:

> ...in the case of sane adult persons, a knowledge of Christ and a voluntary acceptance of him is essential in order to a personal interest in his salvation.[68]

Secondly, with regard to the heathen who are outwith the scope of the preaching of the gospel, the Confession seems unequivocal as to their fate: unless they 'come to Christ' they cannot be saved,

> ...be they ever so diligent to frame their lives according to the light of nature, and the law of that religion they do profess; and

---

64. See *Proceedings, op. cit.*, May 8, 1879, p. 638.

65. *Westminster Confession of Faith, op. cit.*, Chapter X, 3. p. 18.

66. *Ibid.*

67. Quoted in R. *Shaw, The Reformed Faith: An Exposition of the Westminster Confession of Faith*, Christian Focus Publication Edition (Inverness, 1974), p. 123. First published in 1845.

68. Hodge, *op. cit.*, p. 176.

to assert and maintain that they may, is very pernicious, and to be detested.[69]

Again, however, it must be conceded that other interpretations are possible, especially with regard to the meaning of the fourth article in the Declaratory Act. Sadly, the *Proceedings and Debates* shed no light on the subject.

Before passing on, it is interesting to compare the reaction in the Free Church when a similar article was proposed for inclusion in its Declaratory legislation. Section four of the legislation stated:

> ...while the Gospel is the ordinary means of salvation for those to whom it is made known, yet it does not follow...that God may not extend His mercy...to those who are beyond the reach of these means.[70]

The objection to the article by the conservative minority was vocal and vehement. When the article was first proposed, Murdoch Macaskill, one of the leaders of the minority, declared in the Assembly:

> If one soul could be saved in this way, why not all? They [the Modern Church] must revise the Bible, and expunge not a little of it, before they could get any footing for their theory, for it is anti-scriptural, anti-Confessional, and therefore most pernicious, and to be detested.[71]

The Free Church Declaratory Act (see Appendix C) was in many ways identical to the United Presbtyerian Act of 1879. It is remarkable that, whereas there is no record of dissent in the United Presbyterian Synod over the nature and content of their proposed Declaratory legislation, the Free Church Assembly

---

69. *Westminster Confession of Faith, op. cit.*, Chapter X, 4, pp. 18f.
70. *Proceedings and Debates of the Free Church, op. cit.*, 1893, pp. 478f.
71. *Ibid.*, 1891, p. 88.

was a ferment of controversy. The proposed legislation was characterised as 'diluted Arminianism',[72] and construed as a device aimed at driving a wedge between Christ's redemption of his elect, and the sovereign love of God which was the source of that redemption.[73] It was also argued that the universalistic emphases in the legislation opened up the way for 'Amyraldianism, Baxterianism, and Neonomianism' to corrupt the orthodoxy of the Church![74] Not content to impugn the theological character of the legislation, the conservative minority assailed it as being 'injurious to vital godliness',[75] 'unscriptural, immoral, and popish',[76] and as a veritable smokescreen aimed at fostering the views of Marcus Dods, A. B. Bruce, and others, so paving the way for the entrance of the 'modern faith'.[77]

It is this intensity of feeling and vocal opposition, so marked in the passing of the Free Church Declaratory Act, that is completely missing in the United Presbyterian Synods of 1878 and 1879.

*c. The Crux of the Legislation*

The crux of the Declaratory legislation, the provision of liberty for ministers who felt bound by the terms of subscription imposed by the Church in relation to the Confession of Faith, lay in the seventh article (see Appendix B). At least three important points were imbedded in this article.

First, the liberty of opinion that ministers were free to avail themselves of was considered a practice with historic precedent. The use of the phrase 'in accordance with the practice hitherto observed in this Church' suggests that the liberty now granted was *de jure*, whereas in the past it had merely been *de facto*. Secondly, the liberty of opinion allowed to ministers was

---

72. *Ibid.*
73. *Ibid.*, p. 87.
74. *Ibid.*, 1893, p. 176.
75. *Ibid.*
76. *Ibid.*
77. *Ibid.*, 1891, p. 89.

qualified. No liberty is allowed with regard to the 'substance of the faith',[78] the scope being limited to minor points of doctrine such as the 'interpretation of the "six days" in the Mosaic account of the creation'. Thirdly, the Church claimed for itself sole authority to decide when liberty becomes licence, and abuses its concession.

Considering the importance of this article in particular, it is remarkable that little has been written analysing its role in the liberalising of Scottish theology. It is fairly obvious from the terms of the article that the Synod did not intend it as an invitation for ministers to maintain a personal *credo*, irrespective of the traditional theological position held by the United Presbyterian Church. As was noted in an earlier part of the chapter, Cairns, for one, recognised the possibility of ministers abusing the terms under which liberty of opinion was to be granted, and accordingly urged the Church to guard zealously against attempts to widen the scope of the concessionary clause. It is difficult, however, not to charge Cairns with exhibiting a degree of theological naiveté in this respect. To place the doctrinal orthodoxy of the Church in precarious dependence upon a 'gentleman's agreement' that those present at the Synod, and the Church's future ministry, would not abuse the limits of the liberty granted, was surely extremely naïve. While it is possible to admire the trust that Cairns placed upon the integrity of the Church's ministry not to abuse the 'here and there' liberty granted by the seventh article, the unwillingness of the Church to prosecute

---

78. A.C. Cheyne, *op. cit.*, p. 214. The ambiguity of the meaning of 'the substance of the faith' was also highlighted during the debates in the Free Church when it came to discuss the possible inclusion of the phrase in the Declaratory legislation. The Free Church legislation spoke of the 'substance of the Reformed Faith'. More than one minister in the Free Church Assembly spoke of the possibility of theological anarchy arising over the ambiguity of the phrase. A Mr Hamilton from Symington thought the phrase meaningless, not least because he claimed to know of one man who did not think that the doctrine of election belonged to the 'substance of the Reformed Faith'! The well-known conservative controversialist, Rev. Kenneth Moody-Stuart of Moffat, claimed that the Church had never in the past been satisfied with such vague expressions (*Proceedings and Debates in the Free Church, op. cit.*, 1892, pp. 169, 109).

an effective policy of church discipline, as demonstrated in the Ferguson case, rendered Cairns' trust all but meaningless.

The lack of any coherent policy of discipline was augmented by the Synod's failure to define, in any way, what it understood by the phrase 'the substance of the faith'. The ambiguity of the phrase is specifically highlighted when placed alongside the Synod's decision to retain Fergus Ferguson in the Church's ministry. That the Synod could find Ferguson guilty on six counts of heresy, and be satisfied with giving him an 'affectionate and solemn admonition', only serves to illustrate the great difficulty involved in defining just what 'the substance of the faith' means.

The Synod's *Proceedings* give no indication of anyone questioning the meaning of the problem phrase. The absence of any definition could possibly be accounted for in two ways. First, it is possible that everyone knew what the substance of the faith was, and was agreed as to its content. Secondly, and much more likely, the absence of any definition was a calculated 'risk' on the part of the Committee which drew up the legislation, and the Synod which sanctioned it – the illusiveness of the phrase being due to the Synod's awareness that anything more definite could initiate a split in the Church between the more liberally inclined younger ministers, and the older, more conservative ones. Whether the Church was trying to reconcile the irreconcilable[79] is a matter for conjecture. The lack of documentary evidence precludes any dogmatic conclusion.

### d. Alteration in the Formula of Subscription

The terms of the Declaratory Act, and in particular the terms of the seventh article, made it necessary for the United Presbyterian Church to alter its Formula of Subscription to the Westminster Confession of Faith.

The revised Formula related the requirement for subscription to the Confession of Faith to the 'liberty of opinion' allowed

---

79. Cheyne, *op. cit.*, p. 214.

ministers in article seven of the Declaratory legislation. While A.T. Innes probably went too far when he maintained that the United Presbyterian Church's Formula of 1847 'abolished' the Formula of Subscription as a meaningful test of ministers' orthodoxy, it would be difficult not to agree with that assessment with regard to the 1879 Formula. The complete lack of definition accorded to the phrase 'the substance of the faith' rendered the new Formula weak and ineffective, if not actually useless. 'Subscription' is no longer required to a *defined* corpus of truth, but only to an indeterminate, undefined 'substance of the faith'.

Although the Westminster Confession of Faith was still retained as the Church's Subordinate Standard of Faith, its historic role as the 'watchdog of theological orthodoxy' was finally put to one side.

# 7

# Summary

It may be helpful to the reader at this stage, before reading the next chapter which considers developments in the Free Church of Scotland, to have a summary of the significant steps in the erosion of Westminster Calvinism among Scottish Seceders. Five such steps are identified.

First, contrary to the accepted views of historians of Scottish Church history, the present study concludes that ministers were given no liberty to qualify publicly their subscription to the Westminster Confession of Faith during the first half of the eighteenth century. A thorough examination of the primary sources, the Presbytery and Synod records, revealed no deviation from the unqualified commitment to the Formula of Subscription required by the Act of 1711.

Second, there has been a tendency among Scottish Church historians to view the Relief Church as always having a less strict approach to matters of doctrine than the other branches of the Secession. In particular, the Relief Church was commonly thought to treat its relationship to the Westminster Standards with less exactitude than the other Secession Churches. However, the present study found that as late as the 1790s, the Relief Church used the strictest form of subscription to the Westminster Confession of Faith. There is no evidence to suggest that the Relief Church was less than thoroughly committed to the Calvinism of the Confession of Faith during the first forty or so years of its existence. It only began to change its attachment to the Standards at a time when the other branches of the Secession were doing so.

Third, perhaps the most important conclusion reached in the present work is that the erosion of Westminster Calvinism within Scottish Presbyterianism occurred earlier than most historians have assumed. The Atonement Controversy of 1841–1845 resulted in the sanctioning of Amyraldianism in the United Secession Church. The 'hypothetical universalism' of Professors Brown and Balmer undermined the specific particularism of the Standards in their exposition of Christ's atonement. The 'double substitution' theory of the professors, as Cunningham called it, was considered by Brown to be generally consistent with the teaching of the Standards – although Balmer expressed his doubts that the two could be reconciled. However, it is impossible to harmonise the two schemes in the light of the Westminster Confession's reiterated emphasis upon the particularity of Christ's atonement.

Westminster Calvinism received a body blow with the official sanctioning of Brown and Balmer's teaching. A climate of thought was evolving which eventually opened up the way for evangelists like D.L. Moody to visit Scotland and preach their Arminian gospel.

Fourth, the Union Controversy of 1863–1873 was significant at least for this reason: a small, but articulate and highly organised, minority in the Free Church was able to frustrate plans for union with the United Presbyterian Church. The eventual success of the minority can be partly traced to their insistence that the United Presbyterians were doctrinally suspect in their understanding of the atonement. Their case was strengthened by the refusal of the main architects of Union to publicly answer their criticisms and suspicions. The Union Controversy was a classic case of deeply held suspicions by a small number undermining the aims and hopes of a powerful majority.

Fifth, it is undeniable that the watershed in the process of the erosion of Westminster Calvinism among Scottish Seceders was reached with the trials of the Rev. Fergus Ferguson, and the passing of the 1879 United Presbyterian Declaratory Act. Ferguson's acquittal by the United Presbyterian Synod in 1878, after being found guilty on six charges of holding erroneous doctrines, pointed to a Church which had departed some way from Westminster Calvinism. The protestations of Cairns and others that the Declaratory legislation of 1879 did not in any way repeal or abrogate anything in the Westminster Standards, must be seen in the light of Ferguson's acquittal the previous year. The so-called 'liberty of opinion' which the Declaratory legislation gave to ministers sealed the fate of Westminster Calvinism in the United Presbyterian Church. To accommodate men like Ferguson, and no doubt others who were less radical, the new revised Formula only required that ministers subscribe an undefined, undeterminate 'substance of the faith', an entity which each individual was left to determine as to its precise nature and bounds. The Formula of Subscription, which was the lynchpin of Westminster orthodoxy, was finally eroded of any real meaning as the guardian of the Church's commitment to the Calvinism of the Confession of Faith.

However much John Cairns hoped against hope that the new Declaratory legislation would settle the persistent calls for creedal change, the very terms of the Act itself ensured that the system of truth to which Cairns himself was committed was in mortal danger.

Although Cairns defended the Calvinism of the Confession, the very defensiveness of his position meant that he was the one who had eventually to give ground. At the very time when Cairns was saying, 'I am not prepared to give up our Calvinism, even for the theology which, in the hands of Wesley and his successors, has made such conquests for Christ',[1] the United Presbyterian Church was committing itself to a course of action which all but sounded the death knell of Calvinism within its bounds.

1. MacEwen, op. cit., p. 668.

# Chronological Outline of Chapter 8

*1889.* The Assembly authorised the setting up of a Committee to report on ways of possible relief for individuals who baulked at subscribing *ex animo* to the Confession. Marcus Dods was overwhelmingly elected Professor of New Testament Exegesis at Edinburgh.

1890. The majority of returns to the Committee's questions to Presbyteries on 'change' against any alteration in the Church's relation to the Confession. Attention in the Committee increasingly focusing on the merits of a Declaratory Act as affording the best means of relief.

*1891.* The proposed Declaratory Act presented to the Assembly by Rainy. Macaskill proposes a countermotion to refuse the Committee's proposals. Overwhelming victory (428-466) for Rainy's motion. Committee's second motion on 'Scripture' objected to as ambiguous, and affording a 'double-sense' (again by Macaskill). Rainy's motion again carries the day (283-251).

The overtures anent the writings of Dods and Bruce overruled and passed from (383-373). Both professors fully vindicated by the Assembly's decision.

*1892.*The Declaratory Act, having been sent down to Presbyteries the previous year under the Barrier Act, becomes law (see Appendix 1). The Committee's proposals for a revision of *'Questions and Formula'* sent to Presbyteries for 'suggestions' under advice of Rainy. Dingwall Presbytery's desire for a 'Pastoral Letter' from the Assembly to allay the fears of their people over the terms of the Declaratory Act is rejected by the Assembly.

*1893.* Controversy over Synodical and Presbyterial records (in the Highlands) containing denunciations of the Declaratory Act. Overtures anent the Declaratory Act from concerned Highland Presbyteries dismissed. Proposed changes in the *'Questions and Formula'* referred to next Assembly. Free Presbyterian Secession.

*1894.* Change in Preamble to *Questions and Formula,* but no change in the Questions themselves. Motion for relief by Balfour rejected by the Assembly.

# 8

# The Making of the Free Church Declaratory Act 1892

The aim of this concluding chapter is to analyse the making of the Free Church Declaratory Act of 1892. Particular attention will be given to the course of the debate, the issues involved, and the various personalities who dominated the Assembly proceedings.

## 1. Relation of the Free Church to the Westminster Confession 1843-1889

The theological conservatism which characterised the beginnings of the Free Church in 1843 was underlined by the *Act Anent Questions and Formula* passed by its General Assembly in 1846.[1] The revised Questions and Formula clearly intimated that subscription to the Confession of Faith had to be both personal, and without reservation. Probationers, for example, were to be asked, 'Do you sincerely own and believe the whole doctrine of the Confession of Faith… and do you own the whole doctrine therein contained as the confession of your faith?'[2]

---

1. *Act XII*, 1846, of the General Assembly of Free Church of Scotland. *Act Anent Questions and Formula*, p. 27f. (John Greig, Edinburgh, 1847).

2. *Ibid.* 'Questions to be put to Probationers before they are licensed to preach the Gospel' (p. 28).

All office-bearers were required to sign the Formula, which underlined the Church's commitment to its Subordinate Standard in terms of personal, wholehearted approbation. The Formula stated:

> I, — , do hereby declare that I do sincerely own and believe the whole doctrine contained in the Confession of Faith, approven by former General Assemblies of this Church, to be the truths of God; and I do own the same as the Confession of my faith…[3]

No laxity was permitted in subscription; the adherence of the first generation of Free Church ministers was, as a result (as far as outward profession went), *ex animo*. Whatever 'difficulties or scruples'[4] individuals felt had to be shelved if they desired ordination, or admitted, with the inevitable result of disbarment from the ministry.[5]

The commitment of the Free Church to the Westminster Confession in the terms outlined above was somewhat modified, however, by the latter half of the Preamble to the *Act anent Questions and Formula* which purported to give 'an explanation'[6] of the Confessional teaching on the duties of nations and rulers to true religion.[7] The Preamble declared that:

---

3. *Ibid.* 'Formula' p. 30. It is also interesting to note that the Church excised part of the 1711 Formula which referred to the Confession's ratification by Acts of Parliament. The 1711 Formula stated: '…approven by General Assemblies of this National Church, and ratified by law in the year 1690, and frequently confirmed by divers Acts of Parliament since that time, to be the truths of God…' cf. A.T. Innes *'Law of Creeds'* (1st ed. 1867), pp. 436f.

4. Prof. Brown's phrase in his motion to the 1889 General Assembly for relief from the strict bonds of adherence to the Confession. See *'Proceedings and Debates of Free Church…'* 1889, p. 137.

5. A. Webster, *'Theology in Scotland' as Reviewed by a Heretic* (London 1915), p.127. Webster mentions the case of Peter Hately Waddell, 'one of the ablest Disruption students'.

6. So Innes, *op.cit.,* p. 436.

7. Westminster Confession of Faith in *'Subordinate Standards…of the Free Church'* (Edinburgh 1955), Chap. 23, 'Of the Civil Magistrate', especially section III.

...the General Assembly, in passing this Act, think it right to declare that, while the Church firmly maintains the same scriptural principles as to the duties of nations and their rulers in reference to true religion and the Church of Christ, for which she has hitherto contended, she disclaims intolerant or persecuting principles, and does not regard her Confession of Faith, or any portion thereof, *when fairly interpreted,* as favouring intolerance or persecution, or consider that her office-bearers, by subscribing it, profess any principles inconsistent with liberty of conscience and the right of private judgment[8] [italics mine].

Although the phrase 'when fairly interpreted' gives a certain elasticity to any examination of the Confession's teaching on the duties of the Civil Magistrate,[9] it is well-nigh impossible to accept the Free Church's interpretation. In fact, the Assembly's preamble, while having all the features of a declaratory statement,[10] to all intents and purposes acted as a qualification of the Confession's teaching. A. T. Innes made the same point when he wrote:

...the Act is seemingly intended to relieve those who would otherwise have scrupled to sign the Confession, by a declaration of the *animus imponentis*; and so far as those who subscribe under its authority are concerned, it seems as truly a qualification of the Confession, and therefore an addition to it...[11]

---

8. Preamble to 1846 *Act anent Questions and Formula, op. cit.*

9. A.R. McEwan in his biography of John Cairns aptly comments thus on the different understandings of the Civil Magistrate in the Free Church and United Presbyterian Church during union talks in the 1860s. 'At the head [of the differences], was placed that intangible person the Civil Magistrate, who, through his very intangibility, has for 150 years had power to create one schism after another in Presbyterianism' (*Life and Letters of John Cairns*, London, 1898, p. 504).

10. This was Prof. Cooper's assessment, *Confessions of Faith and Formulas* (Glasgow 1907), p. 93.

11. Innes, *op. cit.,* pp. 436-437. An interesting comment on this Preamble is found in a letter of John Cairns to a friend, Rev. Dr King, during the talks on Union between the Free and United Presbyterian Churches. '...a most helpful agreement appeared, and Dr. Candlish rather surprised us by saying that, even if a man thought the Confession intolerant, he was so protected by the Act of 1846 that he might sign it with a clear conscience' (Cairns, *op. cit.*, p. 526 [March 21 1867]).

In a certain sense, the Act of 1846 practically gave a degree of relief to those who could not accept the Confession's teaching *simpliciter*, and allowed them to sign the Formula and answer the Questions in the light of the Preamble to the Act – a situation that was to a large extent paralleled in the eventual relation between the 1892 Declaratory Act, and the revised Preamble to Questions and Formula of 1894.

Although the 1846 Act gave a degree of latitude to those prospective office-bearers who could not subscribe the Confession *ex animo* and *simpliciter*, the terms of the Questions and Formula and the theological conservatism of the first generation of Disruption leaders gave to the Confession an almost sacrosanct position as the Free Church's theological standard. This wholehearted, and in the main unreserved, commitment of the Free Church to the Confession tended to give the impression that the Church placed their Standard almost above criticism. Lord Sands, for example, when reviewing the relation of the Scottish Churches to the Confession, wrote that 'practically if not theoretically, tacitly if not avowedly, ... [the Westminster Confession of Faith] was regarded as inspired and infallible. Criticism was banned.'[12]

Such an analysis, however, fails to appreciate that the Free Church (at least in theory) never held to any static or uncritical assessment of its Confession. At the 1866 General Assembly of the Free Church, the Moderator, Dr Wilson, clearly set out the Church's relation to its Confession of Faith:

> ...no confession of faith can ever be regarded as a final and permanent document. She [the Church] must always vindicate her right to revise, to purge, to add to it... we believe in the progressive advancement of the Church into a more perfect knowledge of the truth.[13]

---

12. Lord Sands, *'Dr Archibald Scott of St. Georges Edinburgh and his times'* (London & Edinburgh, 1919), p. 109.

13. A.T. Innes, *Studies in Scottish History*, p. 257. See also *Proceedings and Debates of Free Church*, 1866.

Even the most dogmatic opponents of the 1892 Declaratory Act never attacked the right of the Church to alter materially its relation to the Confession. While they objected to the Act on the basis that it contravened the 'plain teaching' of Scripture, no-one advocated the infallibility or dogmatic definitiveness of the Confession.[14]

Dr Wilson's utterance can be regarded as significant for two reasons. First, it gave credence to the Free Church's desire for union with the United Presbyterian Church during a period when union talks were increasingly coming under fire. Secondly, it acted as a harbinger of coming developments by stressing the Free Church's commitment to discovering new light from Scripture; 'truth' was not static and finally formulated, but developing and capable of clearer and fuller understanding.

When the overtures from thirty-three Presbyteries anent the Westminster Confession of Faith reached the 1889 General Assembly of the Free Church,[15] the public and official relation of the Church to its Confession was still one of total subscription – excepting the measure of relief afforded by the 1846 Preamble. The fact that an overwhelming majority declared themselves in favour of changing the *status quo,* and of providing a measure of liberty for those who could not subscribe to some aspects of Confessional teaching, can only be explained in the light of the growing challenge to the Calvinism of the Confession during the previous fifty years.

## 2. The Growing Challenge to Westminster Calvinism

It is beyond the scope of this chapter to do other than indicate the extent and nature of the growing challenge to the accepted Calvinism of the Westminster Confession during the post-Disruption period. At least six areas of challenge can be enumerated.

---

14. *Proceedings,* op. cit., 1889, p. 133, for this view. To have argued otherwise would have been to contradict the express teaching of the *Confession,* cf Ch. XXXI, section IV, *op. cit.*

15. *Ibid.* p. 133f.

First, the Atonement Controversy in the United Presbyterian Church (1841-1845) highlighted the growing acceptance of the Amyraldian, or 'double-reference', theory of the atonement among those who subscribed to the Westminster Confession.[16] The importance of this controversy with regard to the erosion of Westminster Calvinism was twofold. In the first place, the accepted language of the Confession,[17] in currency for two centuries, was departed from: universal categories playing an increasing part in the thinking of theologians. Secondly, this 'modified Calvinism'[18] of the Secession Church was considered by Cunningham, and latterly Candlish, as presenting no theological bar to union between the Free Church and the United Presbyterian Church. Cunningham declared in 1861, 'There is nothing in the formula of the United Presbyterian Church to which I have any objection; I could sign it myself.'[19]

The growing popularity of the 'double-reference' theory as against the traditionally held particular, or limited, extent of the atonement paved the way, through its emphasis upon universal categories, for the contention of some that the Confession, or at least the traditional interpretation of the Confession, was imbalanced in its treatment of the atonement.

Secondly, the so-called *Sabbath War* of 1865-1866[20] was instrumental in challenging the Churches to reconsider their understanding of the sanctity of the Sabbath. The two issues

---

16. See for details A. Robertson, *The History of the Atonement Controversies in the Secession Church* (Stow, 1846), pp. 181-183. Also Brown and Balmer's defence against the libel. The Amyraldian or 'double-reference' theory claims that Christ's atonement had a universal as well as a particular reference. He died for the World 'sufficiently' but for the elect 'efficaciously', a theory which moved somewhat away from the accepted Confessional teaching on the subject.

17. Cf Westminster Confession, *op. cit.,* Chap. 8, sec. VI and VIII.

18. A.M. Fairbairn. 'The Westminster Confession of Faith and Scotch Theology' in *The Contemporary Review,* Vol XXI (London 1873), p. 80.

19. McEwan, *op. cit.,* p. 500. Cunningham's famous statement made in the light of union talks in Australia between Free and United Presbyterian Churches.

20. R.D. Brackenridge, 'The Sabbath War of 1865-1866...' in *S.C.H.S. Records Vol. 16,* 1969, pp. 22f. D. Macleod, *Memoirs of Norman Macleod* (London, 1876, 2 vols), pp. 188f.

which came to the fore during this controversy revealed something of the pressure that faced any Church which intended to stick by the letter of the Confession in its teaching on the Sabbath. In the first place, the North British Railway's response to those who condemned their running of Sunday trains in February 1865 – that trains were a necessity in an increasingly industrialised society[21] – was an argument that was difficult to challenge. The Presbytery of Glasgow's acceptance of Sunday horse-drawn trams due to the 'altered conditions and exigencies of modern society'[22] indicated the acceptance, albeit grudging, of the Church to reappraise its understanding of the Confession's teaching in the light of new developments.

The other issue to rise during the controversy was more pointedly theological. Norman Macleod's attitude to the Sabbath was governed, not primarily by the fourth Commandment and its antecedent creation ordinance, but by the teaching of Jesus and the Apostles. Although he continued to uphold the importance of Sabbath observation, he did so on directly New Testament grounds, emphasising the importance of not imputing a legal framework to the rest, renewal, and freedom of the Christian Lord's Day.[23] Macleod also advocated a degree of liberty for subscribers on points which did not enter the substance of the faith.[24] The observation of the Sabbath had become a badge of theological orthodoxy, and the challenge offered to its long-standing sanctity was in reality a challenge to the Westminster Confession's interpretation of Scripture on the subject. Brackenridge makes the same point:

> more than anything else, however, the 'Sabbath War' focussed attention on the meaning and significance of the subordinate standards of the Church.[25]

---

21. Brackenridge, *op. cit.*, p. 25.

22. *Ibid.*, p. 31, quoting *'Glasgow Herald'*, February 6, 1879.

23. MacLeod, *op. cit.*, pp. 188-189, cf p. 201.

24. *Ibid.*, Vol II, p. 191.

25. Brackenridge, *op. cit.*, p. 33.

A third major area of challenge to traditional Westminster Calvinism in Scotland was the United Presbyterian Church's Declaratory Act 1879.[26] Although the Church claimed the Act was purely 'Declaratory',[27] most historical commentators recognise that in fact the Act was virtually a reconstruction and recasting of the symbolical theology of the Confession.[28] Certainly the Declaratory Act repudiated intrusive, compulsory, and intolerant principles in upholding true religion;[29] the Confession's teaching on the exclusive reference of the atonement to the elect was denied;[30] and the destiny of the heathen was put in terms that could never be squared with the Confession's teaching.[31] J.S. Candlish understood the significance of the Act when he wrote:

> This Act is of importance, as making it plain that the Calvinism to which subscribers adhere is not the extreme doctrine that some have held, but moderate evangelistic Calvinism...[32]

The acceptance by the United Presbyterian Church of this 'modified' Calvinism and the resulting degree of liberty it now offered to potential office-bearers[33] heralded a new era in Scottish Churches' relations to the theology of the Westminster Confession.[34]

Fourthly, the years after 1850 witnessed an unparalleled re-assessment of the foundations and accepted beliefs of the

---

26. See *Proceedings of United Presbyterian Assembly* 1879 and *Subordinate Standards of United Presbyterian Church*, pp. 91-93. John Cairns. *Speech on the Subordinate Standards'* (Edinburgh, 1878). See C.G. McCrie, *Confessions of the Church of Scotland* (Edinburgh, 1907), pp. 280f. for assessment of the Act as more than Declaratory.

27. Cairns, *op. cit.*, p. 6: 'We propose nothing in the way of repeal or abrogation or recall of the Standards...' See also McEwan, *op. cit.*, p. 674.

28. McCrie, *op. cit.*, p. 286.

29. United Presbyterian Church Declaratory Act in Standards, 5th Article.

30. *Ibid.* 1st Article.

31. *Ibid.* 4th Article.

32. J.S. Candlish, *Relations of Presbyterian Churches to the Confession of Faith* (Glasgow 1886), p. 18.

33. United Presbyterian Declaratory Act, 7th Article, 'Liberty of Opinion'.

34. Whether it heralded a new era or simply marked the official acceptance of what had gone before would need greater elaboration.

Christian faith. The importance and influence of the *Critical Movement* upon Scottish theology was immense, and men of the calibre of William Robertson Smith, A. B. Davidson, A. B. Bruce, and Marcus Dods sought to re-evaluate their understanding of Scripture and theology in the light of the new discoveries breaking forth from exegetical and archaeological enquiry. It is not the place here to assess the relative strengths and weaknesses of the new theories and hypotheses, but their impact upon accepted, traditionally held views of Scripture, and of course the Confession, was great. Robertson Smith's work challenged the current orthodox understanding of the nature and inspiration of Scripture;[35] his acceptance of the multi-source theory of Pentateuchal authorship, and his 'daring' views on the supposed historicity of the Old Testament, immediately made him a target for heresy hunters.[36]

The 'father' of Higher Criticism in Scotland was A.B. Davidson and he kept an unusually low profile during the years when Robertson Smith's teaching was being examined by the courts of the Church,[37] although he was responsible for introducing his young pupil to the German theories.[38] The immediate significance of the influence of the Critical Movement was in its challenge to the traditional interpretation given to the Westminster Confession's article on Scripture. It is only possible to understand the flow of debate and the excited nature of individual contributions during the years 1889–1894 in the Free Church Assembly when we see them against this backcloth. Whether Robertson Smith's contention that his understanding of the inspiration of Scripture was identical to that of the Reformers[39] was correct or not, the

35. Summarised in his *Britannica* articles 1878–1880. Also see his *Answer to the Form of Libel* (1878).

36. Eg. Job may be parabolic; Ruth 'a graceful idyll'. Also McCrie, *op. cit.,* pp. 181f.

37. Libel brought by Aberdeen Presbytery.

38. It is interesting the Davidson's article in the 1888 *Chambers Encylopaedia* on 'Bible', Vol. II, pp. 117-129, was almost identical to Robertson Smith's 1875 article in the *Britannica*.

39. He claimed this *in Answers to Form of Libel*, pp. 18-44. See also T.M. Lindsay's article in *The Expositor,* Vol X., 1894, pp. 241ff. on 'Prof. W. Robertson-Smith's Doctrine of Scripture'.

prevailing orthodox interpretation was given a severe challenge. The election in 1889 of Marcus Dods to the New Testament Chair in New College seemed to many the final demise of the traditionally held confessional teaching on the inspiration and inerrancy of Scripture.

A fifth sphere of challenge to Westminster orthodoxy was in the rise to prominence of *natural sciences* as a major field of study. It was not that the study of the sciences 'created' unbelief in the Christian faith, but rather that it provided 'new and prestigious arguments' to replace the older philosophical ones.[40] The great work of Darwin was not so much to create the evolutionary hypothesis as to popularise it, and give it a degree of empirical validity. Although many Churchmen thought that 'evolution' offered no serious threat to the Christian faith (embracing themselves its central tenets),[41] it became obvious that the main theses of the theory challenged accepted and traditional norms of belief, especially in the areas of *creation, man, sin,* and *revelation*.[42] Theologians began to use the evolutionary hypothesis as a tool in their attempts to understand the origin and development of biblical religion, concluding that revelation was an evolving and, at best, incomplete reality. The great surge of optimism concerning man's 'upward progress', and science's innate ability to conquer the environmental and physical evils in the world, was recognised as a powerful challenge to the Westminster Confession's view of man and society. The Confession's emphasis upon man's 'total depravity'[43] was increasingly considered by many as erring upon

---

40. Drummond and Bulloch, *Church in Victorian Scotland 1843-1874* (Edinburgh, 1975), p. 215.

41. 'Rabbi' Duncan considered that evolutionary thought offered no 'very terrible results to the theologians' – in Drummond and Bulloch, *Ibid.* p. 232. Churchmen of the stature of Chalmers and the Duke of Argyll considered 'evolution' a not too outrageous proposition either.

42. T. H. Huxley, *Lectures on Evolution* (London, 1876); R. H. Hutton, *Aspects of Relig & Scientific Thought* (London, 1875); M. Arnold, *God and the Bible* (London, 1875). Margaret Oliphant, *Principal Tulloch* (Edinburgh, 1888), Noel Annan, 'Strands of Unbelief' in *Studies in Social History* (ed J.H. Plumb); M. Arnold, *Literature and Dogma* (London, 1873).

43. Westminster Confession, *op cit.*, Art 6 sec II, IV.

the pessimistic, and man's achievements and abilities were given greater prominence in the literature of the period.[44]

Finally, the arrival of Dwight Lyman Moody, an American evangelist, in Scotland in November 1873, introduced a new kind of 'expansive' evangelism to the Scottish Church that was Arminian in its theological orientation. Moody preached to vast crowds and was almost universally praised. W. G. Blaikie, Professor of Apologetics and Pastoral Theology at New College (from 1868 to 1897), commented, 'never, probably, was Scotland so stirred; never was there so much expectation'.[45]

Moody's visits to Scotland (he returned in 1881-1882 and 1891-1892) helped to transform the face of the Church in Scotland. With the enthusiastic support of Andrew and Horatius Bonar, and other Free Church conservatives, Moody's preaching of God's universal love appeared to challenge the teaching of the Westminster Confession of Faith, with its more particularistic emphasis on God's love for his elect.

Moody's preaching attracted the opposition of John Kennedy of Dingwall. Kennedy was not a hyper-Calvinist, but he viewed Moody's preaching and his evangelistic methods with the greatest concern, especially the Arminian theology that buttressed Moody's preaching. In 1874 he published, 'Hyper-Evangelism "Another Gospel" Though a Mighty Power'. While not a lone voice, Kennedy's opposition was swallowed up by the almost nationwide enthusiasm for the 'revival'.

P. Carnegie Simpson, the biographer of Robert Rainy, wrote, interestingly in a chapter entitled, 'An Era of Transition': 'Moody's preaching of a "free Gospel" to all sinners did more to relieve Scotland generally... of the old hyper-Calvinistic doctrine of election and of what theologians call a "limited atonement" and to bring home the sense of the love and grace of God towards

---

44. See Huxley, *op. cit.*

45. Quoted in Ian Hamilton, 'Moody, Dwight Lyman' in *Dictionary of Scottish Church History and Theology*, Organising Editor Nigel M.de S. Cameron (T&T Clark, Edinburgh, 1993), p. 605.

all men, than did even the teaching of John Macleod Campbell.'[46] For Simpson, 'It was an invaluable thing in this transition period of Scottish religion that, when it was unlearning much of its Calvinism, it should be learning these things afresh.'[47]

It is against this background of change and challenge that agitation arose in the Free Church for a reassessment of the Church's relation to its Confessional Standards. The ethos of the period was one of decided flux, as well as expanding horizons. The growing missionary movement, given impetus by the beginnings of Pan-Presbyterian gatherings,[48] challenged the Church to a wider and less parochial vision. A.R. McEwan considered that foreign missions '…combined with an appreciation of the more scientific knowledge of non-Christian religions to create a rebellion against the dogmas of the Confession…'[49] The desire of missionaries to preach in universal and not particular categories was thought to be a major influence in the formulating of the Free Church's Declaratory Act in 1892.

## 3. The Making of the Declaratory Act

a. The formal setting-up of a Committee to consider ways and means whereby individuals' 'difficulties and scruples'[50] over the terms of the Confession could be relieved, wwas ostensibly the result of Presbyterial overtures to the 1889 General Assembly on that subject. Twenty-one Presbyteries submitted overtures indicating dissatisfaction with the prevailing relation of the Church to its Subordinate Standard.[51] The desire for change as evidenced in the Presbyterial overtures was crystallised in the motion presented to the Assembly by Professor David Brown of Aberdeen.[52] Brown's motion called for the establishing of a

---

46. P. Carnegie Simpson, *The Life of Principal Rainy* (Hodder and Stoughton, London, 1909), Vol. 1, 408.

47. *Ibid.*, 409.

48. The first gathering was in 1878.

49. McEwan, *op. cit.*, p. 665.

50. *Proceedings and Debates of Free Church, op. cit.*, 1889, p. 137.

51. There is some confusion over the exact number. William Balfour says twenty-one Presbyteries (see *Proceedings*, 1889, p. 133), and Prof. Bruce says twenty-two Presbyteries (p. 148).

Committee to examine the dissatisfaction that some felt with the Confession, and to propose ways in which individual scruples could be relieved. Brown, himself, was against any relaxation in the terms of subscription,[53] but he considered the Confession overly logical in its system of doctrine, and containing more than was necessary as a competent test for prospective office-bearers.[54] The terms of Brown's speech in defence of his motion provided a model for the vast majority of those which followed. Although advocating change, the Professor expressly stated that he had no intention of interfering with the distinctive Calvinistic principles of the Confession – change meant affording a degree of liberty for those who could not give their wholehearted approbation to the Confession in its entirety, not the removal of the 'Calvinistic theology' which governed the Standard.

Brown's motion was vigorously opposed on the Assembly floor by William Balfour,[55] who acted as the chief spokesman for the traditional or Constitutional position in the Church. Balfour's arguments will be examined in due course; but it is important to note that his arguments, and those who subscribed to his position, were not in any way connected with the thought that the Westminster Confession was either immutable or perfect. His arguments, though varied, essentially stemmed from the belief that the proposed changes contravened Scripture, and consequently subverted the Calvinistic doctrines of the Confession.[56]

In proposing his own countermotion that there was neither the need nor the desire for change, Balfour drew attention to the number of overtures openly critical of the current relation be-

---

52. *Ibid.*, p. 137.

53. *Ibid.*, p. 137.

54. *Ibid.*, p. 138.

55. Balfour was from 1849 until his death in 1895 minister of Holyrood Free Church in Edinburgh, and he was a leading member of the constitutional or traditional position in the Church.

56. See particularly, *Proceedings, op. cit.,* 1889, p. 153 (William Balfour); *Ibid.*, 1889, p. 150 (Dr Scott); *Ibid.*, 1891, p. 88 (Murdoch Macaskill); *Ibid.*,1891, pp. 112-114 (William Balfour).

tween Church and Confession. To argue, as Brown and Adams – who seconded his motion – had done, that there was a 'widespread desire for change' when only twenty-one out of seventy-three Presbyteries had sent in overtures to the Assembly, was, according to Balfour, quite incredible. However, when the vote was taken an overwhelming majority supported Brown's motion (413 to 130),[57] and no time was lost in setting up a Committee to implement the terms of the Professor's proposal.[58] The Assembly's remit to the Committee was in the following terms:

> The General Assembly having taken up the overtures regarding the Confession of Faith, and recognising alike the importance and difficulty of the question thus raised, and the indications of a present call to deal with it, hereby resolve to appoint a Committee to make enquiry, and consider carefully what action it is advisable for the Church to take, so as to meet the difficulties and relieve the scruples referred to in so large a number of overtures – it being always understood that this Church can contemplate the adoption of no change which shall not be consistent with a cordial and steadfast adherence to the great doctrines of the Confession.[59]

One of the most interesting moves by those who opposed any change in the Church's relation with the Confession was that of 'official protest'. Before the overtures anent the Confession were debated at the 1889 Assembly, twenty-nine ministers and elders recorded a protest which in substance declared that in taking part in discussions on the status of the Confession they did not 'in any way admit the lawfulness of altering the relation of the Church to the Westminster Confession of Faith'.[60] The

---

57. *Proceedings op., cit.*, 1889, p. 154.

58. Rainy and Dr Adam were appointed joint-chairmen. Adam died in early 1891. *Proceedings, Ibid.*, p. 234, give all the names on the Committee. Great pains, so Rainy declared, were taken to ensure that all parties were represented.

59. *Proceedings*, 1890, 'Report of the Committee on the Confession of Faith', No XLII, p. 1.

60. *Ibid.*, 1889, p. 132.

value of this action was probably twofold. In the first place it clearly established their position in the Courts of the Church – issuing, as it were, a demarcation line of theological and ecclesiastical orthodoxy. Secondly, it provided clear evidence of their position should, for some reason, the civil courts be involved in determining the relation of the Free Church as it existed to what it was at its foundation in 1843.

b. Before any attempt is made to examine the flow of debate and range of argument during the years 1889 to 1894, it will prove helpful to note in the *chronological outline* at the beginning of this chapter, the making of the Declaratory Act, so giving a degree of perspective and context to the theological debates.

Although the Declaratory Act became law in 1892, it was not until 1894 that the controversy surrounding it began to lessen in intensity. During the five years of debate over the Church's relation to the Confession two main positions and policies were advocated: a small, but vocal, number battled to retain the status quo, and preserve the terms of the Church's 250-year commitment to the Confession;[61] while the vast majority, under the guiding influence of Robert Rainy, advocated some measure of relief and relaxation in the Confessional bonds. Attention will now be directed to the arguments of those who desired to introduce a more flexible relation between the Free Church and its Confessional Standard.

c. The reasons advanced during the course of debate by those in favour of some degree of change were many and varied. As in any party or grouping, homogeneity was not the order of the day. Those who favoured change often did so for different reasons, and from different theological perspectives. Men as moderate, and essentially conservative, as Rainy, Brown, and James Denney, found themselves in the same boat as more extreme and liberally

---

61. Their highest vote in Assembly during these years was 130, but normally it was no more than the mid-sixties.

minded spirits such as James Smith,[62] Sheriff Cowan,[63] and Walter. C. Smith.[64] It is necessary to stress the heterogeneous composition of those who advocated change in order not to impute the motives of some as the motives of all. The polemic and shibboleths which characterised both sides during the debates were often little more than rhetorical devices rather than calculated theological statements – although it is true that a certain measure of perspective and clarity is often lost during hightened theological controversy. While the conservative group who advocated the retention of the status quo characterised the other side as crypto Arminians[65] who were encouraging 'laxity of faith',[66] their opponents lost no opportunity in indulging in the same polemical outbursts.[67]

The main reasons advocated by those who desired some measure of relief in the Church's relation to its Confession were threefold.

## 1. Nature of the Confession

During the five years of debate over the Confessional status of the Free Church, speeches were made criticising the composition and style, length, complexity, and logical exactness of the Westminster Confession. One of the notable critics was James Smith of Tarland.[68] During the opening debates in the 1889 Assembly, Smith practically condemned the Confession. His criticisms were all-embracing, imputing coldness, over logicality, lack of vigour, and lack of light and warmth to the Confession.[69]

---

62. Smith of Tarland thought that 'Confessions were necessary evils' (*Proceedings*, 1899, p. 143).

63. Sheriff Cowan of Paisley said, 'Predestination is a repulsive doctrine' (*Ibid.*, p. 150).

64. Walter C. Smith wanted to excise parts of the Confession (*Ibid.*, p. 152).

65. Dr Scott, *Ibid.*, p. 150; cf. Balfour, p. 154; and Macaskill, *Proceedings*, 1891, p. 88.

66. Macaskill, *Proceedings*, 1891, p. 85.

67. Prof. Inverach vilified Macaskill by likening him to an insect seeking to putrify already open sores (*Proceedings*, 1892, p. 197).

68. A quite radical opponent of the length, complexity, and thoroughness of the Confession.

69. *Proceedings*, 1889, p. 143.

To Smith, Confessions were 'necessary evils'[70] and as such should be accorded toleration but nothing more. The extremism of Smith gained little support in the Assembly, although some of his stinging attacks on the Confession reappeared in more moderate guise in the speeches of others who advocated change.

In addition to Smith's unhappiness with the very nature of the Confession, other more notable figures maintained that the inordinate length of the Standard necessitated the need for some measure of reappraisal and change. Professors Bruce and Brown both commented on the over-meticulous nature of the Confession. Brown maintained that the Westminster divines put more into the Confession than was warranted as a test for potential office-bearers,[71] and Bruce argued that the present situation was calling for a new, shorter creed containing the essence of the Gospel.[72]

While Bruce and Brown were reticent to excise parts of the Confession,[73] Walter C. Smith exhibited no reticence whatever in advocating the radical revision of the Confession's contents. Smith passionately believed that the Church's Confession would be immeasurably improved if certain aspects were removed.[74] Along with his namesake from Tarland he stressed that much in the Confession was there for 'logical completeness', and not because Scripture dictated it.

It is surprising to note that only James Smith commented upon the unusual historical context which produced the Westminster Confession. Smith's contention that the Confession was framed during 'Popish and Arminian controversies'[75] provided the basis of his arguments for radical and wholesale revision. A new era had dawned long since, and new expressions of truth were necessary to commend the gospel to the age.

---

70. *Ibid.,* p. 143.

71. *Ibid.,* pp. 137-138.

72. *Ibid.,* p. 149.

73. Bruce thought the present age was not fitted to creed making (*Ibid.,* p. 149).

74. *Ibid.,* p. 152.

75. *Ibid.,* p. 143.

## 2. *Relation between the Confession and the present faith of the Church*

At the back of most of the overtures which indicated dissatisfaction with the Church's relation to its Confession was the apparent conflict in the minds of many between the teaching of the Confession and the present faith of a large number in the Church. Contrary to those who argued that the present faith of the Church must always be qualified by, and judged by, the Confession,[76] Rainy, Bruce, Adam, and many others endeavoured to hammer out some sort of compromise. In seconding Professor Brown's motion for the setting up of a Committee to examine the need for relief, Dr Adam spoke of the large number of men who wanted change – 'they wish to have their convictions and creed in harmony'[77] – and who wanted to be honest with the world in the terms of their subscription to the Confession.

The theological maelstrom of the previous two decades had done much to detach a number of the younger men from the convictions of their fathers. In fact, the Declaratory Act could be seen as a device to straddle the gulf that had arisen between the traditional beliefs of the Free Church and the new ideas that were percolating through the membership. When he proposed the acceptance of the Presbyteries' decision on the Declaratory Act in 1892, Rainy declared that by the Declaratory Act 'We are winning a great many men … who might otherwise have been in danger of being thrown into a relation of agnosticism to our Confession and to all Confessions. We are really doing what is fitted to reconcile them…'[78]

Along similar lines, Professor Bruce, commenting upon the number of overtures expressing dissatisfaction with the Confession argued that:

---

76. Balfour's view (*Ibid.* p. 134); cf. Alex Forbes, pp. 141–142: 'The Creed regulates faith not vice-versa.'

77. *Ibid.* p. 139.

78. Rainy, *Proceedings,* 1892, p. 148.

*Ipso facto,* the form of subscription was virtually suspended by these overtures, and those who signed henceforth their names to the form of adherence to the Confession of Faith did so with that knowledge, and from that knowledge derived a certain relief to the scruples of conscience.[79]

Although Bruce's view here would be almost impossible to justify, the point he is making is nonetheless clear: the living faith of the Church qualifies the Church's Standard and in so doing (practically if not legally) ameliorates the tensions which had formerly existed. This practical concern to provide some means whereby the Church might commend itself to those who could never subscribe *ex animo* to the Confession was the guiding principle behind Professor Brown's motion in 1889. This willingness to 'meet difficulties and relieve scruples' was attacked by the 'traditionalists' as a sure means of encouraging laxity in the faith and of giving an undue place to human reasoning in the witness of the Church. Some at least were under no illusion as to the sources of these 'liberal' and 'injurious'[80] opinions – Germany, the land of rationalism and doubt.[81]

### 3. Theological Inadequacies in the Confession

Although Rainy argued that the proposed Declaratory Act was aimed at dispelling possible misunderstandings over the Confession's teaching on certain points,[82] the arguments advanced in its support centred more upon the failure of the Confession to reflect truly the teaching of Scripture than upon its ambiguity or lack of clarity. During the course of debate those who advocated change challenged the Confession's theological method,[83]

---

79. Bruce, *Ibid.* 1888, p. 148.
80. Dr Winter of Dyke, *Ibid.* 1893, p. 171.
81. Balfour, *Ibid.* 1889, p. 134.
82. Rainy, *Ibid.* 1891, p. 79.
83. *Ibid.* 1889, p. 138. Brown argued that the Confession adopted 'the logical and not the lateral method of conveying divine truth'. Also he considered the Confession's order wrong in placing Chapter 3 ('on God's Eternal Decrees') before Chapter 6 ('On Fall of Man').

its teaching on man,[84] the relation between sovereignty and love in the divine economy,[85] predestination,[86] and the position of children dying in infancy.[87]

When the proposed Declaratory Act was challenged and opposed by the traditionalists it is not difficult to appreciate the hiatus in their approach and thinking. While the Act was considered to be purely declaratory and explanatory by those who advocated its acceptance,[88] it was seen against this background of theological challenge to the Confession's teaching by those who wanted no change whatever, and as a result opposed as being contra-Confessional. It is not, therefore, a helpful exercise simply to examine the terms of the Declaratory Act and conclude that it was, or was not, against the Confession's teaching on certain points – a procedure that McCrie follows in his otherwise instructive and helpful work on Confessions.[89] Rather, the nature and content of the debates on the Confession during the years after 1889 provides a necessary and indispensable context from which to analyse the Declaratory Act. The reaction of the traditionalists to the Act must be considered in this light. This is not merely to commend their approach and arguments, but to underline the importance of examining context as a determining factor in ascertaining the proper evaluation of the terms of the Declaratory Act.

## 4. Reasons Given for the Retention of the Status Quo.

The reasons advanced by those who endeavoured to retain the Church's long-standing relation to its Confession took two

---

84. Rainy himself argued that the Confession's doctrine of man was 'too black'. He quoted Chalmers and Pascal on man's 'greatness' as well as his 'meanness' (*Ibid.* 1891, p. 81).

85. W. C. Smith, (*Ibid.* 1889, p. 152) argued that 'love was subordinate to sovereignty in the Confession'.

86. Sheriff Cowan, *Ibid.* p. 150, called Predestination 'a repulsive doctrine'.

87. Principal Brown's motion, *Ibid.* p. 137. He considered that there was more in the Confession than was warranted (e.g. elect infants).

88. See *Proceedings*, 1893, p. 167 (Rainy – and others).

89. Cf. McCrie, *op. cit.*, pp. 293f.

forms. Up until the introduction of the proposed Declaratory Act to the Assembly in 1891 the arguments had been of a general nature. William Balfour argued against the competency of Brown's motion in 1889, emphasising that only twenty-one out of seventy-three Presbyteries had indicated dissatisfaction with the Church's relation to the Confession. He considered the proposals for change to be an agitation against the Calvinism of the Confession,[90] and was therefore against them. Dr Scott of Aberlour made a similar point when he imputed 'Arminian and Rationalistic'[91] motives to those who were advocating a measure of change and relief. The thrust of the general position of the traditionalists was embodied in the speech of Alex Forbes of Drumblade at the 1889 Assembly.[92] Forbes argued that the Confession stood as the Church's guardian against error and human ingenuity, and as such regulated the faith of the Church. Where the faith of the Church contravened the teaching of the Confession the former must 'bow the knee' and conform to the Church's Standard.

When the proposed Declaratory Act was presented to the 1891 Assembly, the arguments of those who advocated no change whatever in the Church's relation to its Confession took on a more definite shape and form. In the debates which followed, discussion centred around: the theological contents of the Act; the lack of Presbyterial oversight of the Act; and the explicit nature of the Act as a piece of 'declaratory' legislation.

*1. The Theological Contents of the Act*
During, and after, discussion on the particular clauses or sections of the proposed Act, five areas were singled out as especially undermining the teaching of the Confession. The emphasis upon *the love of God* 'as standing in the forefront of the revelation

---

90. Balfour, *Proceedings,* 1889, p. 153.
91. Scott, *Ibid.* p. 150.
92. Forbes, *Ibid.* pp. 140f.
93. See Declaratory Act, section 1, in Free Church Acts of Assembly, 1982.

of Grace'[93] was looked upon as a liberalising device aimed at driving a wedge between Christ's redemption for his elect, and the sovereign love of God which was the source of that redemption.[94] Murdoch Macaskill went even further and argued that the terms of the statement in the Act reduced God's love 'to a vague, universal benevolence',[95] without effect or purpose.

Another area of controversy was over the Act's reference to the *work of the Holy Spirit* in relation to man's fallenness. Although the Act stated in no uncertain terms that fallen man is 'unable without the aid of the Holy Spirit to return to God', it added a 'qualification' that was attacked by the traditionalists, namely: 'yet (he is) capable of affections and actions which in themselves are virtuous and praiseworthy'.[96] Macaskill considered this clause as nothing less than 'diluted Armininianism'.[97] Although Rainy sought to show that the word 'aid' was used in its strongest Augustinian sense,[98] the statement in the Act was considered a direct challenge to the Confession's teaching on man's complete fallenness, and the sovereign regenerating work of the Holy Spirit.

Thirdly, Macaskill and Balfour both attacked the Act's understanding of *God's dealing with the heathen and imbeciles.* Section three of the Act declared:

> ...while the Gospel is the ordinary means of salvation for those to whom it is made known, yet it does not follow... that God may not extend his mercy...to those who are beyond the reach of these means...[99]

Macaskill, who took the lead in challenging the terms of the proposed Act, asserted that there could be no salvation apart from hearing the name of Jesus. His objection was based on the

---

94. *Proceedings,* 1891, p. 87 (Macaskill).

95. *Ibid.* p. 87.

96. Declaratory Act of Free Church, *op. cit.,* section 4.

97. *Proceedings,* 1891, p. 88.

98. *Ibid.* 1892, p. 151 (Rainy).

99. Declaratory Act, *op. cit.,* section 4.

assumption, later accepted by Rainy, that the above statement referred not so much to imbeciles as to intelligent heathen. Macaskill summed up his objection in this way:

> If one soul could be saved in this way, why not all? They [the Modern Church] must revise the Bible, and expunge not a little of it, before they could get any footing for their theory, for it is anti-Scriptural, anti-Confessional, and therefore most pernicious, and to be detested.[100]

A fourth area of contention was over the Act commitment to allow *'diversity of opinion'* on points which did not enter the substance of the Reformed Faith contained in the Confession.[101] More than one speaker spoke of the possibility of theological anarchy arising over this issue.[102]

However, it was the Act's proposed means for settling what was, and what was not, of the substance of the faith that provoked the major conflict over this final clause. The Act proposed that 'the Church' retain the full authority to discriminate in matters of theological controversy, 'and thus to guard against any abuse of this liberty to the detriment of sound doctrine, or to the injury of her unity and peace'.[103] Macaskill argued that the Church was usurping the place of Scripture as final arbiter in matters of faith, arrogating to itself the functions of 'popery',[104] and in a speech of highly emotional polemic, Major Macleod (an elder from Dalkeith) made the same point.[105]

The theological inadequacies of the Act, as understood by the traditionalists, were highlighted at every point in the debates

---

100. *Proceedings,* 1891, p. 88.

101. Declaratory Act, *op. cit.,* section 6.

102. Mr Hamilton of Symington, *Proceedings,* 1892, p. 169, thought the clause 'meaningless'. He knew of one man who thought 'election' was not part of the substance of the faith. Mr Moody-Stuart of Moffat said the Church had never in the past been satisfied with such vague expressions (p. 109).

103. Declaratory Act, *op. cit.,* section 6.

104. *Proceedings,* 1892, p. 161 (Macaskill).

105. *Ibid.* 1893, p. 178.

– often in language which could only exacerbate dissension and ill feeling. Dr Winter of Dyke considered the Act 'injurious to vital godliness';[106] Mr McNeilage of Govan thought the Church was heading for Socinianism;[107] and Major Macleod summed up the Act as 'unscriptural, immoral and popish'.[108] William Balfour, who refrained from using the wilder language of many who supported him, nonetheless thought the Act a 'subterfuge', a veritable smokescreen to foster the views of Dods, Bruce, and others, paving the way for the entrance of the 'modern faith'.[109]

### 2. Lack of Presbyterial Oversight

John McEwan, who was one of the members of the Confession of Faith Committee, gave some impetus to the traditionalists' arguments when he challenged the procedure under which the Declaratory Act had become law. McEwan contended that Presbyteries were given no suitable opportunity to examine, comment upon, and offer amendments to the proposed Act under the terms of the Barrier Act – the method whereby the Act had been submitted to the Presbyteries.[110] When challenged as to why he never dissented from the Committee's findings, McEwan retorted that it never occurred to him that its report to the Assembly would have been, *ipso facto*, turned into an overture under the Barrier Act – certainly an uncommon procedure, and one that provoked a not inconsiderable antagonism and opposition. The Presbyteries were accordingly left either to reject or accept the overture. Such a situation was felt to be intolerable by McEwan and he strove to have the whole issue remitted to the Presbyteries for further analysis and reassessment, an action he considered in keeping with

---

106. *Ibid.* p. 176. He also thought the Act opened up the way for 'Amyraldianism, Baxterianism and Neonomianism' – terms which would baffle and amuse modern-day Assemblies!

107. *Ibid.* p. 176.

108. *Ibid.* p. 176.

109. *Ibid.* 1891, p. 89 (Balfour).

110. *Ibid.* 1892, pp. 155–158. McEwan's argument was based upon this legal technicality, and its basis has now been disputed. Further study upon the subject would be needed to clarify the position.

the original terms and purpose of the Barrier Act.

McEwan's speech during the 1892 Assembly was marked by its irenic quality, and his motion gained considerable support. However, Rainy's motion that the Assembly pass the Declaratory Act overture as a Declaratory Act without further re-examination was passed by 346 to 195 votes.

*3. Nature of the Declaratory Act*

The antagonism engendered against the Declaratory Act was rooted in the belief that it did not fulfil the function it was devised for. Without exception, the traditionalists considered the Act a deliberate attempt to alter the Church's faith. Underlying nearly all the speeches opposing the Act was the belief that it was not, nor could ever be, declaratory or explanatory of the Church's Standards. This was the emphasis in Macaskill's major speech in the 1892 Assembly when he attempted a last-ditch stand against the Act becoming the law of the Church.[111]

The nature of the Act ensured that a degree of relief and liberty was available to those who scrupled to sign the Confession *simpliciter*. This state of affairs, however, gave rise to a serious controversy in the Church. In 1891 Macaskill had cautioned the Assembly that the proposed Act would be a serious burden upon the consciences of those who adhered *ex animo* to the Confession,[112] and the 1893 Assembly was practically taken up, throughout its course, with the problem.[113]

Although the Declaratory Act was not intended to be binding upon all in the Church, it became evident that in practice it was not possible to subscribe the Confession irrespective of the Act. The Assembly's decision over the case of the Dornoch Presbytery Records in 1893 indicated that no opportunity would be allowed office-bearers publicly to clarify their position vis-à-

---

111. *Ibid.* pp. 159ff.

112. *Ibid.* 1891, p. 85.

113. *Ibid.* 1893, pp. 55f. The case of Dornoch Presbytery Records (pp. 61f.). The motion over the Synod of Glenelg sanctioning statements in Presbyterial records condemning the Declaratory Act.

vis the new Act. The Questions were to be answered *simpliciter* without any qualification as to the individual's refusal to invoke the relief offered by the Declaratory Act.[114]

The decision of the Assembly was considered by the Highland ministers as a most provocative act. Many of these men, and their congregations, gave approbation to the 'whole doctrine' of the Confession, but now they were faced with a situation whereby their consent to its teaching was expressed in the same way as those who used the relief offered by the Declaratory Act. It was this situation which provided the background to the ten overtures anent the Declaratory Act presented at the 1893 Assembly. The overtures (all from Highland Presbyteries) maintained that the Act was neither optional, as had originally been maintained by Rainy, or declaratory, and as such should be rescinded. Certainly the discussion over the Dornoch case, and others in the Assembly, seemed to indicate that the relief offered by the Declaratory legislation was proving a burden to those who were perfectly content with subscribing *ex animo* to the Confession.

Rainy, however, continued to maintain that the Act placed no obligation upon any in the Church, and that it was in essence a declarative measure, in no way 'inconsistent with our Confessional position'.[115] Rainy's insistence that the Act was indeed optional and not binding is difficult to square with the Assembly proceedings, and the way in which individuals and Presbyteries were chastised for making public their refusal to sign the Confession in the light of the relieving legislation. Permissiveness seemed to be only in name, not in reality. Rainy's motion that the overtures be passed from gained overwhelming support (415 to 120). Although the 1894 Assembly witnessed

---

114. *Ibid.* p. 55. Rev. James MacDonald's statement in the Dornoch Records was pronounced an illegal act. He had stated: 'I am to sign the Confession of Faith *simpliciter*, and wholly irrespective of the Declaratory Act passed by the last Assembly, as signed at my licence and by other members of the Presbytery' (*Minute of the Presbytery*, 27 July 1892).

115. *Proceedings,* 1893, p. 167 (Rainy).

more overtures aimed at rescinding the Act, the strength seemed all but sapped from those who opposed it. Balfour's final dissent crystallised the feelings and objections of the traditionalists to the new state of affairs:

> We dissent from this resolution (to pass from the overtures) – first, because it fails in any measure to meet the reasonable objections of those who are opposed to the Declaratory Act, on the grounds that it appears to them to sanction views of doctrine unauthorised by the Standards, injurious to vital godliness, and inconsistent with a *bona fide* subscription to the formula; and second, because it appears to confirm the Declaratory act not merely as a statement of private opinion, but as a law of the Church, binding upon the Church courts in the administration of discipline.[116]

The passage of the Declaratory Act through successive Assemblies was complicated by two other issues which helped to colour individuals' understanding of the relieving legislation. The 1891 Assembly which gave its consent to the Committee's proposals for a Declaratory Act was presented with a second motion by the Convener on the Confession's article on *Scripture*.[117] Ostensibly the motion declared that there was no need to alter the Confession's teaching on the subject, hence its absence from the contents of the declarative measure.[118] Most probably the Committee in proposing their motion were endeavouring to defuse any potential flare-up over the Church's view of the inspiration of Scripture. However, their motives in so doing were challenged in the Assembly. James Denney considered the Committee was overstepping its remit from the Assembly in proposing such a motion, and fostering 'a sham unanimity' among the Committee members of which he was one. A Mr

---

116. *Ibid.* 1894, pp. 91–92.
117. Cf. the motion, *Proceedings,* 1891, pp. 83f.
118. Many expected that the Confession's article on Scripture would be tampered with. When it was left intact, the imputation of 'double-meaning' was given to the Committee's deliverance.

Adam from Kelso thought the deliverance 'a smokescreen to foster the views' of Marcus Dods. Both Balfour and Macaskill considered the motion guilty of a 'double-sense', and advocated a reaffirmation of the doctrine of verbal, plenary inspiration.[119] It is clear from the speeches made during the debate that the election of Dods to the New Testament Chair at Edinburgh, and the widespread support given to Dods and A.B. Bruce in the Church,[120] coloured the traditionalists' understanding of the Committee's deliverance. It would be difficult, if not impossible, for the most ardent supporter of verbal inspiration to quibble with the statement unless deviousness and underhand motives were applied to its framers – Balfour, Macaskill, and Scott all imputed such deviousness to Rainy and his Committee! Macaskill's motion that the Committee insert into its statement on Scripture an affirmation of its inerrancy and perfection was rejected by 283 votes to 51 votes.[121]

The other issue which greatly complicated matters was the Committee's proposal to alter the 1846 Questions and Formula. The purpose of this was somewhat to liberalise the commitment that individuals were bound to give to the Questions and Formula, thus bringing it into line with the relief offered by the Declaratory Act. When the Committee reported to the 1892 Assembly, it proposed that the approbation given to the 'whole doctrine' of the Confession be corrected to read 'the doctrine of the Confession',[122] as the former obligation was no longer embodied in any of the larger Presbyterian Churches which adhered to the Confession.[123] Rainy declared that 'the intention to impose so stringent an obligation is now disclaimed almost universally'.[124] The Committee further recommended that

---

119. *Proceedings,* 1891, pp. 113f.

120. Later in the Assembly the motion against their writings was overruled by 383 to 73 votes.

121. *Ibid.* 1891, pp. 113f.

122. See proposed changes in *Questions, Proceedings,* 1892. Report of the Committee No XXXVII, Appendix II, p. 6.

123. *Ibid.* p. 3.

124. *Ibid.* p. 3.

the proposed Act be sent to Presbyteries for suggestions and comment.

The major opposition to the proposed Act again came from John McEwan, one of the Committee's members. In his dissent he objected to the alteration suggested in the second Question, i.e. the removal of the word 'whole', and to the adoption of the second clause in the revised Preamble, which allowed the Questions to be answered in the light of the Declaratory Act.[125] McEwan's objection was all but unanimously overruled by the Assembly, only eleven recording their support on a show of hands. However, the ferment in the Highlands over the proposed legislation ensured that further action would be taken. Due to lack of time and opportunity for discussion, Rainy recommended to the 1893 Assembly that the Committee's Report be remitted to the next Assembly – an astute piece of ecclesiastical politics by Rainy that was destined, however, to fall by the wayside. (The Committee did, however, make public the returns from Presbyteries concerning the proposed changes. sixty-three Presbyteries sent returns – why no more? – twenty-one disapproving and fourty-two approving – twenty-seven *simpliciter*, and fifteen with amendments.)

The stage was thus set for the 1894 Assembly to ratify the proposed Act, thus adopting 'the one thing that remains to be done to complete the action in regard to the Declaratory Act intended by the Church'.[126] However, the widespread discontent with the proposals, especially in the Highlands, the fact of the Free Presbyterian secession, and the small, but vocal, opposition in the Assembly, caused the Committee to reconsider the proposals. When the motion came before the Assembly, the Committee proposed that if the Church accepted the liberalising Preamble to the Questions, then the Questions themselves might remain untouched. The Preamble stated:

Whereas the Declaratory Act, 1892, was passed 'to remove

---

125. *Ibid.* p. 8.
126. *Proceedings,* 1894. Report of Committee No XXXIII, p. 1.

difficulties and scruples which have been felt by some in reference to the declaration of belief required from persons who receive licence or are admitted to office in this Church', the Assembly hereby declare that the statements of doctrine contained in the said Act are not thereby imposed on any of the Church's office-bearers as part of the Standards of the Church, but that those who are licensed or ordained to office in this Church, on answering the Questions and subscribing the Formula, are entitled to do so in view of the said Act.[127]

Although the Questions were thus saved from revision, their terms and substance were all but emasculated. The Preamble stood as an open-ended qualification of their meaning. A shell of orthodoxy might remain, but the authority of the *prima facie* value of the Questions to the traditional wholehearted commitment to the Confession was undermined.

This understanding of the situation was, however, disputed. The standard Free Church (post-1900) text on the history of the period makes the point that the 'Act' of 1894 (i.e. the Preamble's content) was in fact only a 'resolution' of the Assembly and as such contained no legislative authority.[128] This interesting comment or interpretation of the legal situation, if it were followed, would mean that a certain hybrid set of circumstances prevailed in the Church. The Formula and Questions remained unaltered, intimating that unreserved commitment to the Confession was still the order of the day; in what light therefore stood the 1892 legislation? McEwan for one considered that the situation was only 'resolved' by the way of secret reservation when individuals answered the Questions: 'It (the Declaratory Act) could not be operative without putting a new meaning into those questions which ministers had to answer when they undertook a charge.'[129]

The uncertainty and ambiguity continued for another six

---

127. *Ibid.* pp. 1–2.

128. Rev. Alexander Stewart and Rev. John Kennedy Cameron, 'The Free Church of Scotland. 1843–1910: A Vindication' (Edinburgh & Glasgow 1910).

129. McEwan, *Proceedings,* 1892, p. 157. Also in Stewart and Cameron, *op. cit.,* pp. 77f.

years, until some of the 'old guard', baulking at the Union with the United Presbyterians, withdrew from the new Church, protesting their undying commitment to the theology and ecclesiology of the founding Fathers of the Disruption.

## 5. Leading Personalities

By far the most dominant figure during the years 1889 to 1894 was Robert Rainy, the Principal of New College and past Moderator. Rainy was sole Convener of the Confession of Faith Committee from 1891–1894 (and joint-Convener with Dr Adam 1889–1890), and as such responsible for presenting the Committee's proposals to successive Assemblies. He made all the major speeches supporting and commending the Committee's recommendations, and his erudition, eloquence, and 'moderation' gained him the overwhelming support of the Church. Rainy worked from a platform of strength. Already recognised as the Church's foremost ecclesiastical diplomat, he harnessed his sense of moderation and balance to a finely tuned mind which had analysed all the issues.

What marked Rainy's speeches during these years was a conciseness of thought allied to clarity of vision (he knew where he was going!) and temperate manner. Rarely did Rainy indulge in the bitter polemic that often characterised the debates. Only once did he seem to overstep his usual moderation when he advented to 'reckless spirits spreading exaggerated views' in the Highlands as cruel and wicked men.[130]

Rainy's biographer, Carnegie Simpson, makes much of Rainy's honesty and clarity, but his impartiality has been challenged by not a few – the official Free Presbyterian account of these years designating him a 'hero-worshipper' of Rainy! The account continues: 'We have seldom read in any biography such lame pleading, so full of sophistry, with a naïve simplicity that does

---

130. *Proceedings,* 1894, p. 81 (Rainy).

131. *History of the Free Presbyterian Church of Scotland 1893–1970* (Committee of Free Presbyterian Church – no date or place of publication, p. 40).

not deceive the reader.'[131] Such an assessment, however, betrays more emotion than historical analysis. Rainy, as far as records can reveal, earnestly sought to do what he considered best for the Church, and in all his exchanges with Macaskill and Balfour he never ceased to be polite and civil.

Murdoch Macaskill, along with William Balfour, led the opposition in the Assembly to Rainy and the proposed Declaratory Act. Macaskill had the 'unfortunate' ability to make enemies with his every utterance, and on more than one occasion he was protected from the wrath of the Assembly by Rainy's timely help and intervention. Macaskill's role as one of the leading spokesmen for those who favoured the retention of the *status quo* was not confined to Assembly debates. The minister from Dingwall was noted for his speeches condemning the Act, and he not only organised, but also spoke at rallies where he condemned the relieving legislation in the blackest of terms. It was these extra-Assembly activities which were the cause of Macaskill being subjected to personal attack and approbrium by his opponents in the Assembly. As noted earlier, Professor Inverach of Aberdeen vilified Macaskill in a speech of great anger, likening him to a creature seeking 'open sores in order to make them bigger',[132] and Candlish and Dods both accused him of gross misquotation and personal misrepresentation.

The irony surrounding Macaskill's part in the attempt to oppose the Declaratory Act was seen in 1900 when he led the bulk of his congregation into the Union. The failure of Macaskill and Balfour to follow through their statements with appropriate action has gained this comment from an interested party: 'One has more respect for (the two ministers who seceded)…than for those who had used the most violent language, and had led their people to the brink of secession and then, at the last moment, themselves drew back.'[133]

Rainy advocated a Church policy of inclusiveness, breadth,

---

132. *Proceedings*, 1892, p. 197.
133. A. Carnegie Simpson, *The Life of Principal Rainy* (London 1909), Vol. II, p. 129.

and toleration. Macaskill and his supporters advocated exclusiveness, strictly adhered to Confessional barriers, and intolerance (in the sense of refusing compromise with those who failed to measure up to their defined standard of wholehearted commitment to the Confession). It would be unfair to imply that the traditionalists held to a policy of 'As it was in the seventeenth century, is now, and evermore shall be', but their actions certainly pointed somewhat in that direction. If an answer to that charge could be anticipated it would be along the lines that the Puritans who compiled the Confession were men who placed themselves under the authority of the Scriptures in a way that was foreign to the modern professors in the Church. As such their interpretation was at all times to be favoured above that of the 'modern prophets'.

Behind the scenes, as it were, other figures exerted a great influence. The election of Marcus Dods to the New Testament Chair at Edinburgh in 1889, the refusal of the Assembly to allow a 'process' against Dods and Bruce in 1890, and the vindication of their writings by the 1891 Assembly did much to influence the debates over the Confession during these years. The professors took little part in the debates, except to defend themselves against what they considered misrepresentation. Their writings had challenged the traditionally held interpretation of areas in the Confession, and had been sanctioned by the Assembly of the Church. Macaskill, for one, recognised their importance and endeavoured, especially during the 1892 Assembly, to discredit their views particularly on the Inspiration and Canon of Scripture.[134]

## 6. The Effect of the Declaratory Act upon the Church

Firstly, ever since the United Presbyterian Church passed their Declaratory Act in 1879, it was obvious to all concerned that if the Free Church genuinely desired union it would have to accommodate its position to the new state of affairs in its sister Church. The Declaratory legislation of 1892 was therefore a

---

134. *Proceedings,* 1892 (Macaskill), pp. 174f. and pp. 191f.

necessary preliminary to a union between the two Churches, and smoothed the way for it.

Secondly, the theological and geographical polarisation in the Free Church which had been developing since the abortive Union talks in the 1860s was intensified and heightened. The vast majority of overtures desiring the repeal of the Declaratory Act came from Highland Presbyteries (no complete list was available – otherwise accurate figures would, I am sure, underline the above statement). A great deal of rancour and polemic had marked the rallies and debates considering the proposed legislation – some of which manifested itself in the Assembly debates – and the battle-lines of the 1900–1904 Controversy were all but mapped out during these years. Finally, a small secession of two ministers and twenty elders left the Free Church and formed the Free Presbyterian Synod,[135] contributing further to the fragmented nature of Presbyterianism in Scotland.

While Rainy and his supporters hailed the Declaratory Act as a reconciling piece of legislation,[136] the opponents of the Act considered it divisive and conducive to illfeeling and error. They never ameliorated their view that the Declaratory Act was contrary to the testimony of Scripture, and subversive of the Calvinistic theology of the Confession. Dr Scott of Aberfour crystallised the feelings of the traditionalists, and in so doing anticipated the final phase of the conflict:

> Viewed practically, the Act was in all respects highly inexpedient – doctrinally, in promoting and protecting error – morally, by fomenting intestine [internecine?] war, by which the Church would be distracted and demoralized – and by originating and fostering questions of property.[137]

---

135. MacFarlane's 'protest', on Rainy's advice, was not accepted by the Assembly. Rainy considered it not simply a dissent, but an express repudiation of the General Assembly's authority (*Proceedings*, 1893, p. 183).

136. *Proceedings*, 1892, p. 148.

137. *Ibid.* p. 164.

# 9

# Conclusion

Do we then have to face the fact that we are living in a post-confessional age, an age when confessions of faith are no longer needed? Are the historic confessions and creeds of the Church simply engines of division? To anyone who takes biblical revelation and religion at all seriously the answer must surely be, no. A number of reasons compel us to argue for the necessity of confessions in the Church's life today.

First, a Confession is an appropriate instrument for identifying the Church as such in the world. A Confession is like a banner under which the Church carries on its activities, telling the world what it is, and what it stands for. In this sense it hardly needs to be said, to quote Abraham Kuyper, that 'a creed is not for the purpose of stating our own surmises or conjectures, but for professing that, of which, on the basis of God's revelation, we possess most certain knowledge'.[1] In this respect, the Reformation confessions and the creeds of the patristic age are one in their concern 'to confess Christ against

---

1. Abraham Kuyper, *Presbyterian and Reformed Review*, 1891, p. 338.

views which in some way or another deny or dishonour him, and so to express and safeguard the unity and purity of the Christian faith against inroads of heresy'.[2]

Second, closely allied to this is the Confession's function as an evangelical testimony to those outside the Church fellowship. Norman Shepherd speaks of this as the Confession's 'apologetic and polemic' function: 'since the gospel has come into the world for the purpose of overthrowing the dominion of the father of lies, it is inevitable that the confession will be both apologetic (directed against error outside the Church) and polemic (directed against deception within the professing Church)'.[3] A Confession therefore serves the purpose of making known succinctly to the Church, as well as to the world, 'the faith once for all delivered to the saints'.

Third, a Confession of Faith serves the ecumenical unity of the Church. Far from being engines of division, creeds and confessions serve the cause of true ecumenism by honestly exemplifying what different denominations understand by the 'faith once for all delivered to the saints'. Unity that is not built upon, and is reflective of God's truth, is not Christian unity.

Some have argued that the cause of ecumenism is best served by having a bond of union centring on an arrangement of biblical texts. However, such an arrangement would not solve the problem of language, i.e. just what do we mean by such statements? Further, the meaning of language is eclectic, it changes from age to age. It was this fact which led James Bannerman to write:

> The unity of the Church as a society of believers requires and justifies human compilations of Divine truth, if it is to be really a unity of faith and not merely a unity of form or formal words.[4]

Fourthly, a Confession of Faith serves to maintain ecclesiastical harmony. Without a Confession of Faith, anarchy not harmony

---

2. Packer, *op. cit.*, 5.

3. Norman Shepherd, 'Scripture and Confession', 22, in *Scripture and Confession*, ed. John H Skilton (Presbyterian and Reformed, 1973).

4. James Bannerman, *op. cit.*, vol. 1, p. 298.

would prevail. This fact necessitates the inclusion, in any meaningful confessional statement, of a number of doctrines, which in themselves do not belong to the substance of the faith – infant baptism and Presbyterian polity, to name but two. A church, or a denomination of churches, has to live in harmony and in administrative unity. To have one church in a denomination practise paedo-baptism, while another rejects the practice, would be a recipe for theological, pastoral, and administrative anarchy.

Fifthly, Confessions assist the Church in maintaining internal discipline. This is especially so with regard to those who hold office in the Church. Subscription to a confession of faith would be required as an assurance that the individual's understanding of the truth is such as to qualify him for leadership and teaching in the Church of Christ.

Sixthly, a Confession of Faith has the capacity to register the ecumenical theological attainments of the Church. One of the sad, even tragic, features of modern evangelical Church life is its practical divorce from the Church of the ages. By God's grace and his good, if sovereign, providence, we have inherited the learning, wisdom, and attainments of the Church over the past two millennia. Through the fires of controversy, and often the literal fires of persecution, the Lord has led his Church to mine the deep quarries of his truth in Holy Scripture. A biblical Confession of Faith will surely then reflect those hard-won attainments and acknowledge that the Church did not begin with us and our generation. T.F. Torrance has wisely written:

> It is only in the combination of historical theology and exegesis that the church can be delivered from preaching its own private conceptions and carry through the disciplined self-criticism which frank and obedient conversation with God requires… A theology that is not essentially ecumenical is a contradiction in terms. We cannot engage in conversation with God by forgetting our fathers, or by separating us from our brothers.[5]

---

5. Thomas F. Torrance, *The School of Faith* (Edinburgh, 1959), lxviii.

It is together 'with all the saints' that we 'comprehend...what is the breadth and length and height and depth...[and] know the love of Christ that surpasses knowledge' (Eph. 3:18-19).

Where departure from a Church's Confession is discerned it would be necessary to demonstrate departure from Scripture before disciplinary measures may be applied. A Confession of Faith is then a most helpful tool in guarding the Church's mission to be 'the pillar and foundation of the truth', in ensuring that what is taught and passed on is indeed 'the pattern of sound words'. *Sola scriptura* and not *nuda scriptura* was the conviction of the Reformers, and, more importantly, of the directly inspired prophets and apostles who penned the sacred writings.

Objections to Confessions of Faith

Usually four objections are raised today against the need for Confessions of Faith. First, they detract from the sufficiency and perfection of the Bible as the Church's supreme rule of faith. This argument completely misses the point. Confessions are 'subordinate' Standards (cf. Westminster Confession of Faith I.X). Confessions are only binding in so far as they are biblical, and are therefore open to revision and modification, and rejection in the light of God's infallible Word.

Second, they limit and hinder the liberty of Church members. But it must surely be obvious that Confessions do not seek to impose any extra burden on Church members that the Bible does not already impose. They no more restrict an individual's liberty than the rails on a railway track restrict the liberty of the train running on it. Commenting on the Thirty-Nine Articles, H.P. Liddon answers the claim that Confessions restrict liberty: 'To complain of a creed as an interference with liberty, is to imitate the savage who had to walk across London at night and who remarked that the lamp posts were an obstruction to traffic.'

Third, Confessions limit the progress and development of theology. This objection might have some truth in it if Confessions were considered the last word in biblical interpretation, 'sacred cows' which must never be altered nor interfaced with. The framers of the Scots Confession were well aware that their Confession was by its very nature provisional:

> Protesting that if any man will note in this our Confession any article or sentence repugning to God's holy Word, that it would please him of his gentleness, and for Christian charity's sake, to admonish us of the same in writing; and we of our honour and fidelity do promise unto him satisfaction from the mouth of God (that is, from his Holy Scriptures) or else reformation of that which he shall prove to be amiss.[6]

James Bannerman was speaking for the Reformed tradition when he wrote:

> Let any part of them (Confessions) be proved from Scripture to be false, and we give it up; for we hold them only because, and insofar as, they are true. We invite every man to go beyond them if he can. We encourage and call upon every student of God's Holy Word to press forward to fresh discoveries of truth, and to open up new views of the meaning of Scripture.... Those who have studied their Bibles longest and most prayerfully are most convinced of that.[7]

Neither the antiquity, past usefulness, nor honoured status of any Confession exempts it from its provisional place in the life of the Church.

Fourth, Creeds and Confessions, and in particular subscription to them, do little if anything, in Jonathan Dickinson's words, to 'detect heresies, resist gainsayers, to propagate the truth; and to keep the church not only a garden enclosed, but a garden of peace'.[8] Dickinson believed that subscription to

---

6. *The Scots Confession (Confessio Scoticana), 1560,* Reprinted by The Church of Scotland Committee on Publications, Edinburgh, 1937, p. 41. See also Westminster Confession of Faith 1.10.

7. James Bannerman, *op. cit.,* p. 320.

8. Quoted in Hart and Meuther, *op. cit.,* p. 43.

a Church Confession was no substitute for the Church itself rigorously examining candidates for the ministry. Subscription had, Dickinson believed, the tendency to overly formalise and cerebralise the life of Christ's Church. He was a strictly orthodox Calvinist. He had no desire to allow unsound men, or even men with liberalising tendencies, into the Church's ministry. The question for Dickinson was, 'What means will best secure an orthodox and experimental ministry in the church?' His answer was a careful, exacting examination of ministerial candidates regarding their doctrine and life.

It can hardly be denied that subscription by itself may have, and indeed has had, the sad tendencies Dickinson feared. The cold hand of Moderatism throughout much of eighteenth-century Scotland illustrated the point well. Men subscribed the Westminster Confession *simpliciter*, without reservation, but many did so while being mentally removed from the Confession's doctrines and spiritually at a distance from the saving grace of God proclaimed in those doctrines. However, subscription to a Confession and the strict, careful examination of ministerial candidates are surely not mutually exclusive. The existence of a Confession of Faith provides the Church with a biblically tested basis out of which to conduct a careful and strict examination of ministerial candidates. Indeed, the strict examination that Dickinson and others preferred would itself have been based on a well-formed, if mentally contoured, Confession. The only alternative would have been to depart from *sola scriptura* and replace it with *nuda scriptura*, requiring candidates simply to affirm certain biblical texts.

Having said that, we cannot escape the fact that Confession-alism is considered by many to be a relic of a bygone era. In the Church of Scotland, commitment to the Westminster Confession of Faith – still, remarkably, the Church's subordinate Standard of Faith – is to a purposefully undefined 'substance of the faith'. Individuals are left to determine for themselves what this substance is, the Church steadfastly refusing to clarify what it means by 'the substance of the faith'.[9] Confessionalism has been effectively replaced by theological subjectivism. This should not surprise us; whenever God's truth is relativised the drift into subjectivism is inevitable.

The Confessionalism which presently prevails can be summed up in the phrase: 'I believe (or more accurately, I will do) whatever the General Assembly is pleased to enact.'[10] The *sine qua non* of remaining a minister within the Church is no longer a commitment to the Church's Confession of Faith, but a commitment to the Church's canon law. The issue that most matters is not, 'What do you believe?' but 'What will you practice?'

This was well illustrated in the late 1980s, when the Church of Scotland discussed a Draft Statement of Faith, produced by the Panel on Doctrine at the instruction of the General Assembly. This Draft Statement was intended to affirm what the Church believes today, and to delineate its place within the one apostolic and catholic Church. While this Draft Statement contained some welcome affirmations, it was an example of the reductionist and ambivalent thinking that prevails within much of the Christian Church today (e.g. there is no mention of God's sovereign power and purpose, the Fall, repentance, faith, the need for and nature of Christ's death, the authority of Scripture, evangelism, hell, to name but a few remarkable omissions). The Panel admitted at the time that they had striven to produce a Statement of Faith that would appeal to all segments of the Church. The aim had not been faithfully to reflect the teaching

---

9. See Ian Hamilton, *The Erosion of Calvinist Orthodoxy* in J. Ligon Duncan (ed), *The Westminster Confession into the 21st Century*, Christian Focus, 2004, pp. 169ff. Here Hamilton provides a summary overview of Confessional decline within the Scottish Church.

10. James Weatherhead, then Principal Clerk to the General Assembly of the Church of Scotland, clarified the law of the Church on women's ordination in June 1987: 'Any decision by a Kirk Session to the effect that women will not be considered for the eldership is…in breach of the law of the Church…While the law stands as it is, there is no provision for conscientious objection to applying it.' According to the Church's Procurator, when opposition to women elders is stated as a matter of policy or principle it is *ultra vires*.

and balance of Scripture, but to reflect the diversity of opinion within the Church. This is a new kind of Confessionalism. No longer is Scripture the focus and definer of our theological perameters; what we confess is determined by the consensual opinions of people.

The response of evangelicals within the Kirk at the time was sadly lacking. By and large the Draft Statement was commended.[11] There was a resolve to present a 'centrist' approach to the question, 'What should be included in such a popular Statement of Faith?' 'It is plainly inappropriate that its character should be one-sided or unbalanced, reflecting sectional interests... The only way to ensure the statement's objectivity and general acceptability within the church is to draft it as a statement of mainstream Christian faith, as manifest in this our national Church.' This declaration was a huge disappointment to some and a sign that evangelicals in the Kirk had drifted from their Reformed moorings and had settled for being a 'wing' of the national Church. *Sola scriptura* was no longer the evangelicals' ultimate and alone authority. What held sway was the desire to remain in the Kirk at all costs. If this meant adopting a statement 'of mainstream Christian faith, as manifest in this our national Church', albeit one that was conspicuous by its glaring doctrinal omissions, then so be it. Unity, or at least toleration, was more important than unyielding commitment to biblical truth, however 'one-sided' others may judge it.

The situation that prevails today within the mainstream Protestant Churches is not conducive to Confessionalism. Once you depart from Scripture as the Church's only rule of faith and life, as the song puts it, 'anything goes'. What is left is a theological Noah's Ark, where everyone believes what is right in his and her own eyes; where Confessionalism is relegated to the individual conscience; where no one view is any more, or less, acceptable than any other view.

---

11. See the response of Rutherford House, the evangelical 'think tank' in the Church.

What remains is a reductionist Confessionalism: a Confessionalism which confesses everything and negates practically nothing. This should not surprise us. When truth is de-propositionalised, denied its absolutist character, and subordinated to the modern god 'tolerance', it is not surprising that Confessions and Creeds which propositionalise God's truth are considered passé. Such documents are an embarrassment to the Church today, and increasingly relegated to the sidelines of history: documents of historical interest, landmarks in the evolution of the Church, relevant to their own day, but out of touch with the realities of today. This kind of thinking may appeal to the inclusivist thinking that pervades much of the Church and society, but it is light years removed from the New Testament with its categorical affirmations of truth, and its equally categorical denial of error.

Until the Church wakens up to its follies, and is returned to a new confidence in Scripture, it seems likely that meaningful Confessionalism will be the preserve of so-called 'fundamentalist' remnants.

Without meaningful and biblically substantive Confessions of Faith the Church will the more easily forget, and ignore, the realities on which it depends. It is not mindless fundamentalism, but faithfulness to the Word of God that compels honest Christians 'to contend for the faith once for all delivered to the saints'. There are few better ways of doing so than by clearly holding out what it is that Christians 'most certainly believe'.

# APPENDIX A

**Proposed Declaratory Statement Anent The Subordinate Standards. May 1978.**

Whereas the formula in which the Subordinate Standards of this Church are accepted requires assent to them as an exhibition of the sense in which the Scriptures are understood: Whereas these Standards, being of human composition, are necessarily imperfect, and the Church has already taken exception to their teaching or supposed teaching on one important subject: And whereas there are other subjects in regard to which it has been found desirable to set forth more fully and clearly the view which the Synod takes of the teaching of Holy Scripture: Therefore, the Synod hereby declares as follows:-

1. That in regard to the doctrine of Redemption as taught in the Standards, and in consistency therewith, the love of God to all mankind, His gift of His Son to be the propitiation for the sins of the whole world, and the free offer of salvation to men without distinction on the ground of Christ's perfect sacrifice, are matters which have been and continue to be regarded by this Church as vital in the system of Gospel truth, and to which she desires to give special prominence.

2. That the doctrine of the Divine Decrees, including the doctrine of Election to Eternal Life, is held in connection and harmony with the truth that 'God will have all men to be saved', and has provided a salvation sufficient for all, adapted to all, and offered to all with the grace of His Spirit in the gospel; and also with the responsibility of every man for his dealing with the free and unrestricted offer of eternal life.

3. That the doctrine of Man's Total Depravity, and of his loss of 'all ability of will to any spiritual good accompanying salvation', is not held as implying such a condition of man's nature as would affect his responsibility under the law of God and the Gospel of Christ, or that he may not experience the strivings and restraining influences of the Spirit of God, or that he cannot perform actions in any sense good; though such actions, as not springing from a renewed heart, are not spiritually good, nor holy, and consequently not such as accompany salvation.

4. That while all who are saved are saved through the mediation of Christ and by the grace of His Holy Spirit, who worketh when, and where, and how it pleaseth Him; and while the duty of sending the Gospel to the heathen who are sunk in a state of sin and misery, and perishing for lack of knowledge, is clear and imperative, the Church does not require the acceptance of her Standards in a sense which might imply that any who die in infancy are lost; nor does she bind those who accept these Standards to hold that God in no case saves without the use of the ordinary means.

5. That this Church holds that the Lord Jesus Christ is the only King and Head of the Church, and 'Head over all things to the Church which is His body', and firmly renews her protest against all compulsory or persecuting and intolerant principles in religion, and declares, as hitherto, that she does not require approval of anything in her Standards that teaches, or may be supposed to teach, such principles.

6. That Christ has laid it as a permanent and universal

obligation upon His Church, at once to maintain her own ordinances and to 'preach the Gospel to every creature'; and has ordained that the means of fulfilling this obligation are to be provided by the free-will offerings of His people.

7. That, in accordance with the practice hitherto observed in this Church, liberty of opinion is allowed on such points in the Standards not entering into the substance of the faith, as the interpretation of the 'six days' in the Mosaic account of the creation: the Church guarding against the abuse of this liberty to the injury of its unity and peace.

# APPENDIX B

**Declaratory Act, Adopted May, 1879**

Whereas the formula in which the Subordinate Standards of this Church are accepted requires assent to them as an exhibition of the sense in which the Scriptures are understood: Whereas these Standards, being of human composition, are necessarily imperfect, and the Church has already allowed exception to be taken to their teaching or supposed teaching on one important subject: And whereas there are other subjects in regard to which it has been found desirable to set forth more fully and clearly the view which the Synod takes of the teaching of Holy Scripture: Therefore the Synod hereby declares as follows:-

1. That in regard to the doctrine of redemption as taught in the Standards, and in consistency therewith, the love of God to all mankind, His gift of His Son to be the propitiation for the sins of the whole world, and the free offer of salvation to men without distinction on the ground of Christ's perfect sacrifice, are matters which have been and continue to be regarded by this Church as vital in the system of Gospel truth, and to which due prominence ought ever to be given.

2. That the doctrine of the divine decrees, including the doctrine of election to eternal life, is held in connection and

harmony with the truth that God is not willing that any should perish, but that all should come to repentance, and that He has provided a salvation sufficient for all, adapted to all, and offered to all in the Gospel; and also with the responsibility of every man for his dealing with the free and unrestricted offer of eternal life.

3. That the doctrine of man's total depravity, and of his loss of 'all ability of will to any spiritual good accompanying salvation', is not held as implying such a condition of man's nature as would affect his responsibility under the law of God and the Gospel of Christ, or that he does not experience the strivings and restraining influences of the Spirit of God, or that he cannot perform actions in any sense good; although actions which do not spring from a renewed heart are not spiritually good or holy – such as accompany salvation.

4. That while none are saved except through the mediation of Christ, and by the grace of His Holy Spirit, who worketh when, and where, and how it pleaseth Him; while the duty of sending the Gospel to the heathen, who are sunk in ignorance, sin, and misery, is clear and imperative; and while the outward and ordinary means of salvation for those capable of being called by the Word are the ordinances of the Gospel: in accepting the Standards, it is not required to be held that any who die in infancy are lost, or that God may not extend His grace to any who are without the pale of ordinary means, as it may seem good in His sight.

5. That in regard to the doctrine of the Civil Magistrate, and his authority and duty in the spheres of religion, as taught in the Standards, this Church holds that the Lord Jesus Christ is the only King and Head of the Church, and 'Head over all things to the Church which is His body;' disapproves of all compulsory or persecuting and intolerant principles in religion; and declares, as hitherto, that she does not require approval of anything in her Standards that teaches, or may be supposed to teach, such principles.

6. That Christ has laid it as a permanent and universal obligation upon His Church, at once to maintain her own ordinances, and to 'preach the Gospel to every creature;' and has ordained that His people provide by their free-will offerings for the fulfilment of this obligation.

7. That, in accordance with the practice hitherto observed in this Church, liberty of opinion is allowed on such points in the Standards, not entering into the substance of the faith, as the interpretation of the 'six days' in the Mosaic account of the creation: the Church guarding against the abuse of this liberty to the injury of its unity and peace.

# APPENDIX C

**Free Church Declaratory Act. Act XII, Anent Confession of Faith (Acts of the General Assembly of the Free Church of Scotland, 1889–1893 [Edinburgh 1893], pp. 478f.)**

Whereas it is expedient to remove difficulties and scruples which have been felt by some in reference to the declaration of belief required from persons who receive licence or are admitted to office in this Church, the General Assembly with consent of Presbyteries, declare as follows:-

That, in holding and teaching, according to the Confession, the Divine purpose of grace towards those who are saved, and the execution of that purpose in time, this Church most earnestly proclaims, as standing in the forefront of the revelation of Grace, the love of God – Father, Son, and Holy Spirit – to sinners of mankind, manifested especially in the Father's gift of the Son to be the Saviour of the world, in the coming of the Son to offer Himself a Propitiation for sin, and in the striving of the Holy Spirit with men to bring them to repentance.

That this Church also holds that all who hear the Gospel are warranted and required to believe to the saving of their souls; and in the case of such as do not believe, but perish in their sins, the issue is due to their own rejection of the Gospel call. That this Church does not teach, and does not regard the Confession as teaching, the foreordination of men to death irrespective of their own sin.

That it is the duty of those who believe, and one end of their calling by God, to make known the Gospel to all men everywhere for the obedience of faith. And that while the Gospel is the ordinary means of salvation for those to whom it is made known, yet it does not follow, nor is the Confession to be held as teaching, that any who die in infancy are lost, or that God may not extend His mercy, for Christ's sake, and by His Holy Spirit, to those who are beyond the reach of these means, as may seem good to Him, according to the riches of His Grace.

That, in holding and teaching, according to the Confession of Faith, the corruption of man's whole nature as fallen, this Church also maintains that there remain tokens of his greatness as created in the image of God; that he possesses a knowledge of God and of duty; that he is responsible for compliance with the moral law and with the Gospel; and that, although unable without the aid of the Holy Spirit to return to God, he is yet capable of affections and actions which in themselves are virtuous and praiseworthy.

That this Church disclaims intolerant or persecuting principles, and does not consider her officebearers, in subscribing the Confession, committed to any principles inconsistent with liberty of conscience and the right of private judgment.

That while diversity of opinion is recognised in this Church on such points in the Confession as do not enter into the substance of the Reformed Faith therein set forth, this Church retains full authority to determine, in any case which may arise, what points fall within this description, and thus to guard against any abuse of this liberty to the detriment of sound doctrine, or to the injury of her unity and peace.

The proposed Declaratory Act was accepted by 54 presbyteries, and rejected by 23 presbyteries.

# Bibliography

## 1. Primary Sources

*Acts of the General Assembly of the Church of Scotland 1638–1842*, Edinburgh, 1843.

*The Acts of the Parliaments of Scotland, Vol III, A.D. MCCCCXXIV – A.D. MDLXVII*, Edinburgh, 1814.

*The Acts of the Parliaments of Scotland and The Government During the Commonwealth. Vol VI, Part II, A.D. MDCXLVIII – A.D. MDCLX* (No place of publication), 1872.

*The Acts of the Parliament of Scotland, Vol. IX, A.D. MDCLXXXIX – A.D. MDCXCV (No place of publication)*, 1822.

*Acts and Proceedings of the General Associate Synod, Vol. IV, 1795–1820* (No place of publication).

*Annals of the Free Church of Scotland (1843–1900)*, ed. by W. Ewing, Vol. I, Edinburgh, 1914.

*The Booke of the Universall Kirk of Scotland*, ed. by A. Peterkin, Edinburgh, 1839.

*Minutes of the Relief Synod 1773–1829,* Vol I (No place of publication).

*Minutes of the United Associate Synod, June 1841,* Glasgow, 1841

*Minutes of the United Associate Synod, May 1842,* Glasgow, 1842.

*Minutes of the United Associate Synod, May 1843,* Glasgow, 1843.

*Minutes of the United Associate Synod, Oct 1843,* Glasgow, 1843.

*Minutes of the United Associate Synod, May 1844,* Glasgow, 1844.

*Minutes of the United Associate Synod, May 1845,* Glasgow, 1845.

*Minutes of the United Associate Synod, July 1845,* Glasgow, 1845.

*Minutes of the United Associate Synod, May 1846,* Glasgow, 1846.

*Minutes of the United Associate Synod, Oct 1846,* Saltcoates, 1846.

*Minutes of the United Associate Synod, May 1847,* Saltcoates, 1847.

*Proceedings and Debates in the General Assembly of the Free Church of Scotland, 1863,* Edinburgh and London, 1863.

*Proceedings and Debates in the General Assembly of the Free Church of Scotland, 1864,* Edinburgh and London, 1864.

*Proceedings and Debates in the General Assembly of the Free Church of Scotland, 1865,* Edinburgh and London, 1865.

*Proceedings and Debates in the General Assembly of the Free Church of Scotland, 1866,* Edinburgh and London, 1866.

*Proceedings and Debates in the General Assembly of the Free Church of Scotland, 1867,* Edinburgh and London, 1867.

*Proceedings and Debates in the General Assembly of the Free Church of Scotland, 1868,* Edinburgh and London, 1868.

*Proceedings and Debates in the General Assembly of the Free Church of Scotland, 1869,* Edinburgh and London, 1869.

*Proceedings and Debates in the General Assembly of the Free Church of Scotland, 1870,* Edinburgh and London, 1870.

*Proceedings and Debates in the General Assembly of the Free Church of Scotland, 1871,* Edinburgh, 1871.

*Proceedings and Debates in the General Assembly of the Free Church of Scotland, 1872,* Edinburgh, 1872.

*Proceedings and Debates in the General Assembly of the Free Church of Scotland, 1873,* Edinburgh, 1873.

*Proceedings and Debates in the General Assembly of the Free Church of Scotland, 1889,* Edinburgh, 1889.

*Proceedings and Debates in the General Assembly of the Free Church of Scotland, 1890,* Edinburgh, 1890.

*Proceedings and Debates in the General Assembly of the Free Church of Scotland, 1891,* Edinburgh, 1891.

*Proceedings and Debates in the General Assembly of the Free Church of Scotland, 1892,* Edinburgh, 1892.

*Proceedings and Debates in the General Assembly of the Free Church of Scotland, 1893,* Edinburgh, 1893.

*Proceedings and Debates in the General Assembly of the Free Church of Scotland, 1894,* Edinburgh, 1894.

*Proceedings of the Synod of the United Presbyterian Church, 1847–1856,* Edinburgh, 1856.

*Proceedings of the Synod of the United Presbyterian Church, Vol. VI (1877–79),* Glasgow, 1880.

*Proceedings of the Synod of the United Presbyterian Church, May 1880,* Glasgow, 1880.

*Register of the Actings and Proceedings of the Presbytery of Dunfermline, Vol. V* (n.d.).

*Register of the Actings and Proceedings of the Presbytery of Dunfermline, Vol. VI* (n.d.).

*Subscription to the Confession of Faith and Formula. From 24 February 1697 to 23 April 1793,* Presbytery of Dunfermline (n.d.).

*Glasgow Presbytery of the United Presbyterian Church. Minutes 1875–78, Vol. VI* (No other information).

## 2. Secondary Sources:

*A. Books:*

Ahlstrom, S.E., *A Religious History of the American People*, New Haven and London, 1972.

Arnold, M., *Literature and Dogma – An Essay Towards a Better Appreciation of the Bible*, London, 1873.

Arnold, M., *God and the Bible – A review of objections to 'Literature and Dogma'*, London, 1875.

Bannerman, J., *Inspiration*, Edinburgh, 1865.

Bannerman, J., *The Church of Christ,* 2 vols., Mack. ed., New Jersey, 1972.

Baxter, R., *Richard Baxter's Confession of Faith,* London, 1655.

Beattie, F.R., *The Presbyterian Standards: An Exposition of the Westminster Confession of Faith and Catechisms*, Richmond, 1896.

Begg, J., *Free Church Presbyterianism in the United Kingdom,* Edinburgh, 1865.

Bonar, H., *Our Ministry: How it Touches the Questions of the Age* (No place of publication; n.d.).

Brown, C., *Philosophy and the Christian Faith,* London, 1969.

Brown, James, *Life of John Eadie,* London, 1878.

Brown, James, *The Life of a Scottish Probationer,* Glasgow, 1889.

Brown, J., *Gospel Truth Accurately Stated and Illustrated,* Edinburgh, 1817.

Brown, John, *Hints to Students of Divinity*, Edinburgh, 1841.

Brown, John, *Commentary on the Book of Hebrews,* Edinburgh, 1862.

Brown, John, *Commentary on Second Peter,* Edinburgh, 1856.

Brown, John, *Discourses and Sayings of our Lord,* Edinburgh, 1850.

Brown, John, *Theological Tracts, Selected and Original,* 3 vols., Edinburgh, 1854.

Brown, John, *Statement made April 1, 1845, Before the United Associate Presbytery of Edinburgh, on asking their advice*, Edinburgh, Glasgow, Dublin, London, 1845.

Brown, John, and Balmer, R., *Statements on Certain Doctrinal Points*, Edinburgh, 1844.

Brown, T., *Church and State in Scotland: A Narrative for the Struggle for Independence.* 1560–1843, Edinburgh and London, 1891.

Caird, E., *Hegel,* London and Edinburgh, 1883.

Caird, E., *Lay Sermons and Addresses*, Glasgow, 1907.

Caird, E., *Evolution of Religion,* 2 vols., Glasgow, 1893.

Caird, John, *Aspects of Life,* Edinburgh and London, 1858.

Caird, John, *An Introduction to the Philosophy of Religion,* Glasgow, 1920, edition.

Cairns, J., *Memoir of John Brown, D.D.,* Edinburgh and London, 1860.

Cameron, N,M,de S. *et al* (eds), *Dictionary of Scottish Church History and Theology* (IVP, Downers Grove, 1993).

Candlish, J. S., *The Relations of the Presbyterian Churches to the Confession of Faith,* Glasgow, 1886.

Candlish, R. S., *The Atonement, Its Reality, Completeness and Extent*, London, Edinburgh, New York, 1861.

Clark, I.M., *A History of Church Discipline in Scotland,* Aberdeen, 1929.

Cockshut, A.O.J., *Anglican Attitudes: A Study of Victorian Religious Controversies*, London, 1959.

Cooper, J., *Confessions of Faith and Formulas of Subscription,* Glasgow, 1907.

Cowan, R.M.W., *The Newspaper in Scotland,* Glasgow, 1946.

*Creed Revision in Scotland: Its Necessity and Scope*, Glasgow, 1907.

Crowther, M.A., *Church Embattled: Religious Controversy in Mid-Victorian England,* Connecticut, 1970.

Cunningham, W*., The Reformers and the Theology of the Reformation,* Banner of Truth Trust edition, London, 1967.

Cunningham, W., *Historical Theology,* 2 vols., Edinburgh, 1870.

Curtis, W.A., *History of Creeds and Confessions of Faith,* Edinburgh, 1911.

Dales, J.B., and Patterson, R.M. (eds.), *Report of the Proceedings of the Second General Council of the Presbyterian Alliance,* Philadelphia, 1880.

Donaldson, J., *Westminster Confession of Faith and the Thirty Nine Articles of the Church of England,* London, 1905.

Drummond, A.L., and Bulloch, J., *The Church in Victorian Scotland. 1843–74,* Edinburgh and St Andrews, 1975.

Drummond, A.L., and Bulloch, J., *The Church in Late Victorian Scotland.* 1874–1900, Edinburgh, 1978.

Edwards, S.J., *Marcus Dods,* Unpublished Edinburgh University Ph.D. thesis, 1960.

Elliott-Binns, L.E., *Religion in the Victorian Era,* London, 1936.

Elliott-Binns, L.E., *English Thought 1860–1900: The Theological Aspect,* London, 1956.

Enwright, W. G., *Preaching and Theology in Scotland in the Nineteenth Century: a study in the context and content of the evangelical sermon,* Unpublished Edinburgh University Ph.D. thesis, 1968.

Fairbairn, A.M., *The Religious Progress in Scotland* (No place of publication), 1861.

Ferguson, F., *Immortality of Man,* Edinburgh, 1875.

Ferguson, F., *Additional Statements in Defence of my Doctrinal Position,* Glasgow, 1878.

Ferguson, F., *Reconstruction of the Creed,* Glasgow, 1877.

Fleming, J.R., *A History of the Church in Scotland. 1843–74,* Edinburgh, 1927.

Fleming, J.R., *A History of the Church in Scotland. 1875–1929,* Edinburgh, 1933.

Forrest, D.W., *Letters of Dr. John Brown,* London, 1907.

Fraser, D., *Life and Diary of Rev. Ebenezer Erskine,* Edinburgh, 1834.

Fraser, D., *Life and Diary of Rev. Ralph Erskine,* Edinburgh, 1834.

Gattis,Lee,www.theologian.org.uk/gattisnet/documents/Shadesofopinion

Gib, A., *The Present Truth: A Display of the Secession Testimony,* Edinburgh, 1774.

Goddard, H.L., *The Contribution of George Smeaton to Theological Thought,* Unpublished University of Edinburgh Ph.D., 1960.

Goodsir, J.T., *The Westminster Confession of Faith Examined on the Basis of the Other Protestant Confessions,* London and Edinburgh, 1868.

Hall, D,W (ed.), *The Practice of Confessional Subscription* (Oak Ridge, Tennessee, 1997).

Hart, D.G. and Muether, J.R. (eds), *Seeking a Better Country* (P and R, New Jersey, 2007).

Henderson, H. F., *The Religious Controversies of Scotland,* Edinburgh, 1905.

Hendry, G. S., *The Westminster Confession Today. A Contemporary Interpretation,* Richmond and London, 1960.

Anon., *History of the Free Presbyterian Church of Scotland (1893–1970),* (No place of publication, n.d.).

Hodge, A. A., *The Confession of Faith,* Banner of Truth ed., London, 1958.

Hutchison, M., *The Reformed Presbyterian Church in Scotland 1680–1876,* Paisley, 1893.

Huxley, T.H., *Science and Christian Tradition,* London, 1894.

*Inauguration of the New College of the Free Church, With Introductory Lectures on Theology, Philosophy, and Natural Science,* London and Edinburgh, 1851.

Innes, A.T., *Law of Creeds,* First ed., Edinburgh and London, 1867, Second ed., Edinburgh and London, 1902.

Innes, A.T, *Studies in Scottish History,* London, 1892.

Innes, A.T, *Chapters of Reminiscence,* London, 1913.

Jones, H., and Muirhead, J.H., *The Life and Philosophy of Edward Caird,* Glasgow, 1921.

Lane, E.D., *Theology of the Westminster Symbols,* Columbus, 1900.

Leckie, J.H., *Fergus Ferguson, his Theology and Heresy Trial,* Edinburgh, 1923.

Lyall, F., *Church and State in Scotland,* Unpublished University of Aberdeen Ph.D., 1972.

Marshall, A., *The Death of Christ, the Redemption of the People; or the atonement regulated by the divine purpose,* Edinburgh, Glasgow, London, 1842.

Marshall, A., *The Catholic Doctrine of Redemption Vindicated,* Glasgow, Edinburgh, London, 1844.

Marshall, A., *Remarks on the Pamphlet Intituled, 'Statements on Certain Doctrinal Points, made October 5th., 1843, Before the United Associate Synod',* Edinburgh, Glasgow, Ayr, 1845.

Marshall, W., *Present State of Doctrine in the United Secession Church,* Glasgow and Edinburgh, 1845.

Martin, H., *Westminster Doctrine of the Inspiration of Scripture,* London, 1877.

Martin, H., *The Atonement in its relation to the Covenant, the Priesthood, and the Intercession,* Edinburgh, 1887.

Matthews, G.D. (ed.), *Alliance of Reformed Churches Holding the Presbyterian System. Proceedings of the Eighth General Council, Liverpool, 1904,* London, 1904.

Mitchell, A.F., *The Westminster Confession of Faith: A Contribution to the Study of its Historical Relations and to the Defence of its Teaching*, Edinburgh, 1867.

Moffatt, J. (ed.), *Letters of Principal James Denney to his Family and Friends*, London, New York, Toronto, n.d.

Moncrieff, H.W., *The Free Church Principles, its Character and History*, Edinburgh, 1883.

Moore, J.D., *English Hypothetical Universalism: John Preston and the Softening of Reformed Theology*, Eerdmans, Grand Rapids, Michigan and Cambridge, UK, 2007.

Morgan, B.Q., and Hohlfeld, *German Literature in British Magazines, 1750–1860*, Wisconsin, 1949.

Mosheim, J.L.V., *An Ecclesiastical History from the birth of Christ to the beginning of the Eighteenth Century*, First ed., 1726, London ed., 1842.

Mozley, J.K., *Some Tendencies in British Theology from the publication of Lux Mundi to the Present day*, London, 1951.

MacAlister, D.M., *The Declaratory Act, A Stumbling-Block*, Edinburgh, 1894.

McCoy, W.L., *John Brown of Edinburgh. 1784–1858: Churchman and Theologian*, Unpublished University of Edinburgh Ph.D., 1956.

McCrie, C. G., *The Confessions of the Church of Scotland*, Edinburgh, 1907.

McCrie, C. G., *The Church of Scotland, Her Divisions and her Reunions*, Edinburgh, 1901.

McCrie, T., *Statement of the Difference between the Profession of the Reformed Church of Scotland as adopted by the Seceders, and the Profession contained in the New Testimony and Other Acts, Lately Adopted by the General Associate Synod*, First ed., 1807; Second ed., Edinburgh 1871.

MacDonald, G., *David Elginbrod*, London, 1863.

MacEwen, A.R., *Life and Letters of John Cairns*, London, 1898.

McKerrow, J., *History of the Secession Church, 2 vols.*, Edinburgh, 1839.

MacKintosh, R., *Essays Towards a New Theology*, Glasgow, 1889.

MacKintosh, R., *Hegel and Hegelianism*, Edinburgh, 1903.

MacLean, D., *Aspects of Scottish Church History*, Edinburgh, 1927.

Macleod, J., *Scottish Theology: in relation to Church History,* Edinburgh, 1974.

MacPherson, H., *Scotland's Battles for Spiritual Independence,* Edinburgh, 1905.

Anon., *Narrative and Testimony agreed upon and enacted by the General Associate Synod,* Edinburgh, 1804.

Oliphant, B.R., *Horatius Bonar 1808–1889; hymn writer, theologian, preacher, churchman. A study of his religious thought and activity,* Unpublished University of Edinburgh Ph.D., 1951.

Oliphant, M., *Principal Tulloch,* Edinburgh, 1888.

Palmer, R.E., *A.A. Bonar (1810-1892); a study of his life, work and religious thought,* Unpublished University of Edinburgh Ph.D., 1955.

Plumb, J.H. (ed.), *Ideas and Beliefs of the Victorians,* London, 1949.

Polhill, E., *Essay on the Extent of the Death of Christ,* Berwick, 1842.

Rainy, R., *Evolution and Theology,* Edinburgh, 1874.

Rainy, R., *Present Position of the Union Question in the Free Church,* Edinburgh, 1868.

Rainy, R., *Delivery and Development of Christian Doctrine,* Edinburgh, 1874.

Reardon, B.M.G., *From Coleridge to Gare. A Century of Religious Thought in Britain,* London, 1971.

Anon., *Re-exhibition of the Testimony,* Glasgow, 1779.

Reid, H.M.B., *The Divinity Professors in the University of Glasgow 1640–1903,* Glasgow, 1923.

Robertson, A., *History of the Atonement Controversy, In Connexion With the Secession Church, From its Origin to the Present Time,* Edinburgh, 1846.

Robertson, A.K., *Revival of Church Worship in the Church of Scotland from Dr. Robert Lee (1804–67) to Dr. H.J. Wotherspoon (1850–1930),* Unpublished University of Edinburgh Ph.D., 1956.

Sands, Lord, *Sir Archibald Scott of St. Georges' Edinburgh and His Times,* Edinburgh and London, 1919.

Schaeffer, F. A., *Escape from Reason,* London, 1968.

Schaff, P., *Creeds of Christendom, III,* New York, 1878.

Selbie, W.B., *Life of A.M. Fairbairn,* London, New York, Toronto, 1914.

Shaw, R., *The Reformed Faith,* Edinburgh, 1974 ed.

Simpson, P.C., *The Life of Principal Rainy, 2 vols.,* London, 1909.

Sjolinder, R., *Presbyterian Reunion in Scotland 1907–1921. Its Background and Development,* Uppsala, 1962.

Smith, T., *Memoirs of Dr. Begg,* II, Edinburgh, 1888.

Stewart, A., and Cameron, J.K., *The Free Church of Scotland. 1843–1910: A Vindication,* Edinburgh and Glasgow, 1910.

Struthers, G., *History of the Relief Church,* Glasgow, 1843.

Anon., *Testimony of the United Associate Synod of the Secession Church,* Edinburgh, 1828.

Tulloch, J., *Movements of Religious Thought in Britain During the Nineteenth Century,* London, 1885.

Walker, J., *James Walker D.D.; Essays, Papers and Sermons,* Edinburgh, 1898.

Walker, N. L., *Robert Buchanan D.D. (An Ecclesiastical Biography),* London, Edinburgh, New York, 1877.

Walker, T. H., *Principal James Denney, D.D., A Memoir and a Tribute,* London, Edinburgh, New York, 1918.

Warfield, B. B., *The Westminster Assembly and its Work,* New Jersey, 1972 ed.

Warfield, B. B., *Studies in Theology,* New York, 1932.

Warr, C.L., *Principal Caird,* Edinburgh, 1926.

Begg, J. (ed.), *The Watchword: A Magazine for the defence of Bible Truth, and the Advocacy of Free Church Principles, Vols. 1–8,* Edinburgh, Glasgow, London, 1867, 1868, 1869, 1870, 1871, 1872, 1873.

Webster, A., *Theology in Scotland: Reviewed by a Heretic,* London, 1915.

Willey, B., *Nineteenth Century Studies,* London, 1949.

Willey, B., *More Nineteenth Century Studies: A Group of Honest Doubters,* London, 1956.

Wilson, W., *Memorials of R.S. Candlish,* Edinburgh, 1880.

Withrow, W.H., *Religious Progress of the Century,* London and Edinburgh, 1902.

Wood, H.G., *Belief and Unbelief since 1850,* Cambridge, 1955.

Woodside, D., *The Soul of a Scottish Church,* Edinburgh, n.d.

Woodside, D. *The Life of Henry Calderwood,* London, 1900.


*B. Pamphlets:*

Anon., *Address to the People of the Free Church of Scotland Called Forth by the Doctrinal Defections Prevailing in that Church*, Edinburgh, 1889.

Bonar, A. A., *The Case Stated,* Glasgow, 1890.

Cairns, J., *Speech on the Subordinate Standards*, Edinburgh, 1878.

Dods, M., *What is a Christian?,* Edinburgh, 1889.

Dods, M., *Recent Progress in Theology,* London and Edinburgh, 1889.

'Clericus', *An Examination of the Sermon by the Rev. Professor Marcus Dods, D.D., entitled 'What is a Christian?'*, Edinburgh, 1890.

Free Presbytery of Lockerbie, *The Free Church Declaratory Act and Proposed Alterations on the Questions and Formula,* Glasgow, 1893.

Anon., *Free Church Declaratory Act. A Criticism and Protest,* Glasgow, 1892.

Anon., *Free Church Policy and Prospects; or, The Position of Professors Dods and Bruce on the History of the Free Church,* Edinburgh, 1890.

Forsyth, J., *Remarks on Dr. Heugh's Irenicum,* Edinburgh, 1845.

Gavin, J., *Church of Scotland and the Formula of Subscription to the Confession of Faith*, Edinburgh, 1909.

Gibson, J., *The Union Question. Re-Statement of the Difference Free Church V Broad Churchism*, Edinburgh and Glasgow, 1870.

Heugh, H., *Irenicum: an enquiry into the real amount of the difference alleged to exist in the Synod of the Secession Church, on the Atonement, and the doctrines connected with it,* Glasgow, 1845.

Howie, R., *Reply to Letter of Professor Blaikie, D.D., LL.D., To Rev Andrew A. Bonar D.D., on Statement issued on the Dods and Bruce Cases,* Glasgow and Edinburgh, 1890.

Kerr, J., *Vivisection in Theology, and its Chief Apologist, Professor Dods, D. D.,* Glasgow, Edinburgh, London, 1890.

Long, H. A., *Analytical Refutation of the Famous Sermon "What is a Christian?", By the Rev. Professor Marcus Dods, D.D., in Nineteen Quotations, Wherein its Arianism is Plainly shown,* Glasgow, 1890.

Macaskill, M., *Dr. Dods and His Apologists: A Criticism of the "New School of Theology",* Edinburgh and Wick, 1890.

Mackintosh, R., *The Obsoleteness of the Westminster Confession of Faith,* Glasgow, 1888.

Moody-Stuart, K., *Why we do not mean to change our Confession of Faith,* Edinburgh, 1889.

Moody-Stuart, K., *The New Declaratory Act and Proposed New Formula of the Free Church of Scotland,* Moffat, 1893.

Anon., *The New Theology as taught and professed in the United Presbyterian Church,* Edinburgh, 1879.

Pearson, G., *The Principles of the United Presbyterian Church, wherein do they differ from other Presbyterian Churches?,* Glasgow, 1877.

Rainy, R., *Explanatory Notes on the Declaratory Act of the Free Church of Scotland,* Edinburgh, 1894.

Anon., *The Religious Condition of the Free Church of Scotland in the Exodus and Jubilee Decades Respectively, Stated and Compared,* Aberdeen, Edinburgh, Glasgow, 1893.

Anon., *Report of the Committee on Union, May 1873* (no other information).

Anon., *Report of the Sub-Committee to bring up a Statement of the Various Doctrinal Findings by the Supreme Courts of the United Church in the Course of its History,* Edinbugh (?), 1877.

Robertson, A., *First Letter to the Rev. Andrew Marshall D.D., LL.D., explaining and enforcing certain propositions embodied in a petition to be presented to the Synod, in condemnation of his views of the subject of the Atonement,* Edinburgh, Glasgow, London, Dublin, 1845.

Robertson, A., *Second Letter to the Rev. Andrew Marshall D.D., LL.D., occasioned by his Overture to the Synod on the present state of doctrine in the United Secession Church,* Edinburgh and Glasgow, 1845.

Robertson, A., *Third Letter to the Rev. Andrew Marshall D.D., in farther condemnation of his views on the subject of the atonement; with proofs drawn from our standards and other official documents,* Edinburgh and Glasgow, 1845.

Storrie, J., *The Scotch Sermons – Analysed and Tested*, Edinburgh, 1881.

Anon., *Theological Jugglery in the Free Church*, Edinburgh, 1890.

Tulloch, J., *Theological Tendencies of the Age*, Edinburgh, 1855.


*C. Articles:*

Anon., 'The Atonement Controversy', *The Ecclectic Review,* XVIII, London, Edinburgh, Glasgow, 1845.

Brackenridge, R.B., 'The "Sabbath War"' of 1865–66: The Shaking of the Foundations, *Scottish Church History Society Records,* XVI, Glasgow, 1969.

Brown, J., 'Notes, Chiefly Historical, On the Question Respecting The Extent of the Reference of the Death of Christ', *United Secession Magazine,* IX, Edinburgh, 1841.

Brase, O., 'F.D. Maurice and the Victorian Crisis of Belief', *Victorian Studies,* III, Indiana, 1960.

Cairns, J., 'Recent Dogmatic Thought in Scotland', *Presbyterian and Reformed Review,* II, New York and Philadelphia, 1891.

Cairns, J., 'Infallibility of the Bible', *North British Review,* XXXV, 1852.

Campbell, I., 'Carlyle and the Secession', *Scottish Church History Society Records,* XVIII, Glasgow, 1972–74.

Cheyne, A.C., 'The Westminster Standards: A Century of Re-appraisal', *Scottish Church History Society Records,* XIV, Glasgow, 1963.

Candlish, R.S., 'On the Atonement Controversy', *Free Church Magazine,* I, Glasgow, Edinburgh, London, 1844.

Candlish, R.S., 'On the Atonement Controversy', *Free Church Magazine,* II, Glasgow, Edinburgh, London, 1845.

Drummond, R.J., 'The Significance of the United Presbyterian Church', *Scottish Church History Society Records,* X, Glasgow, 1950.

Fairbairn, A.M., 'David Friederick Strauss: a Chapter in the History of Modern Religious Thought', *Contemporary Review,* XXVII, London, 1876.

Fairbairn, A.M., 'David Friederick Strauss: a Chapter in the History of Modern Religious Thought', *Contemporary Review,* XXVIII, London, 1876.

Fairbairn, A.M., 'The Westminster Confession of Faith and Scotch Theology', *Contemporary Review,* XXI, London, 1873.

Humphrey, E.P., 'Inspiration, Authenticity and Interpretation of the Scriptures', *Report of Proceedings of the Second General Council of the Presbyterian Alliance,* ed. by J.B. Dales and R.M. Patterson, Philadelphia, 1880.

Anon., 'John Caird As A Thinker, Sermon-Writer and Divine', *United Presbyterian Magazine.*

Lindsay, T. M., 'The Doctrine of Scripture: The Reformers and the Princeton School', *Expositor,* I, London, 1895.

Lindsay, T. M., 'Professor W. Robertson Smith's Doctrine of Scripture', *Expositor,* X, London, 1894.

Lindsay, T. M., 'The Critical Movement in the Free Church of Scotland', *Contemporary Review,* XXXIII, London, 1878.

Murphy, H.R., 'The Ethical Revolt Against Christian Orthodoxy in Early Victorian England', *American Historical Review,* LX, 1955.

Murray, J., 'The Theology of the Westminster Confession of Faith', *Scripture and Confession,* ed. by J.H. Skilton, Philadelphia, 1973.

Macleod, J., 'Theology in the early days of the Secession', *Scottish Church History Society Records,* VIII, Glasgow, 1944.

Rainy, R., 'Modern Theological Thought', *Report of the Proceedings of the Second General Council of the Presbyterian Alliance,* ed. by J.B. Dales and R.M. Patterson, Philadelphia, 1880.

Roberts, W.H., 'The Barrier Act of the Church of Scotland', *Presbyterian and Reformed Review,* II, New York and Philadelphia, 1891.

Robertson Smith, W., 'Review of Recent Dutch Periodicals', *British and Foreign Evangelical Review,* LXXVII, London and Edinburgh, 1871.

Tulloch, J., 'Dean Stanley and the Scotch Moderates', *Contemporary Review*, XX, London, 1872.

Anon., 'Religious Intelligence', *United Presbyterian Magazine*, XXIII, Glasgow, Edinburgh, London, 1879.

Anon., 'The Doctrine of Universal Atonement Examined', *United Secession Magazine*, IX, Edinburgh, 1841.

Walker, M. L., 'Recent Theological Drifts in Scotland', *Presbyterian and Reformed Review*, IV, Philadelphia, 1893.

Walker, M. L., 'Ecclesiastical Situation in Scotland', *Presbyterian and Reformed Review*, V, Philadelphia, 1894.

Watts, R., 'The Scripture Doctrine of Inspiration', *Report of the Proceedings of the Second General Council of the Presbyterian Alliance*, ed. by J.B. Dales, and R.M. Patterson, Philadelphia, 1880.

# UNITY &
# DIVERSITY

## THE FOUNDERS OF
## THE FREE CHURCH OF SCOTLAND

### SANDY FINLAYSON

# Unity & Diversity
*The Founder of the Free Church of Scotland*
## Sandy Finlayson

It has been many years since there has been a popular level book, which has looked at the life and ministry of some of the 'fathers' of the Free Church of Scotland. This book looks at the life and ministry of a number of the key figures in the Disruption era and late 19th Century Free Church. Beginning with Thomas Chalmers, each chapter has a biographical sketch of a key figure with an emphasis on why these men mattered in their time and what they still have to say to us in the 21st century. All of the men portrayed were committed to the advancement of the Gospel in Scotland and further afield. While they shared a commitment to the Confession of Faith and reformed theology, this was expressed in unique ways by each of these men. Hence both unity and diversity is on view in these fascinating pages.

> At this moment in church history the people of God sorely need to be reminded that following Christ means being willing to part with cherished denominational identities and connections, church buildings, and even houses and secure salaries. This welcome book includes a picture of each of these founding fathers of the Free Church of Scotland and - to a man - they all look as sober as hot, black coffee in a styrofoam cup. As we are in no danger of overdoing their earnestness, spending a few hours with such steely-eyed men can safely serve to remind us of what it means to stake one's life and livelihood on the lordship of Jesus Christ. Sandy Finlayson has written a clear, lively book that concedes when these churchmen were wrong without thereby obscuring their passionate stand for the Gospel.
>
> Timothy Larsen ~ McManis Professor of Christian Thought,
> Wheaton College, Wheaton, Illinois

Alexander (Sandy) Finlayson is Library Director and Professor of Theological Bibliography at Westminster Theological Seminary in Philadelphia. Sandy holds degrees from the University of Toronto and Tyndale Theological Seminary in Canada, where he was also Library Director for eleven years. Sandy served as an elder in the Toronto congregation of the Free Church of Scotland for ten years. He is married to Linda, who writes books for children, and they have one son.

**ISBN 9781845505509**

"...a fine and fresh account of a great and godly minister of the gospel."

Eric Alexander

# AWAKENING
## THE LIFE & MINISTRY OF
## ROBERT MURRAY McCHEYNE

David Robertson

# Awakening
*The Life & Ministry of Robert Murray McCheyne*
## David Robertson

"Was Mccheyne for real?"; "Was he just famous because he died so young?"; "Does he have anything to teach us today?"

In this book, David Robertson, the present-day minister of McCheyne's church, St Peter's in Dundee, Scotland, seeks to answer these and other questions. Through the use of published sermons, private papers and historical material, this contemporary devotional biography traces McCheyne's life and influence from his upbringing, conversion and training for the ministry to the revival that occurred in St Peter's in 1839 and his early death. The contemporary relevance of McCheyne for today's church is demonstrated and the glory of God is seen in this wonderful story of what He can do with one 'consecrated sinner'.

"The freshest presentation of McCheyne available"
Ligon Duncan ~ Senior Minister,
First Presbyterian Church, Jackson, Mississippi

"Having used Robert Murray McCheyne's 1842 Bible Reading Calendar for many years, and having admired his hunger for holiness, I am very glad that David Robertson has written this new biography."
John Stott ~ Rector Emeritus, All Souls Church,
Langham Place, London

"...a fine and fresh account of a great and godly minister of the gospel. David Robertson gives us new insight into McCheyne's personal life, and his preparation for preaching, his deep social concern and his absolute devotion to the glory of God as the ultimate motive of everything he did."
Eric Alexander ~ Conference speaker
Formerly minister St George's Tron, Glasgow for 20 years.

David Robertson is Free Church of Scotland Monthly editor, columnist, author and pastor of St Peter's Free Church of Scotland, Dundee.

**ISBN 9781845505424**

CHRISTIAN
HERITAGE

Includes an introduction to the life and theology
of the Erskine brothers by Joel R. Beeke

# The Beauties of

# *Ebenezer Erskine*

Selected from his complete works
by
## Samuel McMillan

# The Beauties of Ebenezer Erskine

## Ebenezer Erskine

Ebenezer and Ralph Erskine were preachers in the 18th century who saw thousands revived and reformed under their ministry. Born at the end of the 17th century, their lives were disrupted by their father Henry's refusal to distance himself from the Covenanters. He was imprisoned for daring to continue his ministry.

Poor health led to Henry's sentence being commuted to exile in England, enabling him to continue to preach in the border counties. It was here that God used him to bring a young Thomas Boston to faith.

Both Ralph and Ebenezer were ordained into the Church of Scotland but Ebenezer was only converted after he was ordained. The difference in the effect of his sermons was remarkable. Thousands flocked to hear him from as far as sixty miles away. When he later ministered in Stirling the whole town was affected.

Erskine also continued to be at the centre of debates within the church. He was formally rebuked by the General Assembly over the 'Marrow' controversy in 1722 and suspended from office over the issue of 'Patronage' in 1732. Ebenezer and three other suspended ministers formed the Associated Presbytery and continued to fight for reform within the Church of Scotland.

Arguments continued, first with George Whitefield (an affair that started with misunderstanding, escalated to intemperate language and was later reconciled) and later within the fledgling denomination over whether or not it was permissible to take an oath.

Despite these diversions Ebenezer's influence on the theological landscape of Scotland was deep. He was a great user of illustrations in his sermons, a pioneer even. He also radiated a warm, experiential, Christ-centred Christianity that was as true of his words as of his life.

**ISBN 9781892777201**

# Christian Focus Publications
publishes books for all ages

Our mission statement –

## *STAYING FAITHFUL*
In dependence upon God we seek to help make His infallible Word, the Bible, relevant. Our aim is to ensure that the Lord Jesus Christ is presented as the only hope to obtain forgiveness of sin, live a useful life and look forward to heaven with Him.

## *REACHING OUT*
Christ's last command requires us to reach out to our world with His gospel. We seek to help fulfil that by publishing books that point people towards Jesus and help them develop a Christ-like maturity. We aim to equip all levels of readers for life, work, ministry and mission.

Books in our adult range are published in three imprints.

*Christian Focus* contains popular works including biographies, commentaries, basic doctrine and Christian living. Our children's books are also published in this imprint.

*Mentor* focuses on books written at a level suitable for Bible College and seminary students, pastors, and other serious readers. The imprint includes commentaries, doctrinal studies, examination of current issues and church history.

*Christian Heritage* contains classic writings from the past.

Christian Focus Publications, Ltd
Geanies House, Fearn,
Ross-shire, IV20 1TW, Scotland, United Kingdom
info@christianfocus.com

www.christianfocus.com